SNAPSHOT

Hill Towns
of
Central Italy

CONTENTS

Siena

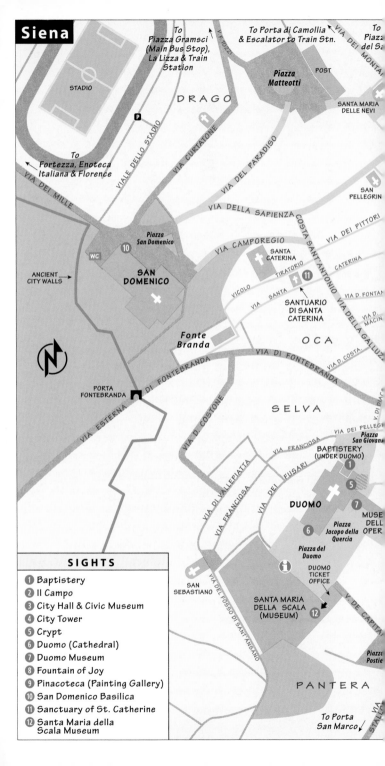

STADIO

DRAGO

To Piazza Gramsci (Main Bus Stop), La Lizza & Train Station

To Porta di Camollia & Escalator to Train Stn.

VIA F. TOZZI

Piazza Matteotti

POST

VIA DEI MONTAN

To Piazza del Sa

SANTA MARIA DELLE NEVI

P

To Fortezza, Enoteca Italiana & Florence

VIALE DELLO STADIO

VIA CURTATONE

VIA DEL PARADISO

VIA DEI MILLE

VIA DELLA SAPIENZA

SAN PELLEGRIN

VIA DEI PITTORI

Piazza San Domenico

VIA CAMPOREGIO

SANTA CATERINA

COSTA SANT'ANTONIO

CATERINA

WC

ANCIENT CITY WALLS

SAN DOMENICO

VICOLO TIRATOIO

VIA SANTA

VIA. D. FONTAN

VIA DELLA GALLUZ

VIA D. MACIN

SANTUARIO DI SANTA CATERINA

11

Fonte Branda

OCA

N

VIA DI FONTEBRANDA

VIA D. COSTA.

PORTA FONTEBRANDA

VIA ESTERNA DI FONTEBRANDA

VIA D. COSTONE

SELVA

VIA DI VALLEPIATTA

VIA FRANCIOSA

VIA DEI PELLEGRI

VIA DI PIAC

Piazza San Giovan

BAPTISTERY (UNDER DUOMO)

1

VIA DEL FUSARI

VIA FRANCIOSA

DUOMO

5

7

MUSE DELL OPER

6

Piazza Jacopo della Quercia

SAN SEBASTIANO

VIA DEL FOSSO DI SANT'ANSANO

Piazza del Duomo

i

DUOMO TICKET OFFICE

SANTA MARIA DELLA SCALA (MUSEUM)

12

V. DE CAPITA

Piazza Postie

PANTERA

VIA STALLC

To Porta San Marco

SIGHTS

1. Baptistery
2. Il Campo
3. City Hall & Civic Museum
4. City Tower
5. Crypt
6. Duomo (Cathedral)
7. Duomo Museum
8. Fountain of Joy
9. Pinacoteca (Painting Gallery)
10. San Domenico Basilica
11. Sanctuary of St. Catherine
12. Santa Maria della Scala Museum

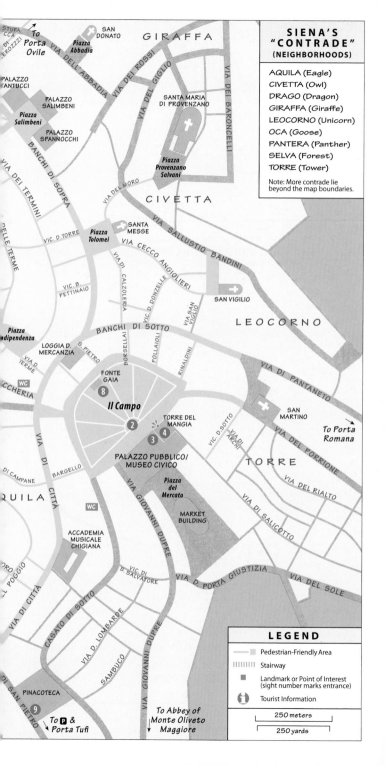

STUFA CCA
DI... EROZZI

To Porta Ovile

SAN DONATO

Piazza Abbadia

GIRAFFA

PALAZZO TANTUCCI

VIA DELL'ABBADIA

VIA DEI ROSSI

VIA DEL GIGLIO

SANTA MARIA DI PROVENZANO

VIA DEI BARONCELLI

PALAZZO SALIMBENI

Piazza Salimbeni

PALAZZO SPANNOCCHI

BANCHI DI SOPRA

VIA DEL MORO

Piazza Provenzano Salvani

VIA DEI TERMINI

DELLE TERME

VIC. D. TORRE

Piazza Tolomei

SANTA MESSE

VIA SALLUSTIO BANDINI

CIVETTA

VIA CECCO ANGIOLIERI

VIA DI CALZOLERIA

VIC. B. PETTINAIO

VIC. D. DONZELLE

VIA SAN VIGILIO

SAN VIGILIO

LEOCORNO

Piazza dipendenza

BANCHI DI SOTTO

LOGGIA D. MERCANZIA

S. PIETRO

POLLAIOLI

RINALDINI

VIA DI FANTANETO

VIA D. TERME

CCHERIA

WC

FONTE GAIA

8

Il Campo

2

TORRE DEL MANGIA

3 4

PALAZZO PUBBLICO/ MUSEO CIVICO

VIC. D. SOTTO

VIA DI ARCHI

SAN MARTINO

To Porta Romana

VIA DEL FORRIONE

TORRE

DI CAMPANE

BARGELLO

VIA DI CITTÀ

AQUILA

Piazza del Mercato

MARKET BUILDING

VIA DEL RIALTO

VIA DI SALICOTTO

WC

ACCADEMIA MUSICALE CHIGIANA

VIA GIOVANNI DUPRE

VIC. DI S. SALVATORE

VIA D. PORTA GIUSTIZIA

VIA DEL SOLE

RO POGGIO

VIA DI CITTÀ

CASATO DI SOTTO

VIA D. LOMBARDE

SAMBUCO

VIA GIOVANNI DUPRE

DI SAN PIETRO

PINACOTECA

9

To P & Porta Tufi

To Abbey of Monte Oliveto Maggiore

SIENA'S "CONTRADE" (NEIGHBORHOODS)

AQUILA (Eagle)
CIVETTA (Owl)
DRAGO (Dragon)
GIRAFFA (Giraffe)
LEOCORNO (Unicorn)
OCA (Goose)
PANTERA (Panther)
SELVA (Forest)
TORRE (Tower)

Note: More contrade lie beyond the map boundaries.

LEGEND

— Pedestrian-Friendly Area

||||||||| Stairway

■ Landmark or Point of Interest (sight number marks entrance)

ℹ Tourist Information

250 meters

250 yards

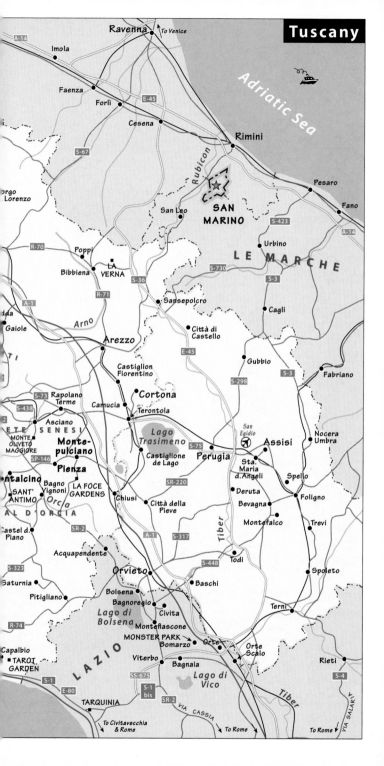

INTRODUCTION

This Snapshot guide, excerpted from my guidebook *Rick Steves Italy,* introduces you to the hill towns of central Italy. Here in Italy's heartland, you'll enjoy an idyllic landscape, time-passed medieval hill towns, and tree-lined meandering backcountry roads. Dine on Italy's heartiest food in an atmospheric farmhouse, and taste a glass of wine poured by a proud vintner whose family's name has been on the bottle for generations.

I've included a mix of towns and cities, some undiscovered, some deservedly popular. Choose among the back-door towns of Volterra and Civita, the wine lovers' towns of Montepulciano and Montalcino, touristy towered San Gimignano, manicured Pienza, classic Orvieto, tradition-steeped Siena, and spiritual, artsy Assisi—or even better, visit them all.

To help you have the best trip possible, I've included the following topics in this book:

• **Planning Your Time,** with advice on how to make the most of your limited time

• **Orientation,** including tourist information (abbreviated as TI), tips on public transportation, local tour options, and helpful hints

• **Sights** with ratings:

▲▲▲—Don't miss

▲▲—Try hard to see

▲—Worthwhile if you can make it

No rating—Worth knowing about

• **Sleeping** and **Eating,** with good-value recommendations in every price range

• **Connections,** with tips on trains, buses, and driving

Practicalities, near the end of this book, has information on money, staying connected, hotel reservations, transportation, and more, plus Italian survival phrases.

To travel smartly, read this little book in its entirety before you go. It's my hope that this guide will make your trip more meaningful and rewarding. Traveling like a temporary local, you'll get the absolute most out of every mile, minute, and dollar.

Buon viaggio!

Rick Steves

HILL TOWNS
OF CENTRAL ITALY

The sun-soaked hill towns of central Italy offer what to many is the quintessential Italian experience: sun-dried tomatoes, homemade pasta, wispy cypress-lined driveways following desolate ridges to fortified 16th-century farmhouses, atmospheric *enoteche* serving famously tasty wines, and dusty old-timers warming the same bench day after day while soccer balls buzz around them like innocuous flies. Hill towns are best enjoyed by adapting to the pace of the countryside. So, slow...down...and savor the delights that this region offers. Spend the night if you can, as many hill towns are mobbed by day-trippers.

PLANNING YOUR TIME

It's a joy to downshift to the more peaceful pace of Italy's small cities...and even smaller hill towns. But how in Dante's name does one choose which to visit? I've covered my favorites in this book. Select among them depending on your interests, time, and mode of transportation.

Siena is the ultimate (and biggest) hill town, with an unrivalled spirit any visitor can enjoy. Like a medieval stage set, its pedestrian-friendly old town is surrounded by its fortified wall. Siena's stunning main square—the gently tilted red-brick Campo—is the city's proud centerpiece.

Northwest of Siena, **Volterra**—with its rustic vitality—is a beautifully preserved jewel. Its out-of-the-way location keeps this town from being trampled by tourist crowds, and its Etruscan history makes for compelling sightseeing. With 14 surviving medieval towers, walled **San Gimignano** is a classic. Because it's easy to

HILL TOWNS

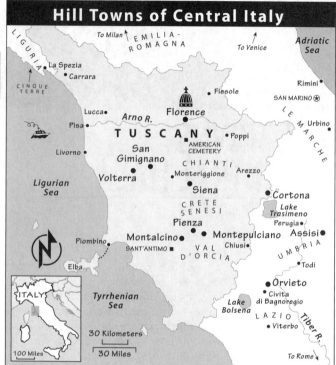

Hill Towns of Central Italy

visit from Florence—about 1.5 hours by bus—midday crowds can overwhelm its charms (but it's an evocative delight early and late).

South of Siena, in the region I call the "Heart of Tuscany," drivers have their pick of hill towns. Ridge-hugging **Montepulciano**'s medieval cityscape resembles a miniature Florence. With several historic wine cellars and easy access to wine country, it attracts wine aficionados, as does **Montalcino,** itself a happy gauntlet of wine shops and art galleries. Fans of architecture and urban design appreciate little **Pienza**'s well-planned streets and squares. To link these towns, see my suggested driving route in the Heart of Tuscany chapter.

To the east, the town of St. Francis, hillside **Assisi,** has a grand basilica and a wistful, saintly serenity. Farther south, cathedral-capped **Orvieto** sits on a grand stone throne a thousand feet above a valley floor, while its tiny neighbor, **Civita,** teeters high over a vast canyon.

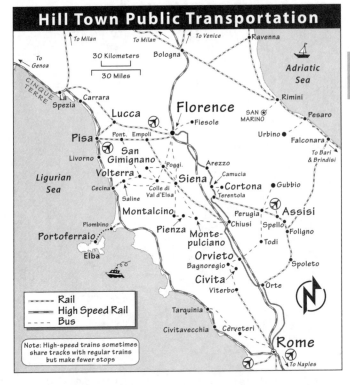

GETTING AROUND THE HILL TOWNS

Most hill towns work best for drivers, but some can be reached by public transportation (see specific chapters for advice on getting around). **Buses** are often the only public-transit choice for linking the smaller towns. **Train stations** are likely to be in the valley below the town center, connected by a local bus.

Exploring the hill towns **by car** can be a great experience.

Wait to pick up your car until the last sizable town you visit (or at the nearest airport to avoid big-city traffic), and carry a good, detailed road map in addition to any digital navigation systems. Smaller roads, such as the super-scenic S-222 connecting Florence and Siena, make for rewarding driving.

Some towns don't allow visitors to drive or park in the city center. Be alert for "ZTL" *(Zona Traffico Limitato)* signs, indicating no cars allowed. Leave your car outside the walls and walk into town. Lots are

HILL TOWNS

usually free and plentiful outside city walls. For more driving tips, see "Practicalities" at the end of this book.

SLEEPING IN A HILL TOWN

For a relaxing break from big-city Italy, settle down in an *agriturismo*—a farmhouse that rents out rooms to travelers (usually for a minimum of a week in high season). These rural B&Bs—almost by definition in the middle of nowhere—provide a good home base from which to find the magic of Italy's hill towns. Many provide memorable meals from locally sourced ingredients. I've listed several good options throughout these chapters.

SIENA

Siena was medieval Florence's archrival. And while Florence ultimately won the battle for political and economic superiority, Siena still competes for the tourists. Sure, Florence has the heavyweight sights. But Siena seems to be every Italy connoisseur's favorite town.

Situated atop three hills, Siena qualifies as Italy's ultimate "hill town." Its thriving historic center, with movie-set lanes cascading every which way, offers Italy's best medieval city experience. Most people visit Siena, just 35 miles south of Florence, as a day trip, but it's best experienced at twilight. While Florence has the blockbuster museums, Siena has an easy-to-enjoy soul: Courtyards sport flower-decked wells, alleys dead-end at rooftop views, and today, even with all the tourists, a strong local spirit pervades.

For those who dream of a Fiat-free Italy, Siena is a haven. Pedestrians rule in the old center of town, as the only drivers allowed are residents and cabbies. Nurse a drink on the main square. Wander narrow streets, tether an imaginary horse to the old metal rings, be stirred by colorful flags. Take time to savor the first European city to eliminate automobile traffic from its main square (1966) and then, just to be silly, wonder what would happen if they did it in your hometown.

PLANNING YOUR TIME

On a quick trip, consider spending two nights in Siena (or three nights with a whole-day side trip into Florence). Whatever you do, be sure to enjoy a sleepy medieval evening in Siena. The next morning, you can see the city's major sights in half a day.

Orientation to Siena

Siena lounges atop a hill, stretching its three legs out from Il Campo. This pedestrianized main square is the historic meeting point of Siena's neighborhoods.

Just about everything mentioned in this chapter is within a 10-minute walk of the square. Navigate by three major landmarks (Il Campo, Duomo, and Basilica of San Domenico), following the excellent system of street-corner signs. The typical visitor sticks to the Il Campo-San Domenico axis. Stray from this main artery. Sienese streets go in anything but a straight line, so it's easy to get lost—but equally easy to get found. Explore.

Siena itself is one big sight. Its individual attractions come in two clusters: the square (Civic Museum and City Tower) and the cathedral (Baptistery and Duomo Museum, with its surprise viewpoint), plus the Pinacoteca for art lovers. Check off these sights, and then you're free to wander.

Tourist Information: The TI, just across from the cathedral, is next to worthless (daily 10:00-18:00; Piazza del Duomo 2, tel. 0577-280-551, www.terresiena.it). The bookshop next to the information desk sells detailed Siena maps.

ARRIVAL IN SIENA
By Train

Siena's small train station is at the base of the hill, on the edge of town. It has a bar/tobacco shop, an intercity bus office (daily 9:00-12:15 & 14:30-18:30), and a newsstand (which sells city bus tickets). Stow bags at Piazza Gramsci where the city bus drops you—see "By Florence-Siena Bus," later. A shopping mall with a supermarket is across the plaza facing the station. WCs are on track 1, past the pharmacy.

Getting from the Train Station to the City Center: To reach central Siena, you can hop a city bus, ride a long series of escalators, or take a taxi. For two or more traveling together, the **taxi** is your best value (€8 to the center, taxi stand just outside station, tel. 0577-49222).

By Escalator or City Bus: To reach either the bus or the escalators, head for the shopping mall across the square (far left corner as you leave). The first of a series of **escalators** climbs through the mall up into the town. From the top of the escalators, it's a 20-minute walk to the town center.

To ride the **city bus,** head to the dreary, concrete, cave-like bus

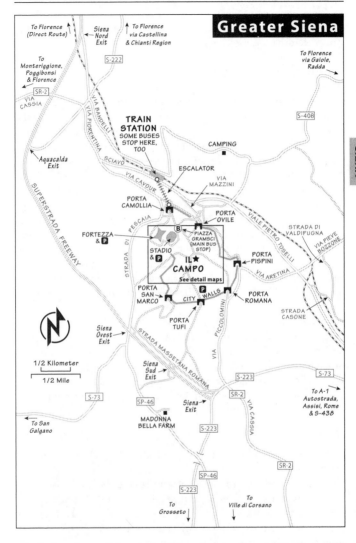

To Florence (Direct Route)
Siena Nord Exit
To Florence via Castellina & Chianti Region

Greater Siena

To Monteriggione, Poggibonsi & Florence

To Florence via Gaiole, Radda

S-222

SR-2

VIA CASSIA

S-408

VIA BANDELLI

VIA FIORENTINA

TRAIN STATION SOME BUSES STOP HERE, TOO

CAMPING

Aquacalda Exit

SCIAVO

VIA CAVOUR

ESCALATOR

VIA MAZZINI

SIENA

STRADA DI PESCAIA

PORTA CAMOLLIA

PORTA OVILE

VIALE PIETRO TOSELLI

STRADA DI VALDIFUGNA

SUPERSTRADA FREEWAY

FORTEZZA & P

Ⓑ

PIAZZA GRAMSCI (MAIN BUS STOP)

VIA PIEVE BOZZONE

STADIO & P

IL★ CAMPO
See detail maps

PORTA PISPINI

PORTA SAN MARCO

P
CITY WALLS

PORTA ROMANA

VIA ARETINA

N

PORTA TUFI

VIA PICCOLOMINI

STRADA CASONE

1/2 Kilometer
1/2 Mile

Siena Ovest Exit

STRADA MASSETANA ROMANA

Siena Sud Exit

VIA

S-223

S-73

S-73

SP-46

Siena Exit

SR-2

VIA CASSIA

To A-1 Autostrada, Assisi, Rome & S-438

To San Galgano

MADONNA BELLA FARM

S-223

SP-46

S-223

SR-2

To Grosseto

To Ville di Corsano

stop below the mall (catch the down elevator from inside the mall's first glass door on immediate right). All buses (big and small) go to Piazza Sale or Piazza Gramsci (both at the edge of the action and within a block of each other). Buy your bus ticket from the train station newsstand, and before boarding, confirm that the bus is going to the center (ask "*Centro?*").

Returning to the Train Station from the City Center: Catch a small shuttle bus directly to the station from Piazza del Sale, or take a big city bus from Piazza Gramsci. Look for *Ferrovia* or

Stazione on schedules and marked on the bus, and confirm with the driver that the bus is going to the *stazione*.

By Florence-Siena Bus

Siena is a pleasant 90-minute express bus ride from Florence (for more on buses, see "Siena Connections," later). Most buses from Florence and other cities arrive in Siena at Piazza Gramsci (or the adjacent Via Tozzi), a few blocks north of the city center. (Some buses only go to the train station; others go first to the train station, then continue to Piazza Gramsci—to confirm, ask your driver, "pee-aht-sah GRAHM-shee?") Downstairs, beneath Piazza Gramsci, you'll find ticket offices, WCs, and a place to store baggage (at the Tiemme office, daily 7:00-19:00, carry-on-size luggage no more than 33 pounds, no overnight storage). If day-tripping, confirm your departure from timetables posted at the platform where you disembark or at the ticket counters downstairs. Late-afternoon buses back to Florence can fill up, so arrive 15 minutes early. From Piazza Gramsci, it's an easy walk into the town center—just head in the opposite direction of the tree-filled park.

By Florence-Siena Taxi

Taxis make the trip from Florence to Siena—hotel to hotel—in about an hour for around €140. (Prices can be soft. Ask a couple of cabbies for their best price. Clearly agree on a price from the start.) If debating the value of this splurge, consider that a couple will spend roughly €40 for two taxi transfers and two train tickets, and the luxury of a hotel-to-hotel cab ride saves you about an hour.

By Car

Siena is not a good place to drive. Park in a big lot or garage and walk into town.

Drivers coming from the autostrada take the *Siena Ovest* exit and follow signs for *Centro*, then *Stadio* (stadium). The soccer-ball signs take you to the stadium lot (Parcheggio Stadio, pay when you leave) near Piazza Gramsci and the huge, bare-brick Basilica of San Domenico. The Fortezza lot is also nearby.

Another good option is the underground Santa Caterina garage (you'll see signs on the way to the stadium lot). From the garage, hike 150 yards uphill through a gate to an escalator on the right, which carries you up into the city. Take a left at the top onto Siena's main street.

If you're staying in the south end of town, try the Il Campo lot, near Porta Tufi.

On parking spots, blue stripes mean pay and display; white stripes mean free parking, but watch for signs that say *solo per gli residenti* (residents only). Signs showing a street cleaner and a day of the week indicate when the street is closed to cars for cleaning. You can park for free in the lot west of the Fortezza; in white-striped spots south of the Fortezza; and overnight in most city lots (20:00-8:00).

Driving within Siena's city center is restricted to local cars and is policed by automatic cameras. If you drive or park anywhere marked *Zona Traffico Limitato (ZTL)*, you'll likely have a hefty ticket waiting for you in the mail back home (if you rented a car, they know how to find you). Check with your hotel in advance if you plan to drop off your bags before parking.

HELPFUL HINTS

Combo-Tickets: Siena often experiments with different combo-tickets, but in general, only three are worth considering: the Opa Si Pass for the Duomo and its related sights; the combo-ticket covering the Civic Museum and Santa Maria della Scala; and the combo-ticket covering the Civic Museum, Santa Maria della Scala, and City Tower. See the "Sights in Siena" section, later, for ticket details.

Markets: Every Wednesday morning a market of clothes, knick-knacks, and food sprawls between the Fortezza and Piazza Gramsci along Viale Cesare Maccari and the adjacent Viale XXV Aprile. Friday mornings see an organic food market in the same location.

Bookstores: For books and magazines in English, try **Libreria Senese** (daily, Via di Città 62) and the **Feltrinelli** bookstore (closed Sun, Via Banchi di Sopra 52).

Cooking Classes: At **Fonte Giusta Cooking School,** you'll prepare a meal (pasta, pizza, meats, dessert) under the instruction of a local chef—and then eat it. Lessons last two hours and cost €50-85, depending upon what you cook (Via Camollia 78, call 0577-40506 or email info@trattoriafontegiusta.com for schedule and details, www.fontegiusta.it).

Laundry: Try **Lavanderia San Pietro** (daily 8:00-22:00, not far from the Duomo at Via San Pietro 70), and **Lavanderia Waterland** (daily 7:00-22:00, north of Il Campo near Porta San Francesco at Via dei Rossi 94).

Tours in Siena

🎧 To sightsee on your own, download my free Siena City Walk audio tour (see page 221).

LOCAL GUIDES

Federica Olla, who leads walking tours of Siena, is a smart, friendly guide with a knack for creative teaching (€55/hour, mini-

Siena at a Glance

▲▲▲**Il Campo** Best square in Italy. See page 16.

▲▲▲**Duomo** Art-packed cathedral with mosaic floors and statues by Michelangelo and Bernini. **Hours:** Mon-Sat 10:30-19:00, Sun 13:30-18:00, Nov-Feb closes daily at 17:30. See page 27.

▲▲**Civic Museum** City museum in City Hall with Sienese frescoes, the *Effects of Good and Bad Government*. **Hours:** Daily 10:00-19:00, Nov-mid-March until 18:00. See page 24.

▲▲**Duomo Museum** Siena's best museum, with cathedral art (Duccio's *Maestà*) and sweeping Tuscan views. **Hours:** Daily 10:00-19:00, Nov-Feb 10:30-17:30. See page 31.

▲**City Tower** Siena's 330-foot tower climb. **Hours:** Daily 10:00-19:00, mid-Oct-Feb until 16:00. See page 25.

▲**Pinacoteca** Fine Sienese paintings. **Hours:** Tue-Sat 8:15-19:15, Sun-Mon 9:00-13:00. See page 26.

▲**Baptistery of San Giovanni** Cave-like building with baptismal font decorated by Ghiberti and Donatello. **Hours:** Daily 10:30-19:00, Nov-Feb until 17:30. See page 33.

▲**Santa Maria della Scala** Museum with much of the original Fountain of Joy, Byzantine reliquaries, and vibrant frescoes depicting day-to-day life in a medieval hospital. **Hours:** Daily 10:00-19:00, Thu until 22:00; closes earlier mid-Oct-mid-March. See page 34.

mum 2 hours, mobile 338-133-9525, www.ollaeventi.com, info@ollaeventi.com).

Anna Piperato, fiercely proud of her adopted hometown of Siena and an expert on Palio culture, leads walking tours in Siena—including a visit to her *contrada*, Lupa—and environs (RS%—10 percent discount, €55/hour, minimum 2 hours, mobile 333-6829-336, www.sienaitalytours.com, anna@sienaitalytours.com).

GSO Guides Co-op is a group of young professionals who offer good tours covering Siena and all of Tuscany and Umbria (€158/half-day, €315/full day, RS%—10 percent discount, they don't drive but can join you in your car, www.guidesienaeoltre.com). Among them, **Stefania Fabrizi** stands out (mobile 338-640-7796, stefaniafabriziguide@gmail.com).

ON FOOT
Walking Tours from the TI
The TI offers walking tours of the old town, including the Duomo. Guides usually conduct their walks (unfortunately) in both English and Italian (€20—pay guide directly, daily April-Oct at 11:00, 2 hours, depart from TI, Piazza del Duomo 2, tel. 0577-280-551).

Siena Info Point Walking Tour
These basic one-hour town walks depart from Siena Info Point's tiny office on Il Campo and end at the Duomo (€15, daily at 11:15, 13:00, and 18:00, just show up). For €5 extra you can extend the tour to the Duomo interior (office open daily 9:30-19:30, mobile 331-742-2646, www.sienainfopoint.com, left of City Hall at Piazza del Campo 72).

Siena City Walks by Roberto
Roberto and his guides offer private three-hour Siena walking tours (€180 for up to 8 people, admissions extra) or joinable group tours (€45/person, admissions extra, minimum 4 people; book online or call 320-147-6590, www.toursbyroberto.com, toursbyroberto@gmail.com).

OTHER TOURS
Tuscany Minibus Tours by Roberto
Roberto Bechi and his guides lead off-the-beaten-path, full-day minibus tours of the countryside surrounding Siena (€100/person, up to eight passengers, pickup at hotel). The first participants to book choose one of seven itineraries—then others join until the van fills. Roberto and his team share the same passion for Sienese culture, Tuscan history, and local cuisine (see website for tour options, RS%—10 percent discount, entry fees extra; also offers multiday tours, booking mobile 320-147-6590, Roberto's mobile 328-425-5648, www.toursbyroberto.com, toursbyroberto@gmail.com). See above and below for Roberto's walking and farm tours; he also provides private van connections to Volterra—see the Volterra & San Gimignano chapter.

Wine Tasting
The Tuscan Wine School offers two foodie experiences in English. The midday food tour (12:00 Mon, Wed, and Sat) focuses on local food culture with tastings (focaccia, cured meats, truffles, gelato) at vendors around town. The afternoon wine-appreciation classes (Mon-Sat at 16:00), held in their classroom, let you taste six Tuscan wines paired with small bites (€45 for either tour, RS%—20 percent discount, Via di Stalloreggi 26, 30 yards from Hotel Duomo, tel. 0577-221-704, mobile 333-722-9716, www.tuscanwineschool.com, tuscanwineschool@gmail.com, Georgia and Milo). They also

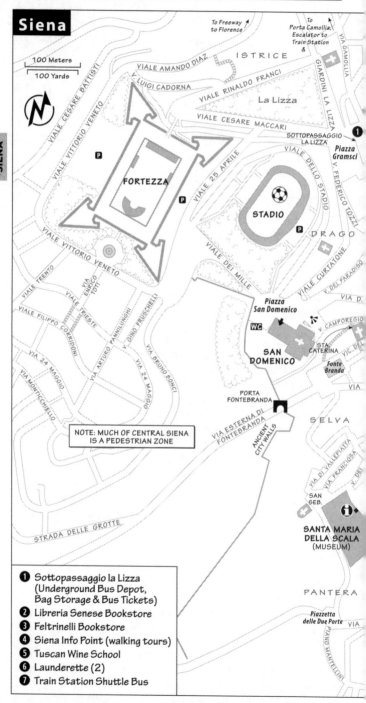

SIENA

Siena

To Freeway
to Florence

To
Porta Camollia,
Escalator to
Train Station &

100 Meters
100 Yards

VIALE AMANDO DIAZ

V. LUIGI CADORNA

VIALE RINALDO FRANCI

La Lizza

ISTRICE

VIALE CESARE BATTISTI

VIALE VITTORIO VENETO

VIALE CESARE MACCARI

SOTTOPASSAGGIO
LA LIZZA

Piazza
Gramsci

FORTEZZA

VIALE 25 APRILE

VIALE DELLO STADIO

STADIO

VIALE VITTORIO VENETO

VIALE DEI MILLE

DRAGO

VIALE TRENTO

VIA ENRICO TOTI

VIALE TRIESTE

VIALE FILIPPO CORRIDONI

VIA ARTURO PANNILUNGHI

VIA GINO FRUSCHELLI

VIA BRUNO BONCI

VIALE CURTATONE

V. DEL PARADISO

VIA D.

Piazza
San Domenico

WC

SAN
DOMENICO

V. CAMPOREGIO

STA.
CATERINA

Fonte
Branda

VIA 24 MAGGIO

VIA MONTICCHIELLO

VIA 24 MAGGIO

PORTA
FONTEBRANDA

VIA ESTERNA DI
FONTEBRANDA

SELVA

NOTE: MUCH OF CENTRAL SIENA
IS A PEDESTRIAN ZONE

ANCIENT
CITY WALLS

SAN
SEB.

VIA DI VALEPIATTA

VIA FRANCIOSA

V. DEL

STRADA DELLE GROTTE

SANTA MARIA
DELLA SCALA
(MUSEUM)

PANTERA

Piazzetta
delle Due Porte

VIA

PIANO MANTELLINI

1 Sottopassaggio la Lizza
   (Underground Bus Depot,
   Bag Storage & Bus Tickets)
2 Libreria Senese Bookstore
3 Feltrinelli Bookstore
4 Siena Info Point (walking tours)
5 Tuscan Wine School
6 Launderette (2)
7 Train Station Shuttle Bus

SIENA

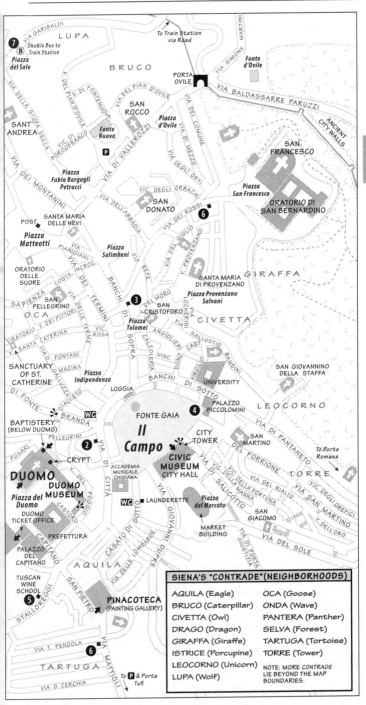

SIENA'S "CONTRADE" (NEIGHBORHOODS)

AQUILA (Eagle)	OCA (Goose)
BRUCO (Caterpillar)	ONDA (Wave)
CIVETTA (Owl)	PANTERA (Panther)
DRAGO (Dragon)	SELVA (Forest)
GIRAFFA (Giraffe)	TARTUGA (Tortoise)
ISTRICE (Porcupine)	TORRE (Tower)
LEOCORNO (Unicorn)	NOTE: MORE *CONTRADE*
LUPA (Wolf)	LIE BEYOND THE MAP BOUNDARIES.

offer countryside food- and wine-oriented tours, convenient for those without their own wheels (www.siena-wine-tour.com).

Farm Visit

Madonna Bella, a farm co-owned by local guide Roberto Bechi, sits just a few minutes outside Siena. Paola welcomes visitors to stop in, enjoy the views, visit the farm, take part in wine and olive-oil tastings, and learn how olive oil and pasta are made. It's best to book ahead if you want to enjoy a food/wine pairing that anyone would consider an abundant lunch (Strada del Tesoro 25—just outside Siena on road SP-46, mobile 393-858-2981, www.madonnabella.com).

SIENA

Siena City Walk

This short self-guided walk laces together Siena's most important sights. If you do the walk without entering the sights, it works great at night when the city is peaceful.

∩ This walk is also available as a free Rick Steves audio tour.
• *Start in the center of the main square, Il Campo, standing just below the fountain.*

❶ Il Campo

This square is the heart of Siena, both geographically and metaphorically—and it's worth ▲▲▲. First laid out in the 12th century, today Il Campo (officially the Piazza del Campo) is the only town square I've seen where people stretch out as if at the beach. At the flat end of its clamshell shape is City Hall, where you can tour the Civic Museum and climb the City Tower. From there the square fans out as if to create an amphitheater. All eyes are on Il Campo twice each summer, when it hosts the famous Palio horse races (see sidebar on page 20).

Originally, this area was just a field *(campo)* outside the city walls (which encircled the cathedral). Bits of those original walls,

which curved against today's square, can be seen above the pharmacy (the black-and-white stones, third story up, to the right as you face City Hall). In the 1200s, with the advent of the Sienese republic, the city expanded. Il Campo became its marketplace and the historic junction of Siena's various com-

peting *contrade* (neighborhood districts). The square and its buildings are the color of the soil upon which they stand—a color known to artists and Crayola users as "burnt sienna."

City Hall (Palazzo Pubblico), with its looming tower, dominates the square. In medieval Siena, this was the center of the city, and the whole focus of Il Campo still flows down to it.

The **City Tower** was built around 1340. At 330 feet, it's one of Italy's tallest secular towers. Medieval Siena was a proud republic, and this tower stands like an exclamation point—an architectural declaration of independence from papacy and empire. The tower's Italian nickname, Torre del Mangia, comes from a hedonistic bell-ringer who consumed his earnings like a glutton consumes food. (His chewed-up statue is just inside City Hall's courtyard, to the left as you enter.)

The open **chapel** located at the base of the tower was built as thanks to God for ending the Black Death of 1348 (after it killed more than a third of the population). These days, the chapel is where Palio contestants are blessed (and where EMTs stand by during the race).

You can visit the Civic Museum inside City Hall and climb the tower (see page 24).

• *Now turn around and take a closer look at the fountain in the top center of the square.*

❷ Fountain of Joy (Fonte Gaia)

This fountain—a copy of an early-15th-century work by Jacopo della Quercia—marks the square's high point. The joy is all about

how the Sienese republic blessed its people with water. Find Lady Justice with her scales and sword (right of center), overseeing the free distribution of water to all. The Fountain of Joy still reminds locals that life in Siena is good. The relief panel on the left shows God creating Adam by helping him to his feet. It's said that this reclining Adam (carved a century before Michelangelo's day) influenced Michelangelo when he painted his Sistine Chapel ceiling. The fountain's original statuary is exhibited at Santa Maria della Scala (see page 34).

• *Leave Il Campo uphill on the widest ramp. With your back to the tower, it's at 10 o'clock. After a few steps you reach Via di Città. Turn left and walk 100 yards uphill toward the imposing white palace with brick crenellations on top.*

Halfway to the palace, at the first corner, notice small plaques on the first level of the building facades—these mark the neighborhood, or **contrada**. If the flags are flying, they reinforce the point.

SIENA

Siena Walk

Piazza Gramsci

To Porta Camollia & Escalator to Train Station

Piazza Matteotti

Piazza Fabio Bargagli Petrucci

To Porta Ovile & Train Station via Road

VIA DEI MONTANINI

VIA DI VALLEROZZI

VIC. DEGLI ORBACHI

SANTA MARIA DELLE NEVI

SAN DONATO

VIA DELL'ABBADIA

VIA DEL GIGLIO

VIA DEI ROSSI

POST

DRAGO

VIALE CURTATONE

V. FED.OZZI

V. DEL PARADISO

ORATORIO DELLE SUORE

V. PIANIGIANI

AGRARIO GROCERY

WALK ENDS

11 Piazza Salimbeni

VIA PROVENZANO

VIA DEL GIGLIO

SANTA MARIA DI PROVENZANO

Piazza Provenzano Salvani

VIA D. SAPIENZA

SAN PELLEGRINO

COSTA DELL'INCROC.

VIA DEL TERMINI

BANCHI DI SOPRA

V. DEL MORO

SAN CRISTOFORO

Piazza Tolomei

LUCHERINI

CIVETTA

V. D. VERGINI

To San Domenico

V. CAMPOREGIO

OCA

SANTA CATERINA

V. DEL TIRATORIO

VIC. DEL

VIA DEI PITTORI

VIA SANTA CATERINA

FONTANI

VIC. ROSA

Piazza Indipendenza

8

9

10

CALZOLERIA

ANGIOLIERI

VISC.

VIA SAL BANDINI

VIRGILIO

UNIVERSITY

PALAZZO PICCOLOMINI

Fonte Branda

SANCTUARY OF ST. CATHERINE

VIA D. GALLUZZA

MACINA

VIA DI FONTEBRANDA

VIA D'ACCETO

LOGGIA

BANCHI DI SOTTO

SELVA

BAPTISTERY (BELOW DUOMO)

PELLEGRINI

WC

RAMP

2

WALK BEGINS 👣

1

CITY TOWER

VIA DEL SALICOTTO

V. FRANCIOSA

V. DEI FUSARI

7

CRYPT

DUOMO

V. DEL CAPITANO

DUOMO MUSEUM

6

Il Campo

CIVIC MUSEUM

CITY HALL

5

Piazza del Duomo

DUOMO TICKET OFFICE

CASTORO

VIA DI POGGIO

3

PALAZZO CHIGI-SARACINI

VIA GIOVANNI DUPRE

Piazza del Mercato

SANTA MARIA DELLA SCALA (MUSEUM)

PREFETTURA

MUSEUM ENTRANCE

CASATO DI SOTTO

WC

MARKET BUILDING

PALAZZO DEL CAPITANO

4

AQUILA

VIA DELLE LOMBARDE

PANTERA

VIA STALLOREGGI

SAN PIETRO

PINACOTECA (PAINTING GALLERY)

ONDA

🧭 N

100 Meters

100 Yards

1 Il Campo	**7** Supporting an Oversized Church
2 Fountain of Joy	**8** Piazza Indipendenza
3 Chigi-Saracini Palace	**9** Loggia della Mercanzia
4 Quattro Cantoni	**10** Banchi di Sopra & Banchi di Sotto
5 Piazza del Duomo & Duomo	**11** Piazza Salimbeni
6 The Unfinished Church	

You are stepping from the *contrada* of the Forest (Selva) into the *contrada* of the Eagle (Aquila). Notice also the once mighty and foreboding medieval **tower house.** Towers once soared all around town, but they're now truncated and no longer add to the skyline—look for their bases as you walk the city.

• *On the left, you reach the big curving facade of the...*

❸ Chigi-Saracini Palace (Palazzo Chigi-Saracini)

This old fortified noble palace is today home to a prestigious music academy, the Accademia Musicale Chigiana. If open, step into the courtyard with its photogenic well (powerful medieval families enjoyed direct connections to the city aqueduct). The walls of the loggia are decorated with the busts of Chigi-Saracini patriarchs, and the vaults are painted in the "grotesque" style popular during the Renaissance. What look like pigeonholes in the other walls are actually for scaffolding, for both construction and ongoing maintenance. The palace hosts a music festival each July and August with popular concerts almost nightly, international talent, and affordable tickets (box office just off courtyard). They offer €7 one-hour tours of the palace's library, art, and musical instruments (Mon-Fri at 11:30 plus Thu-Fri at 16:00, closed Sun, call to request English tour; Via di Città 89, tel. 0577-22091, www.chigiana.it).

• *Walk uphill to the next major intersection...*

❹ Quattro Cantoni

The intersection known as Quattro Cantoni (Four Corners) offers a delightful perch from which to study the city. The modern column (from 1996) with a Carrara marble she-wolf marks one of the three original hills upon which the city was built. You are still in the Eagle district (see the fountain and the corner plaque)—but beware. Just one block up the street, a ready-to-pounce panther—from the rival neighboring district—awaits.

Only the very rich could afford stone residences. The fancy facades here hide their economical brick construction behind a stucco veneer. The stone tower on this corner had only one door—30 feet above street level and reached by ladder, which could be pulled up as necessary. Within a few doors, you'll find a classy bar, an elegant grocery store, and a *gelateria*.

Take a little side trip, venturing up Via di San Pietro. Interesting stops include the window with Palio video clips playing (at #1), Simon and Paula's art shop with delightful Palio and *contrada* knickknacks (#5), a weaver's shop (#7), the recommended La Vecchia Latteria *gelateria* (#10), an art gallery (#11), and four enticing little osterias. At the end of the block you'll reach the best art museum in town, the **Pinacoteca** (for a self-guided tour of its interior, see page 26).

SIENA

Siena's *Contrade* and the Palio

Siena's 17 historic neighborhoods, or *contrade*—each with a parish church, well or fountain, and square—still play an active role in the life of the city. Each is represented by a mascot (porcupine, unicorn, wolf, etc.) and unique colors worn proudly by residents.

Contrada pride is evident year-round in Siena's parades and colorful banners, lamps, and wall plaques. If you hear the thunder of distant drumming, run to it for some medieval action—there's a good chance it'll feature flag throwers. Buy a scarf in *contrada* colors, and join in the merriment of these lively neighborhood festivals.

Contrada rivalries are most visible twice a year—on July 2 and August 16—during the city's world-famous horse race, the **Palio di Siena.** Ten of the 17 neighborhoods compete (chosen by rotation and lot), hurling themselves with medieval abandon into several days of trial races and traditional revelry. Jockeys—usually from out of town—are considered hired guns, no better than paid mercenaries. Bets are placed on which *contrada* will win...and lose. Despite the shady behind-the-scenes dealing, on the big day the horses are taken into their *contrada*'s church to be blessed. ("Go and return victorious," says the priest.) It's considered a sign of luck if a horse leaves droppings in the church.

On the evening of the race, Il Campo is stuffed to the brim with locals and tourists. Dirt is brought in and packed down to create the track's surface, while mattresses pad the walls of surrounding buildings. The most treacherous spots are the sharp

• *Back at the Four Corners, head up Via del Capitano, passing another massive Chigi family palace (at #1). Up next, at the end of the street, is the...*

❺ Piazza del Duomo and the Duomo

The pair of she-wolves atop columns flanking the cathedral's facade says it all: The church was built and paid for not by the pope but by the people and the republic of Siena.

This 13th-century Gothic cathedral, with its striped bell tower—Siena's ultimate tribute to the Virgin Mary—is heaped with statues, plastered with frescoes, and paved with art.

The current structure dates back to 1215, with the major decoration done during Siena's heyday (1250-1350). The lower story, by Giovanni Pisano (who worked from 1284 to 1297), features remnants of the fading Romanesque style (round arches over the doors), corners, where many a rider has bitten the dust.

Picture the scene: Ten snorting horses and their nervous riders line up near the pharmacy (on the west side of the square) to await the starting signal. Then they race like crazy while spectators wave the scarves of their neighborhoods.

Every possible vantage point and perch is packed with people straining to see the action. One lap around the course is about a quarter of a mile; three laps make a full circuit. In this no-holds-barred race—which lasts just over a minute—a horse can win even without its rider (jockeys ride precariously without saddles and often fall off the horses' sweaty backs).

When the winner crosses the line, 1/17th of Siena—the prevailing neighborhood—goes berserk. Winners receive a *palio* (banner), typically painted by a local artist and always featuring the Virgin Mary (the race is dedicated to her). But the true prizes are proving that your *contrada* is *numero uno,* and mocking your losing rivals.

All over town, sketches and posters depict the Palio. This is not some folkloric event—it's a real medieval moment. If you're packed onto the square with 15,000 people, all hungry for victory, you may not see much, but you'll feel it. Bleacher and balcony seats are expensive, but it's free to join the masses in the square. Go with an empty bladder as there are no WCs, and be prepared to surrender any sense of personal space.

While the actual Palio packs the city, you can more easily see the horse-race trials—called *prove*—on any of the three days before the main event (usually at 9:00 and after 19:00, bleacher seats may be available). Good sources for more information include IlPalio.org and ComitatoAmiciDelPalio.it.

topped with the pointed arches of the new Gothic style that was seeping in from France. The upper half, in full-blown frilly Gothic, was designed and built a century later.

The six-story bell tower (c. 1315) looks even taller, thanks to an opti-

cal illusion: The white marble stripes get narrower toward the top, making the upper part seem farther away.

The interior is a Renaissance riot of striped columns, remarkably intricate inlaid-marble floors, a Michelangelo statue, evocative Bernini sculptures, and the amazing Piccolomini Library. (If you want to enter now, you'll need a ticket from the office in the piazza corner, to the right; for a self-guided tour of the interior, see page 28.)

Facing the cathedral is Santa Maria della Scala, a huge building that housed pilgrims and, until the 1990s, was used as a hospital. Its labyrinthine 12th-century cellars—carved from sandstone and finished with brick—go down several floors and, during medieval times, stored supplies for the hospital upstairs. Today, the exhibit-filled hospital and cellars can be a welcome refuge from the hot streets (for a self-guided tour, see page 34).

• *Walk along the right side of the church toward its rear end. This is part of what was once intended to be an extension of the Duomo.*

❻ The Unfinished Church

Grand as Siena's cathedral is, it's actually the rump of a failed vision. After rival republic Florence began its grand cathedral (1296), proud Siena planned to build an even bigger one, the biggest in all Christendom.

To the right, find the unfinished wall with see-through windows (circa 1330). From here you can envision the audacity of this vision.

Picture it: Today's cathedral would have been just a transept. Worshippers would have entered the church from the far end of the piazza through the unfinished wall. (Look way up at the highest part of the wall. That viewpoint is accessible from inside the Duomo Museum.) Some of the nave's green-and-white-striped columns were built, but the space between them is now partially filled in with brick. White stones in the pavement mark where a row of pillars would have been.

But this grand vision underestimated the complexity of constructing such a building without enough land. That, coupled with the devastating effects of the 1348 plague, killed the city's ability and will to finish the project. Many Sienese saw the Black Death as a sign from God, punishing them for their pride. They canceled their plans and humbly faded into the background of Tuscan history.

• *Take note of the Duomo Museum, housing the church's art (see page 31). To continue our walk, exit the piazza through the doorway in a wall, heading to the back end of the church. After a few steps, pause at the top of the marble stairs leading down.*

❼ Supporting an Oversized Church

From here you can see how the church sticks out, high above the lower street level. Because there wasn't enough flat ground, builders propped up the overhanging edge with the church's subterranean features—the Crypt and Baptistery. (Both the Baptistery and the Crypt are worth entering; see page 33.)

• *Descend the stairs, nicknamed "The Steps of St. Catherine," as she would have climbed them each day on her walk from home to the hospital where she worked (Santa Maria della Scala). Below the Baptistery, jog right, then left, through a tunnel down Via di Diacceto. Just ahead, pause on the bridge (originally a drawbridge) to enjoy a beautiful view (to the left) of the towering brick Dominican church in the distance. Then continue straight up the lane until you reach the next big square.*

SIENA

❽ Piazza Indipendenza

This square celebrates the creation of a unified Italy (1860) with a 19th-century loggia sporting busts of the first two Italian kings. Stacking history on history, the neo-Renaissance loggia is backed by a Gothic palace and an older medieval tower.

• *Head right downhill one block (on Via delle Terme), back to the grand Via di Città, and take a few steps to the left to see another, fancier loggia.*

❾ Loggia della Mercanzia

This Gothic-Renaissance loggia was built about 1420 as a kind of headquarters for the union of merchants. Siena's nobility purchased the loggia, and eventually it be-came the clubhouse of the local elites. To this day, it's a private, ritzy, and notoriously out-of-step-with-the-times men's club. The "Gli Uniti" above the door is a "let's stick together" declaration.

• *Next to the loggia, steep steps lead down to Il Campo, but we'll go left and uphill on Via Banchi di Sopra. Pause at the intersection of...*

❿ Banchi di Sopra and Banchi di Sotto

These main drags are named "upper row of banks" and "lower row of banks." They were once lined with market tables *(banchi)*, and vendors paid rent to the city for a table's position along the street. If the owner of a *banco* neglected to pay up, thugs came along and literally broke *(rotto)* his table. It is from this practice—*banco rotto*, broken table—that we get the English word "bankrupt."

In medieval times, these streets were part of the Via Francigena, the main thoroughfare (busy with pilgrims, merchants, and crusaders) linking Rome with northern Europe. Today, strollers—out each evening for their *passeggiata*—fill Via Banchi di Sopra. Join the crowd, strolling past Siena's finest shops.

A block or so farther up the street, Piazza Tolomei faces the imposing Tolomei family palace (now an imposing bank). This is a center for the Owl *contrada*. The column in the square, topped by the she-wolf, marks another of Siena's three hills.

• *Continue on Banchi di Sopra to Piazza Salimbeni; this gets my vote for Siena's finest stretch of palaces.*

❶ Piazza Salimbeni

The next square, Piazza Salimbeni, is dominated by Monte dei Paschi, the head office of a bank founded in 1472. It's amazing to think this bank has been in business on this square for over 500 years. Originally Monte dei Paschi was a kind of community bank for common people. The statue in the center of the square honors Sallustio Antonio Bandini, a reformer who helped develop a system that let people secure firm title to their land.

Directly across from Piazza Salimbeni, the steep little lane called Costa dell'Incrociata leads straight (down and then up) to the Basilica of San Domenico (it's worth the hike; see page 35). Also nearby (behind the cute green newsstand) is the most elegant grocery store in town, Consorzio Agrario di Siena (see page 45).

• *With this walk under your belt, you've got the lay of the land. The city is ready for further exploration—the sights associated with City Hall and the Duomo are all just a few minutes away. Enjoy delving deeper into Siena.*

Sights in Siena

IL CAMPO AND NEARBY

The gorgeous red-brick square known as Il Campo—worth ▲▲▲—is the best in Italy (for more on the square itself, see page 16). It's also home to City Hall (with the Civic Museum and City Tower) and other sights.

▲▲City Hall (Palazzo Pubblico) and Civic Museum (Museo Civico)

Siena's fine Gothic City Hall is still the seat of city government. With its proud tower, this building symbolizes a republic independent from the pope and the Holy Roman Emperor. It also represents a rising secular society, one that appeared first in Tuscany in late medieval times, then spread throughout Europe as humanism took hold during the Renaissance.

City Hall has a fine and manageable museum on its top floor. You'll see the large assembly hall where democracy was forged, adorned with some of Siena's most historic frescoes. There's memorabilia from the birth of the nation of Italy.

The highlight is a room of medieval-era frescoes depicting fascinating examples of governance—good and bad. Strolling the halls, you'll get a glimpse into the city-as-utopia, when this proud town understandably considered itself the vanguard of Western civilization.

Cost and Hours: Museum-€10, €14 combo-ticket with Santa Maria della Scala, €15 combo-ticket with City Tower, €20 combo-ticket includes City Tower and Santa Maria della Scala, ticket office is straight ahead as you enter City Hall courtyard; open daily 10:00-19:00, Nov-mid-March until 18:00, last entry 45 minutes before closing; videoguide-€5 in bookshop, tel. 0577-292-232, www.comune.siena.it.

Visiting the Museum: Start in the Sala del Risorgimento, with dramatic scenes of the 19th-century unification of Italy. Make your way to the chapel, where the city's governors and bureaucrats prayed, then enter the Sala del Mappamondo.

On one end of the room is the beautiful *Maestà* (*Enthroned Virgin*, 1315), by Siena's great Simone Martini (c. 1280-1344). This is a groundbreaking work. It's Siena's first fresco showing a Madonna not in a faraway, gold-leaf heaven, but under the blue sky of a real space that we inhabit.

On the opposite end of the room is the famous *Equestrian Portrait of Guidoriccio da Fogliano* (1330; traditionally attributed to Simone Martini), which depicts a mercenary commander surveying the siege fort, with the catapult that helped Siena win.

Next is the Sala della Pace, where the Council of Nine, who ruled Siena from 1287 to 1355, met. To remind them of their responsibility to rule wisely, they were surrounded by a fascinating fresco series showing the *Effects of Good and Bad Government,* by Ambrogio Lorenzetti (1337-1340).

Notice the better-preserved fresco (on the long wall to the right) depicting the beneficial effects of good government. Compare the whistle-while-you-work happiness against the crime, devastation, and societal mayhem of a community ruled by politicians with more typical values.

You can cap your visit by climbing the **stairs to a grand view** of the city and its surroundings. (For a less impressive view, you could skip the stairs and simply peek behind the curtains in the Sala della Pace.)

▲City Tower (Torre del Mangia)

The tower's nearly 400 steps get pretty skinny at the top, but the reward is one of Italy's best views. For more on the tower, see page 17.

Cost and Hours: €10, €15 combo-ticket with Civic Mu-

seum, €20 combo-ticket with
Civic Museum and Santa Maria
della Scala, daily 10:00-19:00,
mid-Oct-Feb until 16:00, last
entry 45 minutes before closing,
closed in rain, free and manda-
tory bag check.

Crowd Alert: Admission
is limited to 50 people at a time.
Wait at the bottom of the stairs
for the green *Avanti* light. Try to avoid midday crowds (up to an
hour wait at peak times).

▲Pinacoteca

If you're into medieval art, you'll likely find this quiet, uncrowded,
colorful museum delightful. The museum (officially the Pinacoteca
Nazionale di Siena) walks you through Siena's art chronologically,
from the 12th through the 16th century, when a revolution in realism was percolating in Tuscany.

Cost and Hours: €4, Tue-Sat 8:15-19:15, Sun-Mon 9:00-
13:00. From Il Campo, walk out Via di Città and go left on Via
San Pietro to #29; tel. 0577-281-161, www.pinacotecanazionale.
siena.it.

Visiting the Museum: In general, the collection lets you follow the evolution of painting styles from Byzantine to Gothic, then
to International Gothic, and finally to Renaissance.

Long after Florentine art went realistic, the Sienese embraced
a timeless, otherworldly style glittering with lots of gold. But
Sienese art features more than just paintings. In this city of proud
craftsmen, the gilding and carpentry of the frames almost compete
with the actual paintings. The exquisite attention to detail gives
a glimpse into the wealth of the 13th and 14th centuries, Siena's
Golden Age. The woven silk and gold clothing you'll see was worn
by the very people who once walked these halls, when this was a
private mansion (appreciate the colonnaded courtyard).

The core of the collection is on the second floor, in Rooms
1-19. Works by Duccio di Buoninsegna (who created the *Maestà*
in the Duomo Museum) feature groundbreaking innovations that
are subtle: less gold-leaf background, fewer gold creases in robes,
translucent garments, inlaid-marble thrones, and a more human
Mary and Jesus. Notice that the Madonna-and-Bambino pose is
eerily identical in each version.

Works by Duccio's one-time assistant, Simone Martini, including his *St. Augustine of Siena*, show the saint's life in realistic
Sienese streets, buildings, and landscapes. In each panel, the saint
pops out at the oddest (difficult to draw) angles to save the day.

(Simone Martini also did the *Maestà* and possibly the Guidoriccio frescoes in the Civic Museum.)

Also look for religious works by the hometown Lorenzetti brothers (Ambrogio is best known for the secular masterpiece, the *Effects of Good and Bad Government*, in the Civic Museum). Two famous small wooden panels, *Città sul Mare (City by the Sea)* and *Castello in Riva al Lago (Castle on the Lakeshore)*, feature a strange, medieval-landscape Cubism. Notice the weird, melancholy light that captures the sense of the Dark Ages.

Several colorful rooms on the first floor are dedicated to Domenico Beccafumi (1486-1551), who designed many of the Duomo's inlaid pavement panels (including *Slaughter of the Innocents*). With strong bodies, twisting poses, and dramatic gestures, Beccafumi's works epitomize the Mannerist style.

DUOMO AND RELATED SIGHTS

Siena's monumental cathedral complex encompasses the Duomo, Duomo Museum (and its panoramic terrace), Baptistery, and Crypt. While it's possible to enter the Duomo itself with an individual ticket, admission to the related sights is possible only with a combo-ticket, the **Opa Si Pass** (valid for 72 hours, includes Duomo admission). The price varies with the time of year: March-mid-Aug-€13, mid-Aug-Oct-€15, Nov-Feb-€8 (admission to the Duomo itself is free in winter).

The **Porta del Cielo** (Heaven's Gate) Pass covers everything in the Opa Si Pass but adds an escorted visit up into the cathedral dome and onto the cathedral's rooftop (€20, available March-Dec). To include Santa Maria della Scala as well, buy the **Acropoli Pass** (€13-20, depending on time of year).

Buying Passes and Tickets: Individual Duomo tickets and the Opa Si Pass can be bought online (www.operaduomo.siena.it) or from the on-site ticket office (facing the cathedral entry, the ticket office, with a fine bookstore, is behind you to the right). The Porta del Cielo and Acropoli passes are sold at the ticket office (not available online), but because of space limitations for the cathedral roof visit, it's smart to reserve these in advance by phone (tel. 0577-286-300) or email (opasiena@operalaboratori.com).

Note that Santa Maria della Scala, directly opposite the Duomo, has its own ticketing scheme (see details later) but shares its ticket office with that for the Duomo (in the corner of Piazza del Duomo).

▲▲▲Duomo (Duomo di Siena)

Siena's 13th-century cathedral and striped bell tower are one of the most illustrious examples of Romanesque-Gothic style in Italy. This ornate but surprisingly secular shrine to the Virgin Mary is

slathered with colorful art inside and out, from inlaid-marble
floors to stained-glass windows.
The cathedral's interior show-
cases the work of the greatest
sculptors of successive eras—Pisano, Donatello, Michelangelo,
and Bernini—and the Piccolomini Library features a series of
15th-century frescoes chroni-
cling the adventures of Siena's
philanderer-turned-pope, Aeneas Piccolomini.

Cost: €6, €9 mid-Aug-Oct and on Sundays when marble
floors are on display, includes cathedral and Piccolomini Library,
covered by Duomo combo-ticket; admission to the Duomo is free
Nov-Feb.

Hours: Mon-Sat 10:30-19:00, Sun 13:30-18:00, Nov-Feb
closes daily at 17:30. Tel. 0577-286-300, www.operaduomo.siena.
it.

Avoiding Lines: If there's a long line to get into the cathedral
(or even to buy a ticket for it), use ticket office desk 1 or 2 to pay
€1 extra for a reserved ticket that lets you use the short "fast entry"
line at the church. Another good alternative is to purchase tickets
online in advance.

Tours: The commentary on the available **videoguide** (€6
church only, €8 for all combo-ticket sights) is informative but dry;
I'd stick with this chapter.

Going to Church: Worshippers attending Mass can enter the
church free; use the entrance to the right of the main one (Mon-Sat
at 9:00 and 10:00, Sun at 8:00, 11:00, 12:15, and 18:30, no Mass
mid-Aug-Oct).

Dress Code: Modest dress is required, but stylish paper pon-
chos are provided for the inappropriately clothed.

Cathedral Roof Visit: To make a 30-minute escorted (but not
guided) visit to the dome's cupola and roof, buy the Porto del Cielo
(Heaven's Gate) combo-ticket (reservation recommended; see
"Buying Passes and Tickets," earlier; escorted visits go each half-
hour, March-Dec Mon-Sat from 10:30-19:00, Sun 13:30-17:30—
but from 9:30 on some Sun).

Θ Self-Guided Tour: Grab a spot on a stone bench opposite the entry to take in this architectural festival of green, white,
pink, and gold. The Duomo sits atop Siena's highest point, with
one of the most extravagant facades in all of Europe. Like a medieval altarpiece, the facade is divided into sections, each frame filled
with patriarchs and prophets, studded with roaring gargoyles, and

topped with prickly pinnacles (for more about the facade, see page 20).

• *Step inside, putting yourself in the mindset of a pilgrim as you take in this trove of religious art.*

Nave: The heads of 171 popes—who reigned from the time of St. Peter to the 12th century—peer down from above, looking over the fine inlaid art on the floor. With a forest of striped columns, a coffered dome, a large stained-glass window at the far end (it's a copy—the original is viewable up close in the Duomo Museum), and an art gallery's worth of early Renaissance art, this is one busy interior. If you look closely at the popes, you'll see the same four faces repeated over and over.

For almost two centuries (1373-1547), 40 artists paved the marble floor with scenes from the Old Testament, allegories, and intricate patterns. The series starts near the entrance with historical allegories; the larger, more elaborate scenes surrounding the altar are mostly stories from the Old Testament. Many of the floor panels are roped off and covered to prevent further wear and tear. But from mid-August through October, the cathedral uncovers them and holds Mass in another church. The second pavement panel from the entrance depicts Siena as a she-wolf. The proud city of Siena is the center of the Italian universe, orbited by such lesser lights as Roma, Florentia (Florence), and Pisa.

The fourth pavement panel from the entrance is the Fortune Panel, with Lady Luck (lower right) arriving on earth, where she teeters back and forth on a ball and a tipsy boat. The lesson? Fortune is an unstable foundation for life. On the right wall hangs a dim **painting of St. Catherine** (fourth from entrance). Siena's homegrown saint had a vision in which she mystically married Christ.

• *On the opposite wall is a marble altarpiece decorated with statues.*

Piccolomini Altar: This was commissioned by the Sienese-born Pope Pius III (born Francesco Piccolomini) but was never used. The altar is most interesting for its statues: one by Michelangelo and three by his students. Michelangelo was originally contracted to do 15 statues, but another sculptor had started the marble blocks, and Michelangelo's heart was never in the project. He personally finished the figure of St. Paul (lower right, clearly more interesting than the bland, bored saints above him).

• *Now grab a seat under the dome. The dome sits on a 12-sided base, but its "coffered" ceiling is a painted illusion.*

Duccio's Stained-Glass Rose Window: At the far end of the church, high up above the altar, is the rose window. Made in 1288 and dedicated to the Virgin Mary, it's a kaleidoscope of colors and intricate designs. This is a copy of the original window (described on page 32).

• *Closer to you is a stone podium sitting atop columns. This is...*

Pisano's Pulpit: The octagonal Carrara marble pulpit (1268) rests on the backs of lions, symbols of Christianity triumphant. Like the lions, the Church eats its catch (devouring paganism) and nurses its cubs. The seven relief panels tell the life of Christ in rich detail. The pulpit is the work of Nicola Pisano (c. 1220-1278), the "Giotto of sculpture," whose revival of classical forms (columns, sarcophagus-like relief panels) signaled the coming Renaissance. His son Giovanni (c. 1240-1319) carved many of the panels, mixing his dad's classicism and realism with the decorative detail and curvy lines of French Gothic.

• *A few steps to the left of the pulpit (in the left transept), find a panel in the floor, the...*

Slaughter of the Innocents Pavement Panel: Herod (left), sitting enthroned amid Renaissance arches, orders the massacre of all babies to prevent the coming of the promised Messiah. It's a chaotic scene of angry soldiers, grieving mothers, and dead babies, reminding locals that a republic ruled by a tyrant will always experience misery.

• *Nearby in the left transept is a small chapel with a well-known statue.*

Donatello's St. John the Baptist: The rugged saint in his famous rags stands in a quiet chapel. Donatello, the aging Florentine sculptor whose style was now considered passé in Florence, came here to build bronze doors for the church (similar to Ghiberti's in Florence). Donatello didn't complete the door project, but he did finish this bronze statue (1457).

• *Cross the church. Directly opposite find the Chigi Chapel (with its ironwork entrance), also known as the...*

Chapel of the *Madonna del Voto*: To understand why Bernini is considered the greatest Baroque sculptor, step into this sumptuous chapel (designed in the early 1660s for Fabio Chigi, a.k.a. Pope Alexander VII). Move up to the altar and look back at the **two Bernini statues:** Mary Magdalene in a state of spiritual ecstasy and St. Jerome playing the crucifix like a violinist lost in heavenly music.

The painting over the altar is the ***Madonna del Voto,*** a Madonna and Child adorned with a real crown of gold and jewels (painted by a Sienese master in the mid-13th century). In typical medieval fashion, the scene is set in the golden light of heaven. Mary has the almond eyes, long fingers, and golden folds in her robe that are found in orthodox icons of the time. Still, this Mary tilts her head and looks out sympathetically, ready to listen to the prayers of the faithful. This is the Mary to whom the Palio is dedicated, dear to the hearts of the Sienese.

In thanks, they give **offerings** of silver hearts and medallions, many of which now hang on the walls to the right and left as you exit the chapel.

• *Cross back to the other side of the church. Next to the altar, look for the door to the...*

Piccolomini Library: Brilliantly frescoed, the library captures the exuberant, optimistic spirit of the 1400s, when humanism and the Renaissance were born. The never-restored frescoes look nearly as vivid now as the day they were finished 550 years ago. The painter Pinturicchio (c. 1454-1513) was hired to celebrate the life of one of Siena's hometown boys—a man many call "the first humanist," Aeneas Piccolomini (1405-1464), who became Pope Pius II. Each of the 10 scenes is framed with an arch, as if Pinturicchio were opening a window onto the spacious 3-D world we inhabit.

The library also contains intricately decorated, illuminated music scores and a statue (a Roman copy of a Greek original) of the Three Graces, who almost seem to dance to the beat. The oddly huge sheepskin sheets of music are from the days before individual hymnals—they had to be big so that many singers could read the music from a distance. Appreciate the fine painted decorations on the music—the gold-leaf highlights, the blue tones from expensive ultramarine (made from precious lapis lazuli), and the miniature figures. All of this exquisite detail was lovingly crafted by Benedictine monks for the glory of God.

• *Our tour is finished. But to truly appreciate the grandeur of the Duomo, exit the church and make a U-turn to the left, walking alongside the church to Piazza Jacopo della Quercia. Had the massive church Siena envisioned been built, the nave would be where the piazza is today. Look through the unfinished entrance facade, note blue sky where the stained-glass windows would have been, and ponder the struggles, triumphs, and failures of the human spirit. (For more on the unfinished church, see page 22.)*

▲▲Duomo Museum
(Museo dell'Opera e Panorama)

Siena's most enjoyable museum, housing the cathedral's art, is located in a corner of the Duomo's grand but unfinished extension (to the right as you face the main facade). Stand eye-to-eye with the saints and angels who once languished, unknown, in the church's upper reaches (where copies are found today).

Cost and Hours: Covered by Duomo combo-ticket, daily 10:00-19:00, Nov-Feb 10:30-17:30, videoguide-€4 (€6/2 people) but you'll do fine with just the commentary in this listing, tel. 0577-286-300, www.operaduomo.siena.it.

SIENA

● **Self-Guided Tour:** Start on the ground floor, which houses the church's original statues, mainly from the facade and exterior. After descending a few steps, turn your back on the hall of statues and wrought-iron gate. You're now face-to-face with **Donatello's Madonna and Child** (c. 1458). In this round, carved relief, a slender and tender Mary gazes down at her chubby-cheeked baby. Her sad eyes say that she knows the eventual fate of her son.

At the opposite end of the room is **Duccio's Stained-Glass Window** (c. 1287-1290). This splendid original window was installed for centuries above and behind the Duomo's altar. Now the church has a copy, and art lovers can enjoy a close-up look at this masterpiece. The rose window—20 feet across—is dedicated (like the church and the city itself) to the Virgin Mary.

The work is by Siena's most famous artist, Duccio di Buoninsegna (c. 1255-1319). Duccio combined elements from rigid Byzantine icons (Mary's almond-shaped bubble, called a *mandorla*, and the full-frontal saints that flank her) with a budding sense of 3-D realism (the throne turned at a three-quarter angle to simulate depth, with angels behind).

Upstairs awaits a private audience with **Duccio's *Maestà*** (*Enthroned Virgin*, 1311). The panels in this room were once part of the Duomo's main altarpiece. Grab a seat and study one of the great pieces of medieval art. Although the former altarpiece was disassembled (and the frame was lost), most of the pieces are displayed here, with the front side (*Maestà*, with Mary and saints; pronounced my-STAH) at one end of the room and the back side (26 Passion panels) at the other.

The painting was revolutionary for the time in its sheer size and opulence, and in Duccio's budding realism, which broke standard conventions. Duccio, at the height of his powers, used every innovative arrow in his quiver. He replaced the standard gold-leaf background (symbolizing heaven) with a gold, intricately patterned curtain draped over the throne. Mary's blue robe opens to reveal her body, and the curve of her knee suggests real anatomy beneath the robe. Baby Jesus wears a delicately transparent garment. Their faces are modeled with light—a patchwork of bright flesh and shadowy valleys, as if lit from the left (a technique Duccio likely learned from his contemporary, Giotto, during a visit to Florence).

The Passion of Christ: The flip side of the altarpiece featured these 26 smaller panels showing colorful scenes from the Passion of Christ.

• *Our museum tour is done, but the finale of your visit is yet to come.*

Eventually you'll climb down the steps and then up about 40 tight and claustrophobic spiral stairs to the first viewpoint. You can continue up another 100 steps of a similar spiral staircase to reach the very top.

Panorama del Facciatone: Standing on the wall from this high point in the city, you're rewarded with a stunning view of Siena...and an interesting

perspective. Look toward the Duomo and remember this: To outdo Florence, Siena had planned to enlarge this cathedral by turning it into a transept and constructing an enormous nave. You're standing on top of what would have been the new entrance facade. Columns would have stood where you see the rows of white stones in the pavement below. Had the church been completed, you'd be looking straight down the nave toward the altar.

▲Baptistery of San Giovanni (Battistero di San Giovanni)

This richly adorned and quietly tucked-away cave of art is worth a look for its cool tranquility and exquisite art, including an ornately painted vaulted ceiling. The highlight is the baptismal font created in the 1420s by a host of early Renaissance all-stars. Made of marble, bronze, and enamel, the overall design was by Jacopo ("Fountain of Joy") della Quercia. On the base, the first bronze panel you encounter was done by Lorenzo ("Gates of Paradise") Ghiberti. To the right, the tiny bronze statues of Lady Faith and (farther right) the Angel of Hope, were done by the great Donatello. Also on the right side, Donatello made the bronze panel depicting John the Baptist's severed head being brought in on a platter, set in a 3-D banquet hall of receding arches. With this font, we're witnessing the start of the Renaissance.

Cost and Hours: Covered by Duomo combo-ticket, daily 10:30-19:00, Nov-Feb until 17:30, located on the back end of the Duomo.

Crypt (Cripta)

The cathedral "crypt" is archaeologically important. The site of a small 12th-century Romanesque church, it was filled in with dirt a century after its creation to provide a foundation for the huge church that sits atop it today. Recently excavated (with modern metal supports from the 1990s), the several rediscovered rooms show off what are likely the oldest frescoes in town (well-described in English).

Cost and Hours: Covered by Duomo combo-ticket, daily

10:30-19:00, Nov-Feb until 17:30, located on the back end of the Duomo.

Other Cathedral-Area Sights
▲Santa Maria della Scala

This museum, opposite the Duomo, operated for centuries as a hospital, foundling home (orphanage), and pilgrim lodging. Many of those activities are visible in the 15th-century frescoes of its main hall, the Pellegrinaio. Today, the hospital and its cellars are filled with fascinating exhibits (well-described in English).

Cost and Hours: €9, €14 combo-ticket with Civic Museum, €20 combo-ticket includes Civic Museum and City Tower, also covered by Acropoli Pass; daily 10:00-19:00, Thu until 22:00; closes earlier mid-Oct-mid-March; on Piazza del Duomo opposite the cathedral, ticket office at corner, tel. 0577-534-571, www.santamariadellascala.com.

Visiting the Museum: It's easy to get lost in this gigantic complex, so stay focused on the main attractions—the fancily frescoed Pellegrinaio Hall (ground floor) and the Fountain of Joy statues (one floor down). Then explore the lower floors.

From the entrance, turn right to enter what was, until the 1970s, Siena's main hospital. Enter the first room on your right, the **Sacristy,** which displays some powerful relics preserved in golden and silver reliquaries. You may see a drop of Jesus' blood in a vial *(sangue di Christo)*, a nail from Jesus' cross *(sacro chiodo)*, a piece of the Virgin's robe *(beata Vergine)*, and lots of saints' bones. They're encased in reliquaries that befit the preciousness of these sacred bits and saintly pieces. Some of the oldest are Byzantine reliquaries made of gold, silver, and precious stones.

Continue down the hallway (browsing exhibits in side rooms) until you reach the sumptuously frescoed **Pellegrinaio Hall.** This was a reception hall for visiting pilgrims before being converted into a hospital room, lined with beds for the sick. The frescoes (mostly by Domenico di Bartolo, c. 1440) show medieval Siena's innovative healthcare and social welfare system in action.

Now head downstairs, following signs to *Fonte Gaia.* These are the original statues from the Fountain of Joy (Fonte Gaia), Siena's landmark fountain on Il Campo. Jacopo della Quercia's early-15th-century masterpiece began crumbling, so in the 19th century, it was dismantled and plaster casts were made. (These casts formed the replica that graces Il Campo today.) Here you'll see the badly eroded original statues and relief panels, paired alongside their casts (labeled "calco").

In the second basement, under the groin vaults of the **Archaeological Museum** (Museo Archeologico), you're alone with piles of ancient stuff, from Bronze Age axes to Roman pottery. The highlight is a group of Etruscan artifacts excavated from tombs dating from the seventh to second century before Christ—the Etruscan heyday. You'll see their coins, figurines, and terra-cotta funeral urns for ashes (often designed with a standard body but a personalized head). The sarcophagi show the deceased reclining atop the lid, a reminder of their lofty social status.

SAN DOMENICO AREA

Basilica of San Domenico (Basilica di San Domenico)

This huge brick church is worth a quick look. Spacious and plain (except for the colorful flags of the city's 17 *contrade*), the Gothic

interior fits the austere philosophy of the Dominicans and invites meditation on the thoughts and deeds of St. Catherine. Halfway up the nave on the right, find a copper bust of St. Catherine (for four centuries it contained her skull), a small case housing her thumb, and her little flagellation whip. In the chapel, surrounded by candles, you'll see Catherine's head (a clay mask around her skull with her actual teeth showing through) atop the altar.

Cost and Hours: Free, daily 7:00-18:30, shorter hours off-season, www.basilicacateriniana.com.

Sanctuary of St. Catherine (Santuario di Santa Caterina)

Step into the cool and peaceful site of Catherine's home. Siena remembers its favorite hometown gal, a simple, unschooled but mystically devout soul who helped convince the pope to return from France to Rome. Pilgrims have visited this place since 1464, and architects and artists have greatly embellished what was probably once a humble home (her family worked as wool dyers). You'll see paintings throughout showing scenes from her life.

Cost and Hours: Free, daily 9:00-18:00 but chapel closes 12:30-15:00, a few downhill blocks toward the center from San Domenico—follow signs to *Santuario di Santa Caterina*—at Costa di Sant'Antonio 6, tel. 0577-288-175.

Sleeping in Siena

Finding a room in Siena is tough during Easter or the Palio (July 2 and Aug 16). Many hotels won't take reservations until the end of May for the Palio, and even then they might require a four-night stay. If tranquility is important to you, ask for a room that's off the street, or consider staying outside the center.

BIGGER HOTELS NEAR IL CAMPO

$$$$ **Pensione Palazzo Ravizza** is elegant, friendly, and well-run, with 40 rooms and an aristocratic feel—fitting for what was once a noble's residence. Guests enjoy a peaceful garden set on a dramatic bluff, along with a Steinway in the upper lounge (RS%, family rooms, rooms in back overlook countryside, air-con, elevator, free parking makes this a good value for drivers, Via Piano dei Mantellini 34, tel. 0577-280-462, www.palazzoravizza.it, bureau@palazzoravizza.it).

$$$ **Hotel Duomo** is dated but well-located, with 20 spacious but overpriced rooms (many with Duomo views—request when booking), a picnic-friendly roof terrace, and a bizarre floor plan (family rooms, air-con, elevator with some stairs, expensive pay parking; Via di Stalloreggi 38, tel. 0577-289-088, www.hotelduomo.it, booking@hotelduomo.it, Alessandro).

SIMPLE PLACES NEAR IL CAMPO

$$ **Piccolo Hotel Etruria,** with 20 simple rooms, is well-located, restful, and a fine value (RS%—use code "RSITA," family rooms, breakfast extra, air-con May-Oct only, elevator, at Via delle Donzelle 3, tel. 0577-288-088, www.hoteletruria.com, info@hoteletruria.com, friendly Leopoldo and Lucrezia). They also rent apartments nearby.

$ **Albergo Tre Donzelle,** run by the same family as Piccolo Hotel Etruria, has 20 homey rooms that may be the best value in the center. Il Campo, a block away, is your terrace (RS%—use code "RSITA," cheaper rooms with shared bath, family rooms, breakfast extra, fans, no elevator; with your back to the tower, head away from Il Campo toward 2 o'clock to Via delle Donzelle 5; tel. 0577-270-390, www.tredonzelle.com, info@tredonzelle.com, Leopoldo and Lucrezia).

$ **Hotel Cannon d'Oro,** a few blocks up Banchi di Sopra, is a bland, labyrinthine slumbermill renting 30 institutional, overpriced rooms (RS%, family rooms, fans, elevator with some stairs, Via dei Montanini 28, tel. 0577-44321, www.cannondoro.com, info@cannondoro.com; Maurizio, Tommaso, and Rodrigo).

B&BS IN THE OLD CENTER

$$ Antica Residenza Cicogna is a seven-room guesthouse with a homey elegance and an ideal location. It's warmly run by the young and charming Elisa and her friend Ilaria, who set out biscotti, vin santo, and tea for their guests in the afternoon. With artfully frescoed walls and ceilings, this is remarkably genteel for the price (air-con, no elevator, Via delle Terme 76, tel. 0577-285-613, mobile 347-007-2888, www.anticaresidenzacicogna.it, info@ anticaresidenzacicogna.it).

SIENA

$$ Palazzo Masi B&B, run by friendly Alizzardo and Daniela, is just below Il Campo. They rent six pleasant, spacious, antique-furnished rooms with shared common areas on the second and third floors of a restored 13th-century building (RS%—use code "RICK," cheaper rooms with shared bath, no elevator; breakfast provided on Il Campo; from City Hall, walk 50 yards down Casato di Sotto to #29; mobile 349-600-9155, www.palazzomasi. com, info@palazzomasi.it). The place is sometimes unstaffed, so confirm your arrival time in advance.

$$ B&B Alle Due Porte is a charming little establishment renting three big rooms with sweet furniture under medieval beams. The shared breakfast room is delightful. Manager Egisto is a phone call and 10-minute scooter ride away (air-con, Via di Stalloreggi 51, mobile 368-352-3530, www.sienatur.it, soldatini@ interfree.it).

$$ Siena Gallery B&B, run by kindhearted Elisabetta and Fabio, is tucked onto the fourth floor of a relatively modern building, offering four contemporary yet simple rooms (air-con, elevator, Via Banchi di Sopra 31, enter at Galleria Odeon—look for green pharmacy sign, mobile 334-3997-8694, www.sienagallery.it, info@ sienagallery.it).

$$ I Terzi di Siena, run by the same family as Siena Gallery B&B, houses nine rooms in an 11th-century building. It's absent an elevator but full of humble charm and noteworthy views (air-con, cheaper rooms with shared bath, apartments available; Via dei Termini 13, mobile 339-6699-143, www.terzidisiena.it, info@ terzidisiena.it).

$$ B&B Siena in Centro is a clearinghouse managing 15 rooms and 5 apartments. Their handy office functions as a reception area for picking up keys. The rooms are generally spacious, quiet, and comfortable (RS%, some with air-con and others with fans, family rooms, reception open 9:00-13:30 & 15:00-22:00, Via di Stalloreggi 16, tel. 0577-48111, mobile 331-281-0136 or 347-465-9753, www.bbsienaincentro.com, info@bbsienaincentro.com, Gioia or Michela).

$ Le Camerine di Silvia, a romantic hideaway perched near a sweeping, grassy olive grove, rents five simple rooms in a converted

16th-century building. A small terrace with fruit trees and a private hedged garden lends itself to contemplation (cash only, view room on request, no breakfast, fans, free parking nearby, Via Ettore Bastianini 1, just below recommended Pensione Palazzo Ravizza, mobile 338-761-5052 or 339-123-7687, www.lecamerinedisilvia. com, info@lecamerinedisilvia.com, Conti family).

NEAR BASILICA OF SAN DOMENICO

SIENA

$$$ Hotel Chiusarelli, with mix of 48 classic and modern rooms in a beautiful, frescoed Neoclassical villa, is just outside the medieval town center on a busy street—ask for a quieter room in back when you reserve (RS%, family rooms, air-con, limited free parking, across from San Domenico at Viale Curtatone 15, tel. 0577-280-562, www.chiusarelli.com, info@chiusarelli.com).

$$$ Hotel Villa Elda rents 11 bright and light rooms in a recently renovated villa. It's classy, stately, and run with a stylish charm (view rooms extra, air-con, no elevator, garden and view terrace, closed Nov-March, Viale Ventiquattro Maggio 10, tel. 0577-247-927, www.villaeldasiena.it, info@villaeldasiena.it).

$$ Albergo Bernini makes you part of a Sienese family in a modest, clean home with 10 traditional rooms. Giovanni, charming wife Daniela, and their daughters welcome you to their spectacular view terrace—a great spot for a glass of wine or a picnic (cheaper rooms with shared bath, family rooms, breakfast extra, fans, on the main Il Campo-San Domenico drag at Via della Sapienza 15, tel. 0577-289-047, www.albergobernini.com, info@albergobernini.com).

$ Alma Domus is a church-run hotel and a great value, featuring 28 tidy, streamlined rooms with quaint balconies, some fantastic views (ask for a room *con vista*), stately public rooms, and a pleasant atmosphere (but nearby church bells can be a drawback). Consider upgrading to a snazzy superior room for slightly more (family rooms, air-con, elevator; from San Domenico, walk downhill toward the view with the church on your right, turn left down Via Camporegio, make a U-turn down the brick steps to Via Camporegio 37; tel. 0577-44177, www.hotelalmadomus.it, info@hotelalmadomus.it, Louis).

FARTHER FROM THE CENTER

$$ Hotel Minerva is your big, impersonal, plain, efficient option. It's got zero personality and mediocre views, but offers predictable business-class comfort in its 56 rooms. It works best for those with cars—its pay parking is reasonable, and it's only a 15-minute walk from the action (RS%, view rooms extra, air-con, elevator, just inside Porta Ovile at the north end of town at Via Garibaldi 72, tel. 0577-284-474, www.albergominerva.it, info@albergominerva.it).

Eating in Siena

Sienese restaurants are a great value by Florentine and Venetian standards. For pasta, a good option is *pici* (PEE-chee), a thick Sienese spaghetti that seems to be at the top of every menu. Reservations are generally wise for dinner.

IN THE OLD TOWN
Fine Dining

$$$$ Osteria le Logge caters to a fancy crowd and offers pricey Tuscan favorites with a gourmet twist, made with seasonal local ingredients. Inside you'll enjoy a gorgeous living-room setting (books, wood, and wine bottles), and outside there's fine seating on a pedestrian street. I find dining inside on the ground floor most romantic (Mon-Sat 12:00-15:00 & 19:00-23:00, closed Sun, two blocks off Il Campo at Via del Porrione 33, tel. 0577-48013, www. osterialelogge.it, Mirko).

$$$$ Ristorante Tar-Tufo offers a spacious setting, a gourmet presentation, a twist of pretense, and contemporary and innovative Tuscan cuisine—much of it garnished with truffles. While you could eat on their terrace with a view of the countryside, I prefer dining inside under dramatic arches (Thu-Tue 12:00-14:30 & 19:00-22:30, closed Wed, a 10-minute walk behind Il Campo at Via del Sole 6, tel. 0577-284-031, www.tar-tufo.com, chef Pino).

$$$ Compagnia dei Vinattieri, a good bet for wine lovers, serves Tuscan dishes with a creative touch. In this elegant space, you can enjoy a romantic meal under graceful brick arches. The menu is small and accessible. Owner Marco is happy to take you down to the marvelous wine cellar (beef is big here, leave this book on the table for a complimentary *aperitivo* or *digestivo,* daily 12:30-15:00 & 19:30-23:00, Via delle Terme 79, tel. 0577-236-568, www. vinattieri.net).

$$ Osteria la Sosta di Violante, beyond the tourist zone, is the best fine-dining value of my listings. You'll share this dreamy little spot with smart locals. For 20 years chefs Duccio and Enrico have offered gourmet food with no pretense—they make sure diners feel right at home. Order with a sense of adventure. Diners with this book cap their meal with complimentary vin santo and *cantucci* (great indoor and outdoor seating, Mon-Sat 12:30-15:00 & 19:00-23:00, closed Sun, walk down Via Banchi di Sotto to Via Pantaneto 115, tel. 0577-43774).

Traditional and Rustic Places

$$ Trattoria Papei is a sprawling place with festive outdoor seating under a big tent and a high-energy interior. It has a casual, rollicking family atmosphere and friendly servers dishing out gen-

Siena Hotels & Restaurants

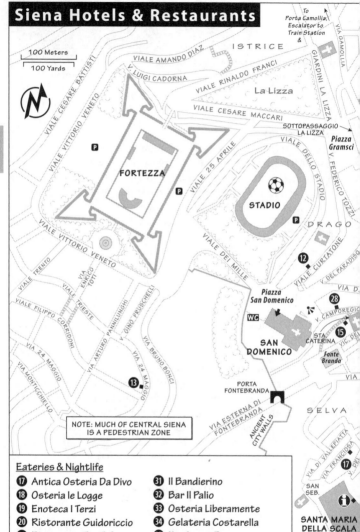

SIENA

Eateries & Nightlife

17 Antica Osteria Da Divo
18 Osteria le Logge
19 Enoteca I Terzi
20 Ristorante Guidoriccio
21 Ristorante Tar-Tufo
22 Compagnia dei Vinattieri
23 Osteria Il Carroccio
24 Trattoria Papei
25 La Taverna Di Cecco
26 Trattoria La Torre; Sapori & Dintorni Conad Grocery
27 Osteria del Gatto
28 Il Pomodorino
29 Osteria il Grattacielo
30 Ristorante Alla Speranza & Bar Paninoteca San Paolo

31 Il Bandierino
32 Bar Il Palio
33 Osteria Liberamente
34 Gelateria Costarella
35 Key Largo Bar
36 Antica Pizzicheria al Palazzo della Chigiana
37 Pizzeria San Martino
38 Pizzeria Poppi
39 Consorzio Agrario di Siena Grocery
40 Morbidi
41 Nannini Pastry Shop
42 La Vecchia Latteria Gelato

Eating in Siena 41

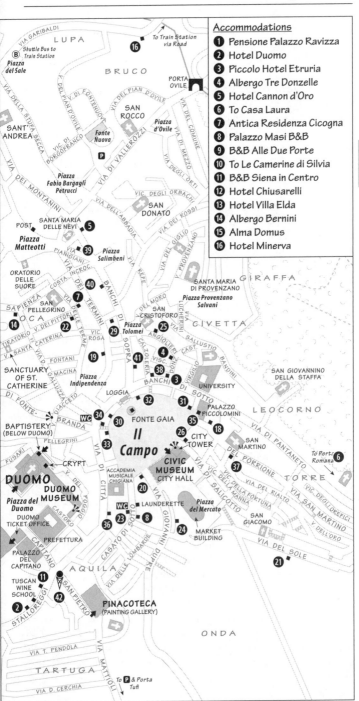

erous portions of rib-stickin' Tuscan specialties and grilled meats (daily 12:00-15:00 & 19:00-22:30, on the market square behind City Hall at Piazza del Mercato 6, tel. 0577-280-894; Amedeo and Eduardo).

$$ Osteria il Carroccio, artsy and convivial, seats guests in a characteristic but tight dining room. They serve traditional "slow food" with innovative flair at affordable prices. To maintain their quality, they have only 35 seats and don't turn the tables—reserve ahead (€30 tasting *menu*—minimum two people, Thu-Tue 12:15-15:00 & 19:15-22:00, closed Wed, Casato di Sotto 32, tel. 0577-41165). They give complimentary vin santo and *cantucci* with this book.

$$ La Taverna di Cecco is a cozy, comfortable little eatery on a quiet back lane where grandma Olga cooks, and earnest Luca and Gianni serve. The elegant place settings feel like nana's finest, and the few tables outside are inviting as well. They offer a simple menu of traditional Sienese favorites along with hearty salads (daily 12:00-16:00 & 19:00-23:00, Via Cecco Angiolieri 19, tel. 0577-288-518).

$$ Trattoria la Torre is an unfussy family-run *casalinga* (home-cooking) place, popular for its homemade pasta. Its open kitchen and 10 tables are packed under one medieval brick arch. Service is brisk and casual—the only menu is posted outside because they like to explain your options individually. Even though located just under the City Tower, it feels more like a local hangout than a tourist trap (Fri-Wed 12:00-15:00 & 19:00-22:00, closed Thu, steps below Il Campo at Via di Salicotto 7, tel. 0577-287-548, Marco).

$ Osteria del Gatto is a classic neighborhood fixture thriving with townspeople and powered by a passion for good Sienese cuisine. Friendly Marco Coradeschi and his staff cook and serve daily specials with attitude. As it's so small and popular, it can get loud (Mon-Sat 12:30-15:00 & 19:30-22:00, closed Sun, 10-minute walk from Il Campo at Via San Marco 8, look for *La Vecchia Osteria* sign, tel. 0577-287-133).

$ Osteria il Grattacielo is a funky hole-in-the-wall with a tight and homey interior and three tables under a tunnel-like arch outside, perfect for a cheap, hearty, memorable yet no-frills meal. Luca, who's clearly found his niche in life, has no menu and just one solid house wine. You'll eat what he's cooking. Lunch is a mixed plate from the bar (be bold and point) or pasta (€10, includes wine). Dinner is three courses—antipasto bar, pasta, and a *secondi*—€15 for Rick Steves readers; €3 extra adds a vin santo and cookies finale (daily 12:00-15:00 & 19:30-21:30, Via dei Pontani 8, mobile 331-742-2835).

Gelato, Tea, and Cocktails in Siena

Evenings are a wonderful time to be out and about in Siena, after the tour groups have left for the day. Join the evening *passeggiata* (peak strolling time is 19:00) along Banchi di Sopra with gelato in hand.

Gelato: There's always a good gelato place nearby (all open daily, generally until late): The gourmet chain Venchi is reliably tasty (across from the Loggia della Mercanzia at Via di Città 28). A good locally owned option is La Vecchia Latteria (a 5-minute walk from Il Campo at Via di San Pietro 10). And, for gelato on Il Campo, drop by the *bar gelateria* Il Camerlengo (at #6, just to the right of City Hall, with a handy WC).

Tea: The Tea Room is an artful ensemble of stone vaults, cozy furniture, romantic lighting, lovingly presented pastries, and a long list of fine teas. Hiding out behind City Hall, it offers a tranquil and relaxing escape (Tue-Sun 17:00-24:00, closed Mon, 200 yards below Il Campo, from the car park banister at the far end of Piazza del Mercato, look down and to the left, at Porta Giustizia 11, tel. 0577-222-753).

***Aperitivo* Happy Hour:** As elsewhere in Italy, you'll find bars all over town attracting an early evening crowd by offering an *aperitivo*—a free buffet of food that's included with the purchase of a drink. For many, this happy-hour special (usually nightly from 18:00-20:00) can make a light dinner. Some good ones to consider are: Morbidi, a trendy and youthful cocktail bar (closed Sun, Via Banchi di Sopra 75); the classic *caffè/pasticceria* Nannini (Via Banchi di Sopra 24, also a branch at Piazza Matteotti 15); and Bar il Palio and Osteria Liberamente, for cocktails and light bites on Il Campo (both described below). A great way to cap any meal or day in Siena is with a drink or dessert on Il Campo.

ON IL CAMPO

If you choose to dine on perhaps the finest town square in Italy, you'll pay a premium, meet waiters who don't need to hustle, and eat mediocre food. And yet I highly recommend it. Consider surveying the scene during your sightseeing day and reserving a table of your choice at the place that feels best to you. (All places listed are open daily for long hours.)

Dining and Drinks on the Square

$$$ Ristorante alla Speranza has primo views and is a decent option for dining on the square (Piazza del Campo 32, tel. 0577-280-190, www.allasperanza.it).

$$$ Il Bandierino is another option for drinks or pizza, with an angled view of City Hall (no cover but a 20 percent service charge, Piazza del Campo 64, tel. 0577-275-894).

$$$ Bar il Palio is the best bar on Il Campo for a before- or after-dinner drink: It has straightforward prices, no cover, and a fine view (Piazza del Campo 47, tel. 0577-282-055).

$$$ Osteria Liberamente, a dynamic little bar with a trendy vibe, is popular with young locals. Consider a drink at *aperitivo* time, from 17:00 on, when drinks come with a small plate of snacks (fine wines by the glass and €7 cocktails, Piazza del Campo 27, tel. 0577-274-733, Pino).

Drinks or Snacks Overlooking Il Campo

These places (all open daily until late) have skinny balconies with benches overlooking the main square for their customers.

$ Gelateria Costarella, on the corner of Via di Città and Costarella dei Barbieri, is a modern cocktail/gelato bar with a great little balcony over Il Campo—which is open to anyone ordering off their pricier menu (Via di Città 33).

$ Bar Paninoteca San Paolo has a youthful English-pub ambience and a row of stools overlooking the square. They have dozens of hearty sandwiches, big salads, and several beers on tap—it's not traditional Italian, but it's quick, filling, and available all day (order and pay at the counter, under the arch on Vicolo di San Paolo, tel. 0577-226-622).

$ Key Largo Bar has a nondescript interior, but two long, upper-story benches in the corner offer a wonderful secret perch. Buy your drink or snack at the bar, climb upstairs, and open the ancient door (no cover and no extra charge to sit on the balcony). Enjoy stretching out, and try to imagine how, during the Palio, three layers of spectators cram into this space—notice the iron railing used to plaster the top row of sardines up against the wall. Suddenly you're picturing Palio ponies zipping wildly around the square's notoriously dangerous corner (on the corner at Via Rinaldini 17, tel. 0577-236-339).

$ Salumeria il Cencio is a simple rustic sandwich shop with a tiny balcony upstairs (enter through back), where, for the take-out price, you can munch your humble meal (daily, near Key Largo Bar at the corner of Il Campo and Via del Porrione, tel. 0577-283-007).

DINING WITH LOCALS, AWAY FROM THE CENTER

A pleasant 10-minute stroll north of Il Campo, Via Camollia—a continuation of the chic Via Banchi di Sopra and Via dei Montanini shopping streets—offers good eating options. **$$ Trattoria Fonte Giusta,** at #102, is a big family-friendly eatery known for its pizza and meat dishes (plenty of streetside tables, daily 12:00-23:00, tel. 0577-40506). My favorite in this area is farther on, at #167—**$$ Osteria il Vinaio.** Festooned with neighborhood memorabilia on the walls, it's an informal place—bright and fun—offering simple dishes at good prices from an inviting menu (Mon-Sat 19:00-22:00, closed Sun, tel. 0577-49615, run by Bobbe and Davide). Beyond that, at #193, is **$$ Osteria Titti,** where friendly Duccio creates a quieter atmosphere, serving Sienese classics in an eclectic and funky setting (Mon-Sat 12:00-15:00 & 19:00-23:00, closed Sun, tel. 0577-285-813).

EATING CHEAPLY IN THE CENTER

Consorzio Agrario di Siena gourmet market is a great place to assemble a cheap yet top-quality meal (salad and smoothie bar at the front, bakery/pizzeria at the back). Take a stool at the excellent pizzeria in the rear, or find a spot on the big comfy stone bench across the way on Piazza Salimbeni (Mon-Sat 8:00-20:30, Sun 9:30-20:00, just off Piazza Matteotti, facing Piazza Salimbeni at Via Pianigiani 9).

Sapori & Dintorni Conad, at the bottom of Il Campo next to the City Tower, is a classy bakery/supermarket/*rosticceria* serving fresh food to go or to eat at one of their tiny tables (daily 8:30-20:00, Piazza Il Campo 80).

DESSERTS AND TREATS

Siena's claim to caloric fame is its panforte, a rich, chewy concoction of nuts, honey, and candied fruits that impresses even fruitcake haters. There are a few varieties: *Margherita,* dusted in powdered sugar, is fruitier, while *panpepato* has a spicy, peppery crust. Locals prefer a chewy, white macaroon-and-almond cookie called *ricciarelli.*

Nannini is the top end, classic café and pastry shop every grandmother has fond memories of. It's ideally located in the center of the evening strolling scene a few blocks off the Campo. For a special dessert or a sweet treat any time of day, stop by. The local specialties are around back at the far end of the bar (Mon-Fri 7:30-21:30, Sat-Sun 8:00-23:00, *aperitivo* happy hour 18:00 until closing, Banchi di Sopra 24). There's also a branch at Piazza Matteotti 15.

Siena Connections

Siena has sparse train connections but is a handy hub for buses to the hill towns. For most, Florence is the gateway to Siena. The bus and train take about the same amount of time, but Siena's bus station is more convenient and central than its train station.

BY TRAIN

Siena's train station is at the edge of town. For details on getting between the town center and the station, see page 8.

From **Siena by Train to: Florence** (direct trains hourly, 1.5 hours), **Pisa** (2/hour, 1.5 hours, some change at Empoli), **Assisi** (10/day, about 4 hours, most involve 2 changes, bus is faster), **Rome** (1-2/hour, 3-4 hours, 1 change), **Orvieto** (12/day, 2.5 hours, change in Chiusi). Train info: Trenitalia.com.

BY BUS

The main bus companies are **Tiemme/Siena Mobilità** (mostly regional destinations, tel. 0577-204-111, www.tiemmespa.it) and **Flixbus** (for long-distance connections, https://global.flixbus.com). On schedules, the fastest buses are marked *rapida*. Many buses depart Siena from Piazza Gramsci (sometimes labeled *Via Tozzi* on schedules); others leave from the train station or right behind it (confirm when you buy your ticket).

Tickets and Information: You can buy tickets in the underground passageway (called Sottopassaggio la Lizza) beneath Piazza Gramsci—look for stairwells in front of NH Excelsior Hotel. You can also get bus tickets from a kiosk at the train station as well as on online. If necessary, you can buy tickets from the driver, but it costs extra.

Tiemme/Siena Mobilità Buses to: Florence (roughly 2/hour—fewer off-season, take the 1.5-hour *rapida/via superstrada* bus—*ordinaria* buses take longer; tickets available at tobacco shops/*tabacchi;* generally leaves from Piazza Gramsci as well as train station), **San Gimignano** (8/day direct, on Sun must change in Poggibonsi, 1.5 hours, from Piazza Gramsci), **Volterra** (4/day Mon-Sat, no buses on Sun, 2 hours, change in Colle di Val d'Elsa, leaves from Piazza Gramsci), **Montepulciano** (6-7/day, none on Sun, 1.5 hours, from train station), **Pienza** (6/day, none on Sun, 1.5 hours, from train station), **Montalcino** (6/day Mon-Sat, 4/day Sun, 1.5 hours, from train station or Piazza del Sale), **Pisa's Galileo Galilei Airport** (3/day, 2 hours, one direct, two via Poggibonsi), **Rome's Fiumicino Airport** (3/day, 3.5 hours, from Piazza Gramsci).

Flixbus Buses to: Rome (13/day, 3 hours, from Piazza Gramsci or the train station, arrives at Rome's Tiburtina station on Metro line B with easy connections to the central Termini train station), **Naples** (6/day direct, 5.5 hours, one overnight bus that departs at 00:20), **Milan** (6-8/day direct, 5-7 hours, arrives at Milan's Lampugnano Metro station for the red line 1), **Assisi** (3/day direct, 2 hours, departs from Siena train station). To reach the town center of **Pisa,** the train is better (described earlier).

VOLTERRA & SAN GIMIGNANO

This fine duo of hill towns—perhaps Italy's most underrated and most overrated, respectively—sits just a half-hour drive apart in the middle of the triangle formed by Florence, Siena, and Pisa. San Gimignano is the region's glamour girl, getting all the fawning attention from passing tour buses. And a quick stroll through its core, in the shadows of its 14 surviving medieval towers, is a delight. But once you've seen it, you've seen it...and that's when you head for Volterra. Volterra isn't as eye-catching as San Gimignano, but it has unmistakable authenticity and surprising depth, richly rewarding travelers adventurous enough to break out of the San Gimignano rut. With its many engaging museums, Volterra offers the best sightseeing of all of Italy's small hill towns.

GETTING THERE

These towns work best for drivers, who can easily reach both in one go. Volterra is farther off the main Florence-Siena road, but it's near the main coastal highway connecting the north (Pisa, Lucca, and Cinque Terre) and south (Montalcino/Montepulciano and Rome). It's a little more than an hour's drive from Pisa or Florence.

If you're relying on public transportation, both towns are reachable—to a point. Visiting either one by bus from Florence or Siena requires a longer-than-it-should-be trek, often with a change (in Colle di Val d'Elsa for Volterra, in Poggibonsi for San Gimignano). Volterra can also be reached by a train-and-bus combination from La Spezia, Pisa, or Florence (transfer to a bus in Pontedera). See each town's "Connections" section for details.

San Gimignano is better connected, but Volterra merits the additional effort. Note that while these towns are only about a

30-minute drive apart, they're poorly connected to each other by public transit.

PLANNING YOUR TIME

Volterra and San Gimignano are a handy yin-and-yang pair. Ideally, you'll overnight in one town and visit the other either as a side trip or en route. Sleeping in Volterra lets you really settle into a charming burg with good restaurants, but it forces you to visit San Gimignano during the day, when it's busiest. Sleeping in San Gimignano lets you enjoy that gorgeous town when it's relatively quiet, but some visitors find it *too* quiet. Ultimately I'd aim to sleep in Volterra, and try to visit San Gimignano as early or late in the day as is practical to avoid crowds. Those with a car may choose to stay in the countryside between the two, visiting Volterra during the day and dining in San Gimignano at night.

Volterra

Encircled by impressive walls and topped with a grand fortress, Volterra perches high above the rich farmland surrounding it. More than 2,000 years ago, Volterra was an important Etruscan city, and much larger than we see today. Greek-trained Etruscan artists worked here, leaving a significant stash of art, particularly cinerary urns. Eventually Volterra was absorbed into the Roman Empire, and for centuries it was an independent city-state. Volterra fought bitterly against the Florentines, but like many Tuscan

towns, it lost in the end and was given a Medici fortress atop the city to "protect" its citizens.

Unlike other famous towns in Tuscany, Volterra feels neither cutesy nor touristy...but real, vibrant, and almost oblivious to the allure of the tourist dollar. Millennia past its prime, Volterra seems to have settled into a well-worn groove; locals are resistant to change. At a town meeting about whether to run a high-speed internet cable to the town, a local grumbled, "The Etruscans didn't need it—why do we?" This stubbornness helps make Volterra a refreshing change of pace from its more aggressively commercial neighbors. Volterra also boasts some interesting sights for a small town, from an ancient Roman theater, to a finely decorated Pisan Romanesque cathedral, to an excellent museum of Etruscan artifacts. And most evenings, charming Annie and Claudia give a delightful, one-hour guided town walk sure to help you appreciate their city (see "Tours in Volterra," later). All in all, Volterra is my favorite small town in Tuscany.

Orientation to Volterra

Compact and walkable, Volterra (pop. 11,000—6,000 inside the old wall) stretches out from the pleasant Piazza dei Priori to the old city gates and beyond. Be ready for some steep walking: While the spine of the city from the main square to the Etruscan Museum is fairly level, nearly everything else involves a climb.

Tourist Information: The helpful TI is on the main square, at Piazza dei Priori 20 (daily 9:30-13:00 & 14:00-18:00, tel. 0588-87257, www.volterratur.it). The TI's excellent €5 audioguide narrates 20 stops (2-for-1 discount with this book). They have bus schedules, and their free *Handicraft in Volterra* booklet is useful for understanding the town's traditional artisans. Check the TI website for details on frequent summer festivals and concerts.

ARRIVAL IN VOLTERRA

By Public Transport: Buses stop at Piazza Martiri della Libertà in the town center. Train travelers can reach the town with a short bus ride from Poggibonsi, which has the nearest train station.

By Car: Don't drive into the town center; it's prohibited except for locals (and you'll get a huge fine). It's easiest to simply wind to the top where the road ends at Piazza Martiri della Libertà. (Halfway up the hill, there's a confusing hard right—don't take it; keep going straight uphill under the wall.) Immediately before the Piazza Martiri bus roundabout is the entry to an **underground garage** (€2/hour, €15/day, keep ticket and pay as you leave) that's within a few blocks of nearly all my recommended hotels and sights.

If the main garage is full, the police may direct you to other pay **lots** that ring the town walls (try the handy-but-small lot facing the Roman Theater and Porta Fiorentina gate). You can also pay to park outside the walls in any street spot marked with blue lines. Behind town, a lot named Docciola is free, but it requires a steep climb from the Porta di Docciola gate up into town.

If you're staying in town, check with your hotel about the best parking options.

HELPFUL HINTS

Volterra Card: This €16 card covers all the main sights—except for the Palazzo Viti (valid 72 hours, buy at any covered sight). If traveling with kids, ask about the family card, an especially good deal (€24 for 1-2 adults and kids under 16).

Market Day: The market is on Saturday morning near the Roman Theater (8:00-13:00, Nov-March it moves to Piazza dei Priori). The TI hands out a list of other market days in the area.

Laundry: The handy self-service **Lavanderia Splash** is just off the main square (daily 7:00-23:00, Via Roma 7, tel. 0588-80030). Their next-door dry-cleaning shop also provides wash-and-dry services that usually take about 24 hours (closed Sun).

Tours in Volterra

▲▲Guided Volterra Walk

Annie Adair and her colleague Claudia Meucci offer a great one-hour, English-only introductory walking tour of Volterra for €10. The walk touches on Volterra's Etruscan, Roman, and medieval history, as well as the contemporary cultural scene (daily April-Oct, rain or shine Mon, Wed, and Fri at 12:30, other days at 18:00; meet in front of alabaster shop on Piazza Martiri della Libertà, no need to reserve, tours run with a minimum of 3 people or €30; www.volterrawalkingtour.com or www.tuscantour.com, info@volterrawalkingtour.com). There's no better way to spend €10 and one hour in this city. I mean it. Don't miss this beautiful experience.

Local Guides

American **Annie Adair** is an excellent guide for private, in-depth tours of Volterra (€60/hour, minimum 2 hours). Her husband **Francesco,** an easygoing sommelier and wine critic, leads a Wine Tasting 101 crash course in sampling Tuscan wines (€60/hour per group, plus cost of wine). Annie and Francesco also offer excursions to a honey farm, alabaster quarry, and winery, or a more wine-focused trip to Montalcino or the heart of Chianti (about €450/day for 2-4 people, larger groups possible, mobile 347-143-5004, www.tuscantour.com, info@tuscantour.com).

Sights in Volterra

I've linked these sights with handy walking directions.

• *Begin at the Etruscan Arch at the bottom of Via Porta all'Arco (about 4 blocks below the main square, Piazza dei Priori).*

▲Etruscan Arch (Porta all'Arco)

Volterra's renowned Etruscan arch was built of massive stones in the fourth century BC. The original city wall was four miles around—twice the size of today's wall. Imagine: This city had 20,000 people four centuries before Christ. Volterra was a key trading center and one of 12 leading towns in the confederation of Etruria. The three seriously eroded heads, dating from the first century BC, show

what happens when you leave something outside for 2,000 years. The newer stones are part of the 13th-century city wall, which incorporated parts of the much older Etruscan wall.

A plaque just outside remembers June 30, 1944. That night, Nazi forces were planning to blow up the arch to slow the Allied advance. To save their treasured landmark, Volterrans ripped up the stones that pave Via Porta all'Arco, plugged up the gate, and managed to convince the Nazi commander that there was no need to blow up the arch. Today, all the paving stones are back in their places, and like silent heroes, they welcome you through the oldest standing gate into Volterra. Locals claim this as the oldest surviving rounded arch of the Etruscan age; some experts believe this is where the Romans got the idea for using a keystone in their arches.

• *Go through the arch and head up Via Porta all'Arco, which I like to call...*

"Artisan Lane" (Via Porta all'Arco)

This steep and atmospheric lane is lined with interesting shops featuring the work of artisans and producers. Because of its alabaster heritage, Volterra developed a tradition of craftsmanship and

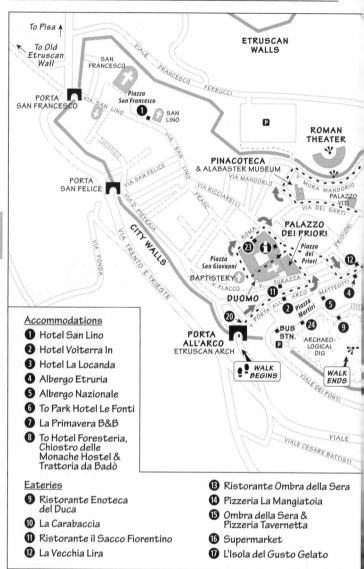

Accommodations
1 Hotel San Lino
2 Hotel Volterra In
3 Hotel La Locanda
4 Albergo Etruria
5 Albergo Nazionale
6 To Park Hotel Le Fonti
7 La Primavera B&B
8 To Hotel Foresteria, Chiostro delle Monache Hostel & Trattoria da Badò

Eateries
9 Ristorante Enoteca del Duca
10 La Carabaccia
11 Ristorante il Sacco Fiorentino
12 La Vecchia Lira
13 Ristorante Ombra della Sera
14 Pizzeria La Mangiatoia
15 Ombra della Sera & Pizzeria Tavernetta
16 Supermarket
17 L'Isola del Gusto Gelato

artistry, and today you'll find a rich variety of handiwork (shops generally open Mon-Sat 10:00-13:00 & 16:00-19:00, closed Sun).

From the Etruscan Arch, browse your way up the hill, checking out these shops and items (listed from bottom to top): alabaster shops (#57 and #45); book bindery and papery (#26); jewelry (#25); etchings (#23); and bronze work (#6).

• *Reaching the top of Via Porta all'Arco, turn left and walk a few steps into Volterra's main square, Piazza dei Priori. It's dominated by the...*

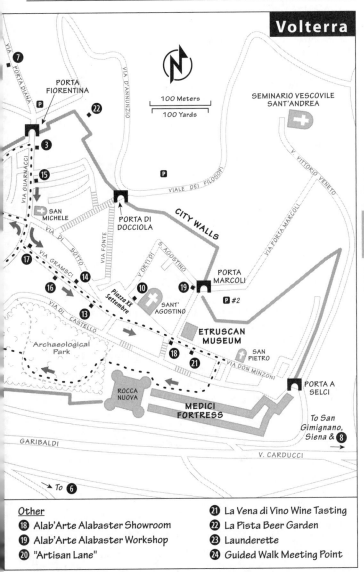

Volterra

PORTA FIORENTINA

PORTA DIANA

VIA D'ANNUNZIO

100 Meters
100 Yards

SEMINARIO VESCOVILE SANT'ANDREA

VIA GUARNACCI

SAN MICHELE

VIALE DEI FILOSOFI

VIA DI SOTTO

PORTA DI DOCCIOLA

CITY WALLS

VIA FONTE

V. ORTI DI S. AGOSTINO

V. VITTORIO VENETO

VIA PORTA MARCOLI

PORTA MARCOLI

VIA GRAMSCI

Piazza XX Settembre

SANT' AGOSTINO

P #2

VIA DI CASTELLO

Archaeological Park

ETRUSCAN MUSEUM

SAN PIETRO

VIA DON MINZONI

ROCCA NUOVA

MEDICI FORTRESS

PORTA A SELCI

To San Gimignano, Siena &

GARIBALDI

V. CARDUCCI

To

Other
18 Alab'Arte Alabaster Showroom
19 Alab'Arte Alabaster Workshop
20 "Artisan Lane"

21 La Vena di Vino Wine Tasting
22 La Pista Beer Garden
23 Launderette
24 Guided Walk Meeting Point

Palazzo dei Priori

Volterra's City Hall, built about 1200, claims to be the oldest of any Tuscan city-state. It clearly inspired the more famous Palazzo Vecchio in Florence. Town halls like this are emblematic of the era of powerful city-states. They were architectural exclamation points declaring that, around here, no pope or emperor called the shots. Towns such as Volterra were truly city-states—proudly independent and relatively democratic. They had their own armies, taxes, and even weights and measures. Notice the horizontal "cane" cut into the City Hall wall (10 yards to the right of the door). For a thousand years, this square hosted a market, and the "cane" was the local yardstick.

Cost and Hours: €6, includes council chambers and tower climb, daily 10:30-17:30, Nov-mid-March until 16:30, tower closed in bad weather.

· *As you face the City Hall, find the little back door in the black-and-white striped wall (to the right), which leads into Volterra's cathedral.*

Duomo

This church is not as elaborate as its cousin in Pisa, but it is a beautiful example of the Pisan Romanesque style. The simple 13th-century facade conceals a more intricate interior (rebuilt in the late 16th and 19th centuries), with a central nave flanked by monolithic stucco columns, painted to imitate pink granite, and topped by a gilded, coffered ceiling. Just past the pulpit midway down the nave (at the Rosary Chapel), check out the *Annunciation*, painted in 1497 by Mariotto Albertinelli and Fra Bartolomeo (both were students of Fra Angelico). The two, friends since childhood, delicately give worshippers a way to see Mary "conceived by the Holy Spirit." Note the vibrant colors, exaggerated perspective, and Mary's *contrapposto* pose—all attributes of the Renaissance.

Cost and Hours: Free, daily 8:00-12:30 & 15:00-18:00, Nov-Feb until 17:00, closed Fri 12:30-16:00 for cleaning.

· *Exit the cathedral through its "front" door and go right, circling all the way around the block to return to Piazza dei Priori. Exit the far end of the square; after one short block, you're standing at the head (on the left) of...*

▲Via Matteotti

The town's main drag, named after the popular Socialist leader Giacomo Matteotti (killed by the fascists in 1924), provides a good cultural scavenger hunt.

At #1, on the left, is a typical **Italian bank security door.** (Step in and say, "Beam me up, Scotty.") Back outside, stand at the corner and look up and all around. Find the medieval griffin torch-holder—symbol of Volterra, looking down Via Matteotti—and imagine it holding a flaming torch. The pharmacy sports the symbol of its medieval guild. Across the street from the bank, #2 is the base of what was a San Gimignano-style **fortified Tuscan tower.** Look up and imagine heavy beams cantilevered out, supporting extra wooden rooms and balconies crowding out over the street. Throughout Tuscany, today's stark and stony old building fronts once supported a tangle of wooden extensions.

As you head down Via Matteotti, notice how the doors show centuries of refitting work. Doors that once led to these extra rooms are now partially bricked up to make windows. Contemplate urban density in the 14th century, before the plague thinned out the population. Be careful: A **wild boar** (a local delicacy) awaits you at #10.

At #12, on the right, notice the line of doorbells: This typical **palace,** once the home of a single rich family, is now occupied by many middle-class families. After the social revolution in the 18th century and the rise of the middle class, former palaces were condominium-ized. Even so, the original family still lives here—apartment #1 is the home of Count Guidi.

On the right at #16, pop in to the **alabaster showroom.** Alabaster, quarried nearby, has long been a big industry here. Volterra alabaster—softer and more translucent than marble—was sliced thin to serve as windows for Italy's medieval churches.

At #19, the recommended **La Vecchia Lira** is a lively cafeteria and restaurant. The **Bar L'Incontro** across the street is a favorite for breakfast and pastries; in the summer, they sell homemade gelato, while in the winter they make chocolates. In the evening, it's a bustling local spot for a drink.

Across the way, side-trip 10 steps up Vicolo delle Prigioni to the fun **Panificio Rosetti** bakery. They're happy to sell small quantities if you want to try the local *cantuccini* (almond biscotti) or another treat.

Continue on Via Matteotti to the end of the block. Notice the bit of **Etruscan wall** artfully used to display more alabaster art (at #51). Nearby is the alabaster **art gallery** of Paolo Sabatini, who specializes in unique, contemporary sculptures (#56A).

Locals gather early each evening at **Osteria dei Poeti** (#57) for some of the best cocktails in town (served with free munchies). The cinema is across the street. Movies in Italy are rarely in *versione originale;* Italians are used to getting their movies dubbed into Italian. To bring some culture to this little town, they also show live broadcasts of operas and concerts (advertised in the window).

Another **Tuscan tower** on the corner (#66) marks the end of the street. This noble house had a ground floor with no interior access to the safe upper floors. Rope ladders were used to get upstairs. The tiny door was wide enough to let in your skinny friends...but definitely not anyone wearing armor and carrying big weapons.

Across the little square stands the ancient **Church of St. Michael.** After long years of barbarian chaos, the Germanic Langobards moved in from the north in the sixth century and asserted law and order in places like Volterra. That generally included building a Christian church over the old Roman forum to symbolically claim and tame the center of town. The church standing here today is Romanesque, dating from the 12th century.

Around the right side, find the crude little guy and the smiling octopus under its eaves—they've been making faces at the passing crowds for 800 years.

• *When you reach the little* piazzetta *with a Romanesque church, turn left down Via dei Sarti. Our next stop—Palazzo Viti—is halfway down the block. But if you want to linger on the square for a bit, drop in for a glass of wine at* **Enoteca Scali** *(at Via Guarnacci 3), where friendly Massimo and Patrizia sell a vast selection of wines and local delicacies in an inviting atmosphere.*

▲Palazzo Viti

Palazzo Viti takes you behind the rustic, heavy stone walls of the city to see how the wealthy lived—in this case, rich from the 19th-century alabaster trade. This time warp is popular with Italian movie directors. With 12 rooms on one floor open to the public, Palazzo Viti feels remarkably lived in—because it is. Behind the ropes you'll see intimate family photos. You'll often find Signora Viti herself selling admission tickets. In high season, your visit may end in the cellar with a short wine tasting.

Cost and Hours: €5, daily 10:00-17:30, by appointment only Nov-March, Via dei Sarti 41, tel. 0588-84047, www. palazzoviti.it, info@palazzoviti.it.

Visiting the Palazzo: The elegant interior is compact and well-described. You'll climb up a stately staircase, buy your ticket, and head into the grand ballroom. From here, you'll tour the blue-hued dining room (with slice-of-life Chinese scenes painted on rice paper); the salon of battles (with warfare paintings on the walls); and the long hall of temporary exhibits. Looping back, you'll see the porcelain hall (decorated with priceless plates) and the inviting library (notice the delicate lamp with a finely carved alabaster lampshade).

The Brachettone Salon is named for the local artist responsible for the small sketch of near-nudes hanging just left of the door into the next room. Brachettone (from *brache,* "pants") is the nickname for the hometown 16th-century artist Daniele da Volterra, who owns the dubious distinction of having painted all those wispy loincloths over the genitalia of Michelangelo's figures in the *Last Judgment* at the Sistine Chapel. (In this drawing, notice a similar aversion to showing the full monty...though everything-but is fair game.) On the table, notice the family wedding photo with Pope John Paul II presiding. In the red room, a portrait of Giuseppe Viti (looking like Pavarotti) hangs next to the exit door. He's the man who purchased the place in 1850. Your visit ends with bedrooms and a dressing room.

Your Palazzo Viti ticket sometimes gets you a fine little cheese, salami, and wine tasting, typically in high season. As you leave the palace, climb down into the cool cellar (used as a disco on some weekends), where you can pop into a Roman cistern, marvel at an Etruscan well, and enjoy a friendly sit-down snack.

• *A block past Palazzo Viti, also on Via dei Sarti, is the...*

Pinacoteca and Alabaster Museum (Pinacoteca e Ecomuseo dell'Alabastro)

The Pinacoteca fills a 15th-century palace with fine paintings that feel more Florentine than Sienese—a reminder of whose domain this town was in. You'll see a stunning altarpiece by Taddeo di Bartolo, once displayed in the original residence. You'll also find roomfuls of gilded altarpieces and saintly statues, as well as a trio of striking High Renaissance altar paintings by Signorelli, Fiorentino, and Ghirlandaio.

The adjoining Alabaster Museum gives a fascinating overview of the local alabaster industry, past and present.

Cost and Hours: €8, daily 9:00-19:00, off-season 10:00-16:30, Via dei Sarti 1, tel. 0588-87580.

• *Exiting the building, circle right along the side of the museum into the tunnel-like Passo del Gualduccio passage; then turn right and walk along the wall, with fine views of the...*

Roman Theater (Teatro Romano)

With this fine aerial view from the city wall promenade, there's no reason to pay to enter this well-preserved, first-century theater

(although it is covered by the Volterra Card). The 13th-century wall that you're standing on divided the theater from the town center...so, naturally, the theater became the town dump. Over time, the theater was forgotten—covered in the garbage of Volterra. It was rediscovered in the 1950s and excavated.

The stage wall (immediately in front of the theater seats) was standard Roman design—with three levels from which actors would appear: one level for mortals, one for heroes, and the top one for gods. Parts of two levels still stand. Gods leaped out onto the third level for the last time around the third century AD, which is when the town began to use the theater stones to build fancy baths instead. You can see the scant remains of the baths behind the theater, including the little round sauna in the far corner with brick supports that raise the heated floor.

From this vantage point, you can trace Volterra's vast Etruscan wall. Find the church in the distance, on the left, and notice the stones just below. They are from the Etruscan wall that followed the ridge into the valley and defined Volterra in the fourth century BC.

• *From the theater viewpoint, continue along the wall downhill to the T-intersection (the old gate, Porta Fiorentina, with fine wooden medieval doors, is on your left). Turn right, making your way uphill on Via Guarnacci back to Via Matteotti. A block up Via Matteotti, you can't miss the wide, pedestrianized shopping street called Via Gramsci. Follow this up to Piazza XX Settembre, walk through that leafy square, and continue uphill on Via Don Minzoni. Watch on your left for the...*

▲▲Etruscan Museum (Museo Etrusco Guarnacci)

Filled top to bottom with rare Etruscan artifacts, this museum—even with few English explanations and its dusty, old-school style—makes it easy to appreciate how advanced this pre-Roman culture was.

Cost and Hours: €8, daily 9:00-19:00, Nov-mid-March 10:00-16:30, audioguide-€3, Via Don Minzoni 15, tel. 0588-86347, www.comune.volterra.pi.it/english.

Visiting the Museum: The museum's three floors feel dusty and disorganized. As there are scarcely any English explanations, consider the serious but interesting audioguide; the information below hits the highlights. There's an inviting public garden out back.

The collection starts on the **ground floor** with a small gathering of pre-Etruscan Villanovian artifacts (c. 1500 BC), with the oldest items to the left as you enter. To the right are an impressive warrior's hat and a remarkable, richly decorated, double-spouted military flask for wine and water. Look down to see Etruscan foundations and a road (the discovery of which foiled the museum's attempt to build an elevator here). It's mind-boggling to think that 20,000 people lived within the town's Etruscan walls in 400 BC.

Filling the rest of the ground floor is a vast collection of stone Etruscan **cinerary urns** (seventh-first century BC). Etruscan urns have two parts: The box on the bottom contained the cremated remains (with elaborately carved panels), while the lid was decorated with a sculpture of the departed. The carved bas-relief scenes and motifs decorating the urns are a prized catalog of Etruscan life and activities.

First pay attention to the people on top. While contemporaries of the Greeks, the Etruscans were more libertine. Their religion was less demanding, and their women were a respected part of both the social and public spheres. Women and men alike are depicted lounging on Etruscan urns. While they seem to be just hanging out, the lounging dead were actually offering the gods a banquet—in order to gain the Etruscan equivalent of salvation. Etruscans really did lounge like this in front of a table, but this banquet had eternal consequences. The dearly departed are often depicted holding blank wax tablets (symbolizing blank new lives in the next world). Men hold containers that would generally be used at banquets, including libation cups for offering wine to the gods. The women are finely dressed, sometimes holding a pomegranate (symbolizing fertility) or a mirror. Look at the faces, and imagine the lives they lived.

Now tune into the reliefs carved into the fronts of the boxes. The motifs vary widely, from floral patterns to mystical animals (such as a Starbucks-like mermaid) to parades of magistrates. Some show journeys on horseback—appropriate for someone leaving this world and entering the next. Some show the fabled horseback-and-carriage ride to the underworld, where the dead are greeted by Charun, an underworld demon, with his hammer and pointy ears.

While the finer urns are carved of alabaster, most are made of limestone. Originally they were colorfully painted. Many lids are mismatched—casualties of reckless 18th- and 19th-century archaeological digs.

Head upstairs to the **first floor.** You'll enter a room with a circular mosaic in the floor (a Roman original, found in Volterra and transplanted here). Explore more treasures in a series of urn-filled rooms.

Fans of Alberto Giacometti will be amazed at how the tall, skinny figure called *The Evening Shadow* (*L'Ombra della Sera,* third century BC) looks just like the modern Swiss sculptor's work—but 2,500 years older. This is an example of the ex-voto bronze statues that the Etruscans created in thanks to the gods. With his supremely lanky frame, distinctive wavy hairdo, and inscrutable smirk, this Etruscan lad captures the illusion of a shadow stretching long, late in the day. Admire the sheer artistry and modernity of the statue.

The museum's other top piece is the *Urn of the Spouses* (*Urna degli Sposi,* first century BC). It's unique for various reasons, including its material (it's in terra-cotta—relatively rare for these urns) and its depiction of two people rather than one. Looking at this elderly couple, it's easy to imagine the long life they spent together and their desire to pass eternity lounging with each other at a banquet for the gods.

Other highlights include alabaster urns with more Greek myths, ex-voto water-bearer statues, kraters (vases with handles used for mixing water and wine), bronze hand mirrors, exquisite golden jewelry that would still be fashionable today, a battle helmet ominously dented at the left temple, black glazed pottery, and hundreds of ancient coins.

The **top floor** features a re-created gravesite, with several neatly aligned urns and artifacts that would have been buried with the deceased. Some of these were funeral dowries that the dead would pack along—including mirrors, coins, hardware for vases, votive statues, pots, pans, and jewelry.

• *After your visit, duck across the street to the...*

▲Alabaster Showroom and Workshop

For a fun peek into the art of alabaster, visit the Alab'Arte showroom, directly across from the Etruscan Museum, and their pow-

dery workshop, a block down the narrow lane (Via Porta Marcoli) next to the museum. Here you can watch Roberto Chiti and Giorgio Finazzo at work. (Everything—including Roberto and Giorgio—is covered in a fine white dust.) Lighting shows off the translucent quality of the stone and the expertise of these artists, who are delighted to share their art with visitors. This is not a touristy guided visit, but something far more special: the chance to see busy artisans practicing their craft.

Cost and Hours: Free, showroom—daily 10:00-13:00 & 15:00-19:00, closes at 17:30 in off-season, closed Nov-Feb, Via Don Minzoni 18; workshop—Mon-Sat 10:00-12:30 & 15:00-19:00, closed Sun, Via Orti Sant'Agostino 28, www. alabarte.com.

▲La Vena di Vino Wine Tasting

La Vena di Vino, just across from the Etruscan Museum, is a fun *enoteca* where Bruno and Lucio have devoted themselves to the wonders of wine and share it with a fun-loving passion. Each day they open six or eight bottles, serve your choice by the glass, pair it with characteristic munchies, and offer fine music (guitars available for patrons) and an unusual decor (the place is strewn with bras). Hang out here with the local characters. According to Bruno, a Brunello is just right with wild boar, and a Super Tuscan is perfect for meditation. Although Volterra is famously quiet late at night, this place is full of action (Wed-Mon 11:30-24:00, closed Tue, Nov-Feb open Fri-Sat only, Via Don Minzoni 30, tel. 0588-81491, www.lavenadivino.com).

• *Volterra's final sight is perched atop the hill just above the wine bar. Climb up one of the lanes nearby, then walk (to the right) along the formidable wall to find the park.*

Medici Fortress and Archaeological Park (Fortezza Medicea and Parco Archeologico)

The archaeological park marks what was the acropolis of Volterra from 1500 BC until AD 1472, when Florence conquered the pesky city. The Florentines burned Volterra's political and historic center, turning it into a grassy commons and building the adjacent Medici Fortress. The old fortress—a symbol of Florentine dominance—now keeps people in rather than out. It's a maximum-security prison housing only about 150 special prisoners.

The park sprawling next to the fortress (toward the town center) is a rare, grassy meadow at the top of a rustic hill town—a favorite place for locals to relax and picnic on a sunny day. Nearby are the scant remains of the acropolis, which can be viewed through the fence for free, or entered for a fee. Of more interest to antiquities enthusiasts is the acropolis' first-century Roman cistern. You can descend 40 tight spiral steps to stand in a chamber that once held about 250,000 gallons of water, enough to provide for more than a thousand people. While not huge, it provides a good look at Roman engineering and reminds you just how important a supply of water was to the survival of a hill town.

Cost and Hours: Park—free, open until 20:00 in peak of summer, shorter hours off-season; acropolis and cistern—€5, daily 10:30-17:30, closes at 16:30 off-season.

Evening Scene

La Pista: Volterra is pretty quiet at night. For a little action during summer evenings you can venture just outside the wall to La Pista, a Tuscan family-friendly neighborhood beer-garden kind of hangout (DJ on weekends, snacks and drinks sold, playground, closed off-season). It's outside the Porta Fiorentina (100 yards to the right in the shadow of the wall).

Passeggiata: As they have for generations, Volterrans young and old stroll during the cool of the early evening. The main cruising is along Via Gramsci and Via Matteotti to the main square, Piazza dei Priori.

Aperitivo: Each evening several bars put out little buffet

Under the Etruscan Sun
(c. 900 BC-AD 1)

Around 550 BC—just before the Golden Age of Greece—the Etruscan people of central Italy had their own Golden Age. Though their origins are unclear, their mix of Greek-style art with Roman-style customs helped lay a civilized foundation for the rise of the Roman Empire. As you travel through Italy—particularly in Tuscany (from "Etruscan")—you'll find traces of this long-lost people. Etruscan tombs and artifacts are still being discovered, often by farmers in the countryside.

The Etruscans were established in central Italy by the early seventh century BC, when a number of settlements sprouted up in sparsely populated Tuscany and Umbria, including today's hill towns of Cortona, Chiusi, and Volterra. Possibly immigrants from Turkey, but more likely local farmers who moved to the city, they became sailors, traders, and craftsmen, and welcomed new ideas from Greece.

More technologically advanced than their neighbors, the Etruscans mined iron ore, smelting and exporting it around the Mediterranean. They drained and irrigated large tracts of land, creating the fertile farmland of central Italy's breadbasket. With their disciplined army, warships, merchant vessels, and (from the Greek perspective) pirate galleys, they ruled central Italy and the major ports along the Tyrrhenian Sea. For nearly two centuries (c. 700-500 BC), much of Italy lived in peace and prosperity under the Etruscan sun.

Judging from the frescoes and many luxury items that have survived, the Etruscans enjoyed the good life: They look healthy and vibrant as they play flutes, dance with birds, or play party games. Etruscan artists celebrated individual people, showing their wrinkles, crooked noses, silly smiles, and funny haircuts.

Scholars today have deciphered the Etruscans' Greek-style alphabet and some individual words, but they have yet to fully understand their language, which is unlike any other in Europe. Much of what we know of the Etruscans comes from their tombs. The tomb was a home in the hereafter, complete with the deceased's belongings. The urn might have a statue on the lid of the deceased at a banquet—lying across a dining couch, spooning with his wife, smiles on their faces, living the good life for all eternity.

Seven decades of wars with the Greeks (545-474 BC) disrupted their trade routes and drained the Etruscan League, just as a new Mediterranean power was emerging: Rome. In 509 BC, the Romans overthrew their Etruscan king, and Rome expanded, capturing Etruscan cities one by one (the last in 264 BC). Etruscan resisters were killed, the survivors intermarried with Romans, and their kids grew up speaking Latin. By Julius Caesar's time, the only remnants of Etruscan culture were its priests, who became Rome's professional soothsayers. Interestingly, the Etrus-

can prophets had foreseen their own demise, having predicted that Etruscan civilization would last 10 centuries.

But Etruscan culture lived on in Roman religion (pantheon of gods, household gods, and divination rituals), art (realism), lifestyle (the banquet), and in a taste for Greek styles—the mix that became our "Western civilization."

Etruscan Sights in Italy

Rome: Traces of original Etruscan engineering projects (e.g., Circus Maximus), Vatican Museum artifacts, and Villa Giulia Museum, with the famous "husband and wife sarcophagus."

Orvieto: Archaeological Museum (coins, dinnerware, and a sarcophagus), necropolis, and underground tunnels and caves.

Volterra: Etruscan gate (Porta all'Arco, from fourth century BC) and Etruscan Museum (urns, pottery, and devotional figures).

spreads free with a drink to attract a crowd. Bars popular for their *aperitivo* include VolaTerra (Via Turazza 5, next to City Hall), L'Incontro (Via Matteotti 19), and Bar dei Poeti (across from the cinema, Via Matteotti 57). And the gang at La Vena di Vino (described under "Sights in Volterra") always seems ready for a good time.

Sleeping in Volterra

Volterra has plenty of places offering a good night's sleep at a fair price. Lodgings outside the old town are generally a bit cheaper (and easier for drivers). But keep in mind that these places involve not just walking, but steep walking.

INSIDE THE OLD TOWN

$$$ Hotel San Lino fills a former convent with 42 modern rooms, all named for the nuns who lived in them. It's at the sleepy lower end of town—close to the Porta San Francesco gate, and about a five-minute uphill walk to the main drag. Although it's within the town walls, it doesn't feel like it: The hotel has a fine swimming pool and view terrace and is the only in-town option that's convenient for drivers, who can reserve pay parking at the on-site garage (RS%, air-con, elevator, closed Nov-Feb, Via San Lino 26, tel. 0588-85250, www.hotelsanlino.com, info@hotelsanlino.com).

$$$ Hotel Volterra In is fresh, tasteful, and in a central yet quiet location. Marco rents 10 bright and spacious rooms with thoughtful, upscale touches and a hearty buffet breakfast (RS%, air-con, elevator, Via Porta all'Arco 41, tel. 0588-86820, www. hotelvolterrain.it, info@hotelvolterrain.it).

$$ Hotel La Locanda feels stately and old-fashioned. This well-located place (just inside Porta Fiorentina, near the Roman Theater and parking lot) rents 18 rooms with flowery decor and modern comforts (RS%, family rooms, air-con, elevator, Via Guarnacci 24, tel. 0588-81547, www.hotel-lalocanda.com, staff@hotel-lalocanda.com, Irina).

$ Albergo Etruria is on Volterra's main drag. They offer a good location, a peaceful rooftop garden, and 19 frilly rooms (RS%, family rooms, some air-con, Via Matteotti 32, tel. 0588-87377, www.albergoetruria.it, info@albergoetruria.it, Paola, Daniele, and Sveva).

$ Albergo Nazionale, with 38 big and aging rooms, is simple, a little musty, popular with school groups, and steps from the bus stop. It's a nicely located last resort if you have your heart set on sleeping in the old town (RS%, family rooms, elevator, Via dei Marchesi 11, tel. 0588-86284, www.hotelnazionale-volterra.it, info@hotelnazionale-volterra.it).

JUST OUTSIDE THE OLD TOWN

These accommodations are within a 5- to 20-minute walk of the city walls.

$$$ Park Hotel Le Fonti, a dull and steep 10-minute walk downhill from Porta all'Arco, can't decide whether it's a business hotel or a resort. The spacious, imposing building, old and stately, has 64 modern, comfortable rooms, half with views. While generally overpriced, it can be a good value if you manage to snag a deal. In addition to the swimming pool, guests can use its small spa (pay more for a view or a balcony, air-con, elevator, on-site restaurant, wine bar, free parking, Via di Fontecorrenti 2, tel. 0588-85219, www.parkhotellefonti.com, info@parkhotellefonti.com).

$ La Primavera B&B feels like a British B&B transplanted to Tuscany. It's a great value just a few minutes' walk outside Porta Fiorentina (near the Roman Theater). Silvia rents five charming, neat-as-a-pin rooms that share a cutesy-country lounge. The house is set back from the road in a pleasant courtyard and with a garden to lounge in. With free parking and a short walk to the old town, this is a handy option for drivers (RS%, fans but no air-con, Via Porta Diana 15, tel. 0588-87295, mobile 328-865-0390, www.affittacamere-laprimavera.com, info@affittacamere-laprimavera.com).

$ Hotel Foresteria, near the Chiostro delle Monache hostel and run by the same organization, has 35 big, utilitarian, new-feeling rooms with decent prices but the same location woes as the hostel described below; it's worth considering for a family with a car and a tight budget (family rooms, air-con, elevator, restaurant, free parking, Borgo San Lazzaro, tel. 0588-80050, www.foresteriavolterra.it, info@foresteriavolterra.it).

¢ Chiostro delle Monache, Volterra's youth hostel, fills a wing of the restored Convent of San Girolamo. It's modern, spacious, and very institutional, with lots of services and a tranquil cloister. Unfortunately, it's about a 20-minute hike from town, in a boring area near deserted hospital buildings (private rooms available and include breakfast, family rooms, reception closed 13:00-15:00 and after 19:00, elevator, free parking, kids' playroom; Via dell Teatro 4, look for hospital sign from main Volterra-San Gimignano road; tel. 0588-86613, www.chiostrodellemonache.com, info@chiostrodellemonache.it).

IN THE COUNTRYSIDE NEAR VOLTERRA

Charming farmhouse accommodations dot the countryside surrounding Volterra, and for drivers, these can be a good value and a fun experience. Some properties offer swimming pools, cooking classes, and more. For locations, see the map on page 48.

$$ Podere Marcampo is an *agriturismo* set in the dramatic landscape surrounding Volterra. Run by Genuino (owner of the recommended Ristorante Enoteca del Duca), his wife Ivana, and their English-speaking daughter Claudia, this peaceful spot has three dark but well-appointed rooms and three apartments, plus a swimming pool with panoramic views. Genuino produces his sangiovese and award-winning merlot on site; you can tour where the wine is made and then sample it in their view tasting room. Cooking classes at their restaurant in town are also available (breakfast included for Rick Steves readers, air-con, free self-service laundry, free parking, about two miles north of Volterra on the road to Pisa, tel. 0588-85393, Claudia's mobile 328-174-4605, www.agriturismo-marcampo.com, info@agriturismo-marcampo.com).

$$ Agriturismo Podere San Lorenzo is a short drive from the walls of Volterra but feels a world away. Mariella rents eight apartments and three rooms in an old farmhouse, clustered around a small church that is now the breakfast room. The grounds are scenic, with a natural swimming pool that looks like an artistic pond. She offers a fixed-price dinner (€30, on request) and cooking classes (breakfast extra, air-con, free self-service laundry, free parking, Via degli Alloi 80, tel. 0588-39080, www.agriturismo-volterra.it, info@agriturismosanlorenzo.it).

$$ Agriturismo il Mulinaccio is a welcoming, family-friendly farm about a 15-minute drive down a dirt road outside Volterra. Alessio and his family rent four apartments and four bed-and-breakfast rooms, all with a cozy style. They also offer dinner, truffle hunts, and a spa/wellness center (air-con, pool, Via Vicinale di Pretenzano 49, mobile 338-149-8432, www.agriturismoilmulinaccio.it, info@agriturismoilmulinaccio.it).

$$ Agriturismo Santa Vittoria sits on the top of a hill, with commanding views into the Volterra countryside. Their four bright apartments, decorated with funky art, have access to a cliffside pool. Their popular restaurant serves up hearty dishes from their farm, served at view tables (breakfast extra, air-con, Localita Molino d'Era, tel. 0588-33071, www.agriturismosantavittoria.com, info@agriturismosantavittoria.com, Katuscia).

Eating in Volterra

Menus feature a Volterran take on regional dishes. *Zuppa alla Volterrana* is a fresh vegetable-and-bread soup, similar to *ribollita*. *Torta di ceci,* also known as *cecina,* is a savory crêpe-like garbanzo-bean flatbread that's served at *pizzerie*. Those with more adventurous palates dive into *trippa* (tripe stew, the traditional breakfast of the alabaster carvers). *Fegatelli* are meatballs made with liver.

$$$$ Ristorante Enoteca del Duca, serving well-presented and creative Tuscan cuisine, offers the best elegant meal in town.

You can dine under a medieval arch with walls lined with wine bottles, in a sedate, high-ceilinged dining room (with an Etruscan statuette at each table), in their little *enoteca* (wine cellar), or in their terraced garden in summer. Chef Genuino, daughter Claudia, and the friendly staff take good care of diners. The fine wine list includes Genuino's own highly regarded merlot and sangiovese. The spacious seating, dressy clientele, and calm atmosphere make this a good choice for a romantic splurge. Their €55 food-sampler fixed-price meal comes with a free glass of wine for diners with this book (Wed-Mon 12:30-15:00 & 19:30-22:00, closed Tue, near City Hall at Via di Castello 2, tel. 0588-81510).

$$ La Carabaccia is unique: It feels like a local family invited you over for a dinner of classic Tuscan comfort food that's rarely seen on restaurant menus. They serve only two pastas and two *secondi* on any given day (listed on the chalkboard by the door), in addition to quality cheese and cold-cut plates. Committed to tradition, on Fridays they serve only fish. They also have fun, family-friendly outdoor seating on a traffic-free piazza (Tue-Sat 12:30-14:30 & 19:30-22:00, Sun 12:30-14:30, closed Mon, reservations smart, Piazza XX Settembre 4, tel. 0588-86239, https://lacarabacciavolterra.it, Patrizia and daughters Sara and Ilaria).

$$ Ristorante il Sacco Fiorentino is a family-run local favorite for traditional cuisine and seasonal specials. While mostly indoors, the restaurant has a few nice tables on a peaceful street (Thu-Tue 12:00-15:00 & 19:00-22:00, closed Wed, Via Giusto Turazza 13, tel. 0588-88537, Cristina).

$$ Trattoria da Badò, a 10-minute hike out of town, is popular with a local crowd for its *cucina tipica Volterrana*. Giacomo and family offer a rustic atmosphere and serve food with no pretense—"the way you wish your mamma cooks." Reserve before you go, as it's often full, especially on weekends (Thu-Tue 12:30-14:30 & 19:30-22:00, closed Wed, Borgo San Lazzero 9—along the main road toward San Gimignano, near the turnoff for the old hospital, tel. 0588-80402, www.trattoriadabado.com).

$$ La Vecchia Lira, bright and cheery, is a classy self-serve eatery that's a hit with locals as a quick and cheap lunch spot by day and a mediocre sit-down restaurant at night (Fri-Wed 11:30-14:30 & 19:00-22:30, closed Thu, Via Matteotti 19, tel. 0588-86180, Lamberto and Massimo).

$$ Ristorante Ombra della Sera is another good fine-dining option for elegant Tuscan cuisine and truffle dishes. While they have a dressy interior, I'd eat here to be on the street and part of the *passeggiata* action (Tue-Sun 12:00-15:00 & 19:00-22:00, closed Mon and mid-Nov-mid-March, Via Gramsci 70, tel. 0588-86663, Massimo and Cinzia).

$$ Pizzeria La Mangiatoia is a fun and convivial place with a Tuscan-cowboy interior and picnic tables outside amid a family-friendly street scene. Enjoy pizzas, huge salads, and kebabs at a table or to go (Thu-Tue 12:00-23:00, closed Wed, Via Gramsci 35, tel. 0588-85695).

Side-by-Side Pizzerias: $ Ombra della Sera dishes out what local kids consider the best pizza in town (Tue-Sun 12:00-15:00 & 19:00-22:00, closed Mon and mid-Nov-mid-March, Via Guarnacci 16, tel. 0588-85274). **$ Pizzeria Tavernetta,** next door, has a romantically frescoed dining room upstairs for classier pizza eating (Wed-Mon 12:00-15:00 & 18:30-22:30, closed Tue, Via Guarnacci 14, tel. 0588-88155).

Picnic: You can assemble a picnic at the few *alimentari* around town and eat in the breezy archaeological park. The most convenient supermarket is **Punto Simply** at Via Gramsci 12 (Mon-Sat 7:30-13:00 & 16:00-20:00, Sun 8:30-13:00).

Gelato: Of the many ice-cream shops in the center, I've found **L'Isola del Gusto** to be reliably high quality, with flavors limited to what's in season (daily, closed Nov-Feb, Via Gramsci 3, cheery Giorgia will make you feel happy).

Volterra Connections

By Bus: In Volterra, buses come and go from Piazza Martiri della Libertà (buy tickets at the tobacco shop right on the piazza or on board). Most connections are with the C.T.T. bus company (www.pisa.cttnord.it) through Colle di Val d'Elsa ("koh-leh" for short), a workaday town in the valley (4/day Mon-Sat, 1/day Sun, 50 minutes); for Pisa, you'll change in Pontedera or Saline di Volterra. Ask at the TI for schedules.

From Volterra, you can ride the bus to these destinations: **Florence** (4/day Mon-Sat, 1/day Sun, 2 hours, change in Colle di Val d'Elsa), **Siena** (4/day Mon-Sat, no buses on Sun, 2 hours, change in Colle di Val d'Elsa), **San Gimignano** (4/day Mon-Sat, 1/day Sun, 2 hours, change in Colle di Val d'Elsa, one connection also requires change in Poggibonsi), **Pisa** (9/day, fewer on Sun, 2 hours, change in Pontedera).

By Train: The nearest train station is in Saline di Volterra, a 15-minute bus ride away (7/day, 2/day Sun); however, trains from Saline run only to the coast, not to the major bus destinations listed here. It's better to take a bus from Volterra to Pontedera (CTT bus

#500, 8/day, 1 on Sun, 1.5 hours), where you can catch a train to **Florence, Pisa,** or **La Spezia** (convenient for the Cinque Terre).

By Car: From Pisa, take the highway known as FI-PI-LI (for "Firenze-Pisa-Livorno") in the direction of Florence, exiting at Pontedera to follow the scenic country road SR-439 toward Ponsacco and on to Volterra. From Florence, leave the city to the south to reach SR-2 toward Siena. Exit just past Poggibonsi onto SR-68 toward Colle di Val d'Elsa, passing San Gimignano on the way to Volterra.

By Private Transfer: For those with more money than time, or for travel on tricky Sundays and holidays, a private transfer to or from Volterra is the most efficient option. **Roberto Bechi** and his drivers can take up to eight people in their comfortable vans (€165 to Siena, €185 to Florence, for reservations call mobile 320-147-6590, Roberto's mobile 328-425-5648, www.toursbyroberto.com, toursbyroberto@gmail.com).

San Gimignano

The epitome of a Tuscan hill town, with 14 medieval towers still standing (out of an original 72), San Gimignano (sahn jee-meen-

YAH-noh) is a perfectly preserved tourist trap. There are no important interiors to sightsee, and the town feels greedy and packed with crass commercialism. The locals seem spoiled by the easy money of tourism, and

most of the rustic is faux. But San Gimignano is so easy to reach and so visually striking that it remains a good stop, especially if you can sidestep some of the hordes. The town is an ideal place to go against the touristic flow—arrive late in the day, enjoy it at twilight, then take off in the morning before the deluge begins. (Or day-trip here from Volterra—a 30-minute drive away—and visit early or late.)

In the 13th century—back in the days of Romeo and Juliet—feuding noble families ran the hill towns. They'd periodically battle things out from the protection of their respective family towers. Pointy skylines like San Gimignano's were the norm in medieval Tuscany.

San Gimignano's cuisine is mostly what you might find in Siena—typical Tuscan home cooking. *Cinghiale* (cheen-gee-AH-lay, boar) is served in almost every way: stews, soups, cutlets, and, my favorite, salami. The area is well-known for producing some of the best saffron in Italy; you'll find the spice for sale in shops and as a flavoring in meals at finer restaurants. Although Tuscany is normally a red-wine region, the most famous Tuscan white wine comes from here: the inexpensive, light, and fruity Vernaccia di San Gimignano.

Orientation to San Gimignano

While the basic ▲▲▲ sight here is the town of San Gimignano itself (pop. 7,800, just 2,000 of whom live within the walls), there are a few worthwhile stops. The wall circles an amazingly preserved stony town, once on the Via Francigena pilgrimage route to Rome. The road, which cuts through the middle of San Gimignano, is named for St. Matthew in the north of town (Via San Matteo) and St. John in the south (Via San Giovanni). The town is centered on two delightful squares—Piazza del Duomo and Piazza della Cisterna—where you find the town well, City Hall, and cathedral (along with most of the tourists).

Tourist Information: The helpful TI is in the old center on Piazza del Duomo (daily March-Oct 10:00-13:00 & 15:00-19:00, Nov-Feb 10:00-13:00 & 14:00-18:00, sells bus tickets to Siena and Florence, tel. 0577-940-008, www.sangimignano.com). They offer occasional countryside tours and a guided city tour (€15, April-Oct Mon, Wed, Fri-Sat at 11:00 and 16:00, Sun at 11:00).

ARRIVAL IN SAN GIMIGNANO

The **bus** stops at the main town gate, Porta San Giovanni. There's no baggage storage in town.

You can't **drive** within the walled town; drive past the *"ZTL"* red circle and you'll get socked with a big fine. Three numbered pay lots are a short walk outside the walls (and connected to town by a shuttle bus in summer; see later): The handiest is Parcheggio Montemaggio (P2), at the bottom of town near the bus stop, just outside Porta San Giovanni (€2/hour, €15/day). Least expensive but a steeper walk into town is the lot below the roundabout and Co-op supermarket, Parcheggio Giubileo (P1; €1.50/hour, €6/day). And at the north end of town, by Porta San Jacopo, is Parcheggio Bagnaia (P3/P4, €2/hour, €15/day). Note that some lots—including the one directly in front of Co-op and the one just outside Porta San Matteo—are designated for locals and have a one-hour limit for tourists.

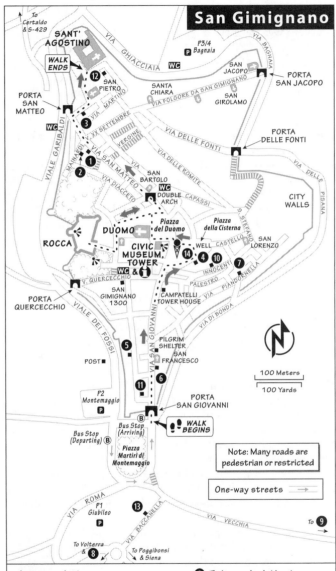

San Gimignano

VOLTERRA & SAN GIMIGNANO

Note: Many roads are pedestrian or restricted

One-way streets ⟶

100 Meters

100 Yards

Accommodations

1 Hotel l'Antico Pozzo
2 Le Undici Lune
3 Locanda il Pino
4 Hotel la Cisterna
5 Palazzo al Torrione
6 Hotel Belsoggiorno (Torrione Check-in)
7 Le Vecchie Mura Camere & Rist.
8 To Locanda dei Logi
9 To Podere Ponte a Nappo

Eateries & Other

10 Dulcis in Fundo Ristorante
11 Trattoria Chiribiri
12 Locanda di Sant'Agostino
13 Supermarket
14 Gelateria Dondoli

HELPFUL HINTS

Market Day: Thursday is market day on Piazza del Duomo and Piazza delle Erbe (8:00-13:00), but for local merchants, every day is a sales frenzy.

Services: A public WC is just off Piazza della Cisterna; you'll also find WCs at the Rocca fortress, near San Bartolo church, just outside Porta San Matteo, and at the Parcheggio Bagnaia parking lot.

Shuttle Bus: A little electric shuttle bus does its laps about hourly all day from Porta San Giovanni to Piazza della Cisterna to Porta San Matteo. Route #1 runs back and forth through town; route #2—which runs only in summer—connects the three parking lots to the town center (€1.20 one-way). When pedestrian congestion in the town center is greatest (Sat afternoons, all day Sun, and May-Sept), the bus runs along the road skirting the outside of town.

San Gimignano Walk

This quick self-guided walking tour takes you across town, from the bus stop at Porta San Giovanni through the town's main squares to the Duomo, and on to the Sant'Agostino Church.

• *Start at the Porta San Giovanni gate at the bottom (south) end of town.*

Porta San Giovanni

San Gimignano lies about 25 miles from both Siena and Florence, a day's trek for pilgrims en route to those cities, and on a naturally fortified hilltop that encouraged settlement. The town's walls were built in the 13th century, and gates like this helped regulate who came and went. Today, modern posts keep out all but service and emergency vehicles. The small square just outside the gate features a memorial to the town's WWII dead. Follow the pilgrims' route (and flood of modern tourists) through the gate and up the main drag.

About 100 yards up, where the street widens, look right to see a pilgrims' shelter (12th century, Pisan Romanesque). The eight-pointed Maltese cross on the facade of the church indicates that it was built by the Knights of Malta, whose early mission (before they became Crusaders) was to provide care for sick and poor pilgrims. It was one of 11 such shelters in town. Today, only the wall of the shelter remains, and the surviving interior of the church houses yet one more shop selling gifty edibles.

• *Carry on past all manner of shops, up to the top of Via San Giovanni. Look up at the formidable inner wall, built 200 years before today's outer wall. Just beyond that is the central Piazza della Cisterna. Sit on the steps of the well.*

Piazza della Cisterna

The piazza is named for the cistern that is served by the old well standing in the center of this square. A clever system of pipes

drained rainwater from the nearby rooftops into the underground cistern. This square has been the center of the town since the ninth century. Turn in a slow circle and observe the commotion of rustic-yet-proud facades crowding in a tight huddle around the well. Imagine this square in pilgrimage times, lined by inns and taverns for the town's guests. Now finger the grooves in the lip of the well and imagine generations of women and children fetching water. Each Thursday morning, the square fills with a market—as it has for more than a thousand years.

• *Notice San Gimignano's famous towers.*

The Towers

Of the original 72 towers, only 14 survive (and one can be climbed—at the City Hall). Some of the original towers were just empty, chimney-like structures built to boost noble egos, while others were actually the forts of wealthy families.

Before effective city walls were developed, rich people needed to fortify and protect their homes themselves. These towers provided a handy refuge when ruffians and rival city-states were sacking the town. If under attack, tower owners would set fire to the external wooden staircase, leaving the sole entrance unreachable a story up; inside, fleeing nobles pulled up behind them the ladders that connected each level, leaving invaders no way to reach the stronghold at the tower's top. These towers became a standard part of medieval skylines. Even after town walls were built, the towers continued to rise—now to fortify noble families feuding within a town (Montague and Capulet-style).

In the 14th century, San Gimignano's good times turned very bad. At the start of that century, about 13,000 people lived within the walls. But in 1348, a six-month plague decimated the population, leaving the once-mighty town with barely 4,000 survivors. Once fiercely independent, now crushed and demoralized, San Gimignano came under Florence's control and was forced to tear down most of its towers. (The Banca CR Firenze building occupies the remains of one such toppled tower.) And, to add insult to injury, Florence redirected the vital trade route away from San Gimignano. The town never recovered, and poverty left it in an architectural time warp. That well-preserved 14th-century cityscape, ironically, is responsible for the town's prosperity today.

• *From the well, walk 30 yards uphill to the adjoining square with the cathedral.*

Piazza del Duomo

Stand at the base of the stairs in front of the church. Since before there was gelato, people have lounged on these steps. Take a

360-degree spin clockwise: The cathedral's 12th-century facade is plain-Jane Romanesque—finished even though it doesn't look it. To the right, the two Salvucci Towers date from the 13th century. (Locals claim that the architect who designed New York City's Twin Towers was inspired by these). The towers are empty shells, built by the wealthy Salvucci family simply to show off. At that time, no one was allowed a vanity tower higher than the City Hall's 170 feet. So the Salvuccis built two 130-foot towers—totaling 260 feet of stony ego trip.

The stubby tower next to the Salvucci Towers is the Merchant's Tower. Imagine this in use: ground-floor shop, warehouse upstairs (see the functional shipping door), living quarters, and finally the kitchen on the top (for fire-safety reasons). The holes in the walls held beams that supported wooden balconies and exterior staircases. The tower has heavy stone on the first floor, then cheaper and lighter brick for the upper stories.

Opposite the church stands the first City Hall, with its 170-foot tower, nicknamed "the bad news tower." While the church got to ring its bells in good times, these bells were for battles and fires. The tower's arched public space hosted a textile market back when cloth was the foundation of San Gimignano's booming economy.

Next is the supersize "new" City Hall with its 200-foot tower (the only one in town open to the public; for visiting info, see the Civic Museum and Tower listing, later). The climbing lion is the symbol of the city. The coats of arms of the city's leading families have been ripped down or disfigured. In medieval times locals would have blamed witches or ghosts. For the last two centuries, they've blamed Napoleon instead.

Between the City Hall and the cathedral, a statue of St. Gimignano presides over all the hubbub. The fourth-century bishop protected the village from rampaging barbarians—and is now the city's patron saint. (To enter the cathedral, walk under that statue.)
• *You'll also see the...*

Duomo (Duomo di San Gimignano/La Collegiata)

The nave of San Gimignano's Romanesque cathedral is lined with frescoes that tell the stories of the Bible—Old Testament on the left and New Testament on the right. Painted by masters of the 14th-century Sienese school, the frescoes are a classic use of teaching through art, with parallel themes aligned: Creation faces the Annunciation, the birth of Adam is opposite the Nativity, and—farther forward—the suffering of Job faces the agony of Jesus. Many scenes are portrayed with a 14th-century "slice of life" setting to help lay townspeople relate to Jesus.

To the right of the altar, the St. Fina Chapel honors the devout, 13th-century local girl who brought forth many miracles on her death. Her tomb is beautifully frescoed with scenes from her life by Domenico Ghirlandaio (famed as Michelangelo's teacher). The altar sits atop Fina's skeleton, and its centerpiece is a reliquary that contains her skull (€4, includes dry audioguide; April-Oct Mon-Fri 10:00-19:30, Sat until 17:30, Sun 12:30-19:30; shorter hours off-season; buy ticket and enter from courtyard around left side, www.duomosangimignano.it).
• *From the church, hike uphill (passing the church on your left) following signs to* Rocca e Parco di Montestaffoli. *Keep walking until you enter a peaceful hilltop park and olive grove, set within the shell of a 14th-century fortress the Medici of Florence built to protect this town from Siena.*

Hilltop Views at the Rocca

On the far side, 33 steps take you to the top of a little tower (free) for the best views of San Gimignano's skyline; the far end of town and the Sant'Agostino Church (where this walk ends); and a commanding 360-degree view of the Tuscan countryside. San Gimignano is surrounded by olives, grapes, cypress trees, and—in the Middle Ages—lots of wild dangers. Back then, farmers lived inside the walls and were thankful for the protection.
• *Return to the bottom of Piazza del Duomo, turn left, and continue your walk, cutting under the double arch (from the town's first wall).*

In around 1200, this wall defined the end of town. The **Church of San Bartolo** stood just outside the wall (on the right). The Maltese cross over the door indicates that it likely served as a hostel for pilgrims. As you continue down Via San Matteo, notice that the crowds have dropped by at least half. Enjoy the breathing room as you pass a fascinating array of stone facades from the 13th and 14th centuries—now a happy cancan of wine shops and galleries.

• *Reaching the gateway at the end of town, follow signs to the right to reach...*

Sant'Agostino Church

This tranquil church, at the far end of town (built by the Augustinians who arrived in 1260), has fewer crowds and more soul. Behind the altar, a lovely fresco cycle by Benozzo Gozzoli (who painted the exquisite Chapel of the Magi in the Medici-Riccardi Palace in Florence) tells of the life of St. Augustine, a North African monk who preached simplicity (pay a few coins for light). The kind, English-speaking friars (often from Britain and the US) are happy to tell you about the frescoes and their way of life. Pace the peaceful cloister before heading back into the tourist mobs (free, April-Oct daily 9:00-12:00 & 15:00-19:00, shorter hours off-season; Sunday Mass in English at 11:00).

Sights in San Gimignano

▲Civic Museum and Tower (Musei Civici and Torre Grossa)

This small, entertaining museum, consisting of three unfurnished rooms, is inside the City Hall (Palazzo Comunale). The main reason to visit is to scale the tower, which offers sweeping views over San Gimignano and the countryside.

Cost and Hours: €9 includes museum and tower; daily 10:00-19:30, Oct-March 11:00-17:30, audioguide-€2, Piazza del Duomo, tel. 0577-990-312, www.sangimignanomusei.it.

Visiting the Museum: You'll enter the complex through a delightful stony courtyard (to the left as you face the Duomo). Climb up to the loggia to buy your ticket.

The main room (across from the ticket desk), called the **Sala del Consiglio** (a.k.a. Dante Hall, recalling his visit in 1300), is covered in festive frescoes, including the *Maestà* by Lippo Memmi (from 1317). This virtual copy of Simone Martini's *Maestà* in Siena proves that Memmi didn't have quite the same talent as his famous brother-in-law. The art gives you a peek at how people dressed, lived, worked, and warred back in the 14th century.

Upstairs, the **Pinacoteca** displays a classy little painting collection of mostly altarpieces. The highlight is a 1422 altarpiece by Taddeo di Bartolo honoring St. Gimignano (far end of last room). You can see the saint, with the town—bristling with towers—in his hands, surrounded by events from his life.

Before going back downstairs, be sure to stop by the **Mayor's Room** (Camera del Podestà, across the stairwell from the Pinacoteca). Frescoed in 1310, it offers an intimate and candid peek into the 14th century. As you enter, look right up in the corner to find a young man ready to experience the world. He hits his parents up for a bag of money and is on his way. Suddenly (above the window), he's in trouble, entrapped by two prostitutes, who lead him into a tent where he loses his money, is turned out, and is beaten. Above the door, from left to right, you see a parade of better choices: marriage, the cradle of love, the bride led to the groom's house, and newlyweds bathing together and retiring happily to their bed.

The highlight for most visitors is a chance to climb the **Tower** (entrance halfway down the stairs from the Pinacoteca). The city's tallest tower, 200 feet and 218 steps up, rewards those who climb it with a commanding view. See if you can count the town's 14 towers. It's a sturdy, modern staircase most of the way, but the last stretch is a steep, ladder-like climb.

▲Campatelli Tower House (Torre e Casa Campatelli)

The Campatelli family, wealthy landowners from Florence, bought an age-old tower and adjacent properties in the 19th century and turned them into a palatial residence. They lived here until 2005, when the last of the family donated it to a nonprofit organization that protects historic buildings and gardens, which then opened it to the public. The house contains family belongings and tells the story of upper-class life in Tuscany, but the highlights are an audiovisual presentation on the history of the city and the chance to peer up through the tower, with a cutaway staircase and floor, to see how the towers in San Gimignano were built.

Cost and Hours: €7, Thu-Tue 10:30-17:30, closed Wed, weekends only off-season, Via San Giovanni 15, tel. 0577-941-419, www.fondoambiente.it/luoghi/beni-fai.

San Gimignano 1300

Artists and brothers Michelangelo and Raffaello Rubino share an interesting attraction in their workshop: a painstakingly rendered 1:100 scale clay model of San Gimignano at the turn of the 14th century. Step through a shop selling their art to enjoy the model. You can see the 72 original "tower houses," and marvel at how unchanged the street plan remains today. You'll peek into cross-sections of buildings, view scenes of medieval life both within and outside the city walls, and watch a video about the making of the model.

Cost and Hours: Free, daily 10:00-18:00, Dec-April until 17:00, on a quiet street a block over from the main square at Via Costarella 3, mobile 327-439-5165, www.sangimignano1300.com.

Sleeping in San Gimignano

Although the town is a zoo during the daytime, locals outnumber tourists when evening comes, and San Gimignano becomes mellow and enjoyable.

NEAR PORTA SAN MATTEO, AT THE QUIET END OF TOWN

If arriving by bus, save yourself a crosstown walk to these accommodations by asking for the Porta San Matteo stop. Drivers can park at the less-crowded Bagnaia lots (P3 and P4), and walk around to Porta San Matteo.

$$$ Hotel l'Antico Pozzo is an elegantly restored, 15th-century townhouse with 18 comfortable rooms, a peaceful interior courtyard terrace, and an elite air (air-con, elevator, Via San Matteo 87, tel. 0577-942-014, www.anticopozzo.com, info@anticopozzo.com; Emanuele, Elisabetta, and Mariangela).

$$ Le Undici Lune ("The 11 Moons") is situated in a tight but characteristic circa-1300 townhouse with steep stairs at the tranquil end of town. Its three rooms and one apartment are colorfully decorated (air-con, Via Mainardi 9, mobile 392-450-5221, le11lune@libero.it, Vincenzo).

$ Locanda il Pino has just seven rooms and a big living room. It's plain but clean and quiet. Run by English-speaking Elena and her family, it sits above their elegant restaurant just inside Porta San Matteo (fans, Via Cellolese 4, tel. 0577-907-003, www.locandailpino.it, locandailpino@gmail.com).

NEAR THE MAIN SQUARE, AT THE BUSY END OF TOWN

$$ Hotel la Cisterna, right on Piazza della Cisterna, feels old and stately. Its 48 rooms range from old-fashioned to contemporary, and some have panoramic view terraces (RS%, air-con, elevator, good restaurant with great view, closed Jan-Feb, Piazza della Cisterna 23, tel. 0577-940-328, www.hotelcisterna.it, info@hotelcisterna.it, Alessio and Paola).

$$ Palazzo al Torrione, on an untrampled side street just inside Porta San Giovanni, is quiet and handy. Their 10 modern rooms, some with countryside views and terraces, are spacious and tastefully appointed (RS%, family rooms, breakfast extra, air-con, pay parking, inside and left of gate at Via Berignano 76; check-in at Hotel Belsoggiorno, 2 blocks away, on the main drag at Via

San Giovanni 91; tel. 0577-940-375, www.palazzoaltorrione.com, info@palazzoaltorrione.com, Vanna).

$ Le Vecchie Mura Camere offers three good rooms above their recommended restaurant along a rustic lane, clinging just below the main square (no breakfast, air-con, Via Piandornella 15, tel. 0577-940-270, www.vecchiemura.it, info@vecchiemura.it, Bagnai family).

IN THE COUNTRYSIDE

$$$$ Locanda dei Logi, in the tiny *borgo* of San Donato—eight minutes from San Gimignano—houses six ultramodern, luxury rooms within a cluster of medieval buildings. Each room is elegantly designed, and all look out over the property's vineyard. Wine lovers can combine an overnight and a tasting of their top-notch wines in their cantina (wine tastings available by appointment, dinner on request, air-con, Localita San Donato 1, mobile 392-506-8229, www.locandadeilogi.it, info@locandadeilogi.it).

$$ Podere Ponte a Nappo, run by enterprising Carla Rossi and her English-speaking sons Francesco and Andrea, has six basic rooms and two apartments in a kid-friendly farmhouse boasting fine San Gimignano views. Located a mile below town, it can be reached by foot in about 20 minutes if you don't have a car. A picnic dinner lounging on their comfy garden furniture next to the big swimming pool as the sun sets is good Tuscan living (RS%—use code "RickSteves," air-con, free parking, tel. 0577-907-282, mobile 349-882-1565, www.accommodation-sangimignano.com, info@rossicarla.it). About 100 yards below the monument square at Porta San Giovanni, find tiny Via Baccanella/Via Vecchia and drive downhill. They also rent a dozen rooms and apartments in town.

Eating in San Gimignano

My first two listings cling to quiet, rustic lanes overlooking the Tuscan hills; the rest are buried deep in the old center.

$$$ Dulcis in Fundo Ristorante, small and family-run, proudly serves modest portions of "revisited" Tuscan cuisine (with a modern twist and gourmet presentation) in a jazzy ambience. This enlightened place uses top-quality ingredients, many of which come from their own farm (Thu-Tue 12:30-14:30 & 19:15-21:45, closed Wed and Nov-Feb, Vicolo degli Innocenti 21, tel. 0577-941-919, Roberto and Cristina).

$$ Le Vecchie Mura Ristorante is welcoming, with good service, great prices, tasty if unexceptional home cooking, and the ultimate view. It's romantic indoors or out. They have a dressy, modern interior where you can dine with a view of the busy stainless-steel kitchen under rustic vaults, but the main reason to come is for the incredible cliffside garden terrace. To reserve a cliffside table, call or drop by: Ask for "front view" (surcharge for outdoor tables, open only for dinner 18:00-22:00, closed Tue, Via Piandornella 15, tel. 0577-940-270, Bagnai family).

$ Trattoria Chiribiri, just inside Porta San Giovanni, serves homemade pastas and desserts at good prices. While its petite size and tight seating make it hot in the summer, it's a good budget option—and as such, it's in all the guidebooks (daily 11:00-23:00, Piazza della Madonna 1, tel. 0577-941-948, Roberto and Maurizio).

$$ Locanda di Sant'Agostino spills out onto the peaceful square, facing Sant'Agostino Church. It's homey and cheerful, serving lunch and dinner daily—big portions of basic food in a restful setting. Dripping with wheat stalks and atmosphere on the inside, it has shady on-the-square seating outside (Thu-Tue 11:00-16:00 & 18:30-23:00, closed Wed, closed Jan-Feb, Piazza Sant'Agostino 15, tel. 0577-943-141, Genziana and sons).

Near Porta San Matteo: Just inside Porta San Matteo is a variety of handy and inviting good-value restaurants, bars, cafés, and *gelaterie.*

Picnics: The big, modern **Co-op supermarket** sells all you need for a nice spread (Mon-Sat 8:30-20:00, closed Sun, at parking lot below Porta San Giovanni). Or browse the little shops guarded by boar heads within the town walls; they sell pricey boar meat *(cinghiale).* Pick up 100 grams (about a quarter pound) of boar, cheese, bread, and wine and enjoy a picnic in the garden at the Rocca or the park outside Porta San Giovanni.

Gelato: To cap the evening and sweeten your late-night city stroll, stop by **Gelateria Dondoli** on Piazza della Cisterna (at #4, tel. 0577-942-244, www.gelateriadondoli.com, sergio@gelateriadondoli.com, Dondoli family). Charismatic Sergio also offers hands-on gelato-making classes in his kitchen down the street.

San Gimignano Connections

Bus tickets are sold at the bar just inside the town gate or at the TI. Many connections require a change at Poggibonsi (poh-jee-BOHN-see), which has the nearest train station. Note that the bus connection to Volterra is four times as long as the drive; if you're desperate to get there faster, you can pay about €70 for a taxi.

From San Gimignano by Bus to: Florence (hourly, fewer on Sun, 1.5-2 hours, change in Poggibonsi), **Siena** (8/day direct, on Sun must change in Poggibonsi, 1.5 hours), **Volterra** (4/day Mon-Sat; 1/day Sun—in the late afternoon and usually crowded—with no return to San Gimignano; 2 hours, change in Colle di Val d'Elsa, one connection also requires change in Poggibonsi).

By Car: San Gimignano is an easy 45-minute drive from Florence (take the A-1 exit marked *Firenze Imprugneta*, then a right past tollbooth following *Siena per 4 corsie* sign; exit the free-way at *Poggibonsi Nord*). From San Gimignano, it's a scenic and windy half-hour drive to Volterra.

THE HEART OF TUSCANY

Montepulciano • Pienza • Montalcino • Heart of Tuscany Drive

If your Tuscan dreams feature vibrant neon-green fields rolling to infinity, punctuated by snaking, cypress-lined driveways; humble but beautiful (and steep) hill towns; and world-class wines to make a connoisseur weep, set your sights on the heart of this region.

An hour south of Siena, this slice of splendor—which specializes in views and wine—is a highlight, particularly for drivers. With an astonishing diversity of towns, villages, abbeys, wineries, countryside restaurants, and accommodations—all set within jaw-dropping scenery—this subregion of Tuscany is a fine place to abandon your itinerary and just slow down.

Even though the area's towns sometimes seem little more than a rack upon which to hang the vine-draped hills, each one has its own endearing personality. The biggest and most interesting, Montepulciano, boasts a medieval cityscape wearing a Renaissance coat, wine cellars that plunge deep into the cliffs it sits upon, and a classic town square. Pienza is a sure-of-itself, planned Renaissance town that gave the world a pope. And mellow Montalcino is (even more than most towns around here) all about its wine: the famous Brunello di Montalcino.

PLANNING YOUR TIME

As this compact region is hemmed in by Italy's two main north-south thoroughfares—the A-1 expressway and SR-2 highway—even those with a few hours to spare can get an enticing taste. But ideally, spend two nights and three full days. Many travelers enjoy home-basing here, appreciating not only the area's many attractions, but also its strategic position for day trips to Siena (less than an hour away), or Volterra, San Gimignano, Florence, and Orvieto (each about 1.5 hours away).

Montepulciano is the most all-around engaging town; it's the best choice for those without a car (though connections can still be tricky). With easy access to the vineyards, Montalcino makes sense for wine pilgrims. For drivers who'd like to home-base in the countryside, I've listed several *agriturismi* and other rural accommodations.

The Heart of Tuscany in Three Days

Here's a smart plan, assuming you're coming from Siena. (If coming from the south, do it in reverse.)

Day One: On your way south from Siena, make a winery stop north of Montalcino before settling into Montepulciano (or your countryside accommodation).

Day Two: Follow my Heart of Tuscany Drive, including a sightseeing-and-gelato stop in Pienza. Have dinner back in Montepulciano, or in the nearby countryside.

Day Three: Your day is free to enjoy and sightsee Montepulciano, or drive to countryside attractions (confirm tour availability at La Foce Gardens in advance). You could head to your next destination this afternoon, or spend a third night.

GETTING AROUND THE HEART OF TUSCANY

By Car: This area is ideal by car. Distances are short, and it's easy to mix-and-match sights.

Navigate by town names and use a good map or—better yet—a mapping app to keep you on track. Some sights and wineries are on tiny back lanes, marked only with easy-to-miss, low-profile signs. In small hill towns, make it a habit to park at the lot just outside town and walk in. White lines indicate free parking; blue lines indicate paid parking (pay at the station, then display the ticket on your windshield); and yellow lines are only for locals.

By Public Transportation: While you can reach many of this chapter's sights by public buses, connections are slow, infrequent, and often require a transfer. Taxis can help connect the dots more efficiently. Montepulciano is the best home base for those without a car (though it's still not entirely convenient).

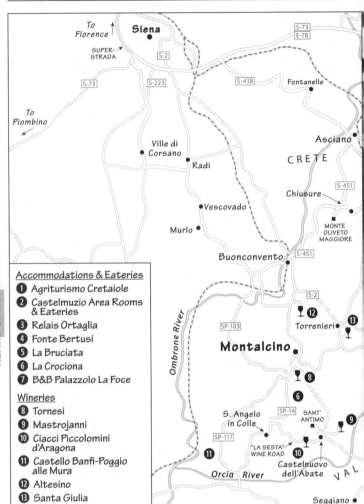

To Florence
Siena
SUPER-STRADA
S-2
S-73
E-78
S-73
S-223
S-438
Fontanelle
To Piombino
Ville di Corsano
Radi
Asciano
CRETE
S-451
Vescovado
Chiusure
Murlo
MONTE OLIVETO MAGGIORE
Buonconvento
S-451
S-2
Ombrone River
SP-103
Torrenieri
Montalcino
S. Angelo in Colle
SP-14
SANT' ANTIMO
SP-117
"LA SESTA" WINE ROAD
Orcia River
Castelnuovo dell'Abate
VAL
Seggiano

Accommodations & Eateries
1 Agriturismo Cretaiole
2 Castelmuzio Area Rooms & Eateries
3 Relais Ortaglia
4 Fonte Bertusi
5 La Bruciata
6 La Crociona
7 B&B Palazzolo La Foce

Wineries
8 Tornesi
9 Mastrojanni
10 Ciacci Piccolomini d'Aragona
11 Castello Banfi-Poggio alle Mura
12 Altesino
13 Santa Giulia

TOURS IN TUSCANY

A good local guide can help you take full advantage of everything this area has to offer. One with a car can save you lots of time and stress.

Antonella Piredda is smart, well organized, and enjoyably opinionated (€60/hour, 3-hour minimum, €350/all day, she can join you in your car or hire a driver for extra, mobile 347-456-5150, www.antonellapiredda.com, antonella.piredda@live.it).

Roberto Bechi runs all-day minibus tours with a passion for local culture, hands-on experiences, and offbeat sights. The price is reasonable, since he assembles groups of up to eight people to

Heart of Tuscany

To Florence

Rapolano Terme

5 Kilometers

5 Miles

S-71

To Cortona

Camucia/Cortona Train Stn.

Camucia

Serre di Rapolano

Sinalunga

S E N E S I

E-78

To Perugia & Assisi

SP-60A

San Giovanni d'Asso

Montisi

Castelmuzio **2** Petroio

A-1
E-35

Montepulciano Train Stn.

U M B R I A

See Heart of Tuscany Drive detail map

SP-146

SAN BIAGIO CHURCH

Montepulciano

4

Pienza

CORSIGNANO CHURCH

5

3

SP-146

Lago di Chiusi

1

San Quirico d'Orcia

S-2

Monticchiello

Chianciano Terme

ETRUSCAN TOMBS

Chiusi

Bagno Vignoni

Rocca d'Orcia

SPEDALETTO CASTLE

SP-53

S-146

Castiglione d'Orcia

LA FOCE GARDENS & **7**

S-478

Chiusi Train Stn.

SS-323

D ' O R C I A

Orcia River

S-2

A-1

To Orvieto & Rome

To Orvieto & Rome

HEART OF TUSCANY

share the experience...and the cost (see website for tour options, RS%—10 percent discount, full-day minibus tours—€100/person, mobile 320-147-6590, www.toursbyroberto.com, toursbyroberto@ gmail.com). For more on Roberto's tours, see page 13.

COUNTRYSIDE ACCOMMODATIONS

A beautiful way to more fully experience this area is to sleep in a farmhouse B&B. For locations, see the "Heart of Tuscany" map. Many of these are working farms (a prerequisite to be officially called an *agriturismo*) and give a great sense of rural family life. Others are just lovely homes in the countryside. The common denominator is the wonderful people you'll meet as your hosts.

Near Pienza

The Isabella Experience: A variety of accommodations and culturally rich experiences in the countryside near Pienza are warmly run by Isabella, her farmer husband Carlo, and their team. Compare options on the website (www.theisabellaexperience.com) or call Isabella (mobile 338-740-9245)—she's happy to answer questions. Here's a rundown:

$$$ Agriturismo Cretaiole is perfect for fully experiencing Tuscany with a group of other travelers. A one-week stay is required (Sat to Sat), which facilitates guests becoming a community of about 20 people—guided by Carlotta—who take part in farm tours, olive oil tastings, pasta-making classes, and more (no air-con or swimming pool, shorter stays may be possible off-season, Carlotta's mobile 338-835-1614).

$$$$ La Moscadella, on the outskirts of Castelmuzio (five miles north of Pienza), provides a more elevated country-hotel experience—with 12 impeccably decorated rooms and a two-bedroom cottage, plus a gourmet-quality restaurant. Run by Isabella and Doriana, La Moscadella also offers à la carte cultural experiences (weeklong stays preferred but may be flexible, air-con, swimming pool; tel. 0577-665-516, Doriana mobile 338-256-6043).

In the village of Castelmuzio, they rent two other properties: **$$$ Le Casine di Castello,** a townhouse with two units; and **$$$$ Casa Moricciani,** a swanky villa with dreamy views and a garden terrace.

More Accommodations Near Pienza: $$$$ Relais Ortaglia, run by Americans Sandy and Phil, rents five pricey rooms in a converted 17th-century farmhouse with modern amenities such as an infinity pool, activities (cooking classes), and a free bottle of prosecco for my readers. Leaving Montepulciano on the main road toward Pienza, watch for the easy-to-miss brown *Ortaglia* sign on the left, just a half-mile past the San Biagio church turnoff (includes breakfast, 2-night minimum, air-con, mobile 391-163-9887, www.relaisortaglia.com, tuscany@ortaglia.it).

$$$ Fonte Bertusi, a classy and artistic guesthouse between Pienza and Cretaiole, is nicely run by young couple Manuela and Andrea, Andrea's artist-father Edoardo, and their attention-starved cats. The eight apartments mix rustic decor with avant-garde creations. The setting is sublime, with a grand sunset-view terrace, a communal barbecue and outdoor kitchen, and a swimming pool (laundry service, just outside Pienza toward San Quirico d'Orcia

Heart of Tuscany at a Glance

▲▲▲**Montepulciano** Hill town with grand vistas, wonderful wine cellars, and a medieval soul that corrals the essence of Tuscany within its walls. See page 88.

▲▲▲**Heart of Tuscany Drive** An unforgettable day lacing together the views, villages, and rural attractions of this region (including both Montepulciano and Pienza). See page 120.

▲▲**Pienza** Unique, pint-sized planned Renaissance town that's amazingly well-preserved, very touristy, and relatively unhilly. See page 103.

▲▲**Montalcino** Touristy "Brunello-ville" wine capital that still exudes a stony charm; aside from the wine, it feels like a second-rate repeat of Montepulciano. See page 111.

▲▲**Sleeping at an *Agriturismo* or Countryside B&B** The best way to experience rural Tuscany: rustic, rural accommodations ranging from fragrant working farms to luxurious retreats. Most are run by families dedicated to making sure their cows and their guests are both well fed. See page 85.

▲**La Foce Gardens** Delightful, unique gardens with gorgeous plantings, engaging history, and fine panoramas. **Hours:** Visit by 45-minute tour only; April-Oct Wed at 15:00, 16:00, 17:00, and 18:00; Sat-Sun at 11:30, 15:00, and 16:30; no tours in winter. See page 124.

▲**Bagno Vignoni** Quirky little spa town that's simply fun to check out, whether you take a dip or not. See page 125.

HEART OF TUSCANY

on the right—just after the turnoff for "Il Fonte," tel. 0578-748-077, Manuela's mobile 339-655-5648, www.fontebertusi.it, info@fontebertusi.it).

$$ La Bruciata is a family-friendly *agriturismo* charmingly tucked in the countryside a five-minute drive outside Montepulciano (on the way to Pienza). Can-do Laura and several generations of her family produce wine and olive oil and rent several tasteful, modern rooms that share a peaceful yard with a swimming pool. From April through October, they prefer one-week stays (pay air-con, farm-fresh meals, cooking classes, Via del Termine 9, tel. 0578-757-704, mobile 339-781-5106, www.agriturismolabruciata.it, info@agriturismolabruciata.it). Leaving Montepulciano toward Pienza, turn off on the left for *Poggiano,* then carefully track brown *La Bruciata* signs (on gravel roads).

Near Montalcino
$$ La Crociona, an *agriturismo* farm and working vineyard, rents seven fully equipped apartments with dated furnishings. Fiorella Vannoni and Roberto and Barbara Nannetti offer cooking classes and tastes of the Brunello wine grown and bottled on the premises (reception open 9:00-13:00 & 14:30-19:30, laundry service, covered pool, hot tub, fitness room, La Croce 15, tel. 0577-847-133, www.lacrociona.com, info@lacrociona.com). The farm is about two miles south of Montalcino on the road to the Sant'Antimo Abbey; don't turn off at the first entrance to the village of La Croce—wait for the second one, following signs to *Tenuta Crocedimezzo e Crociona*. A good restaurant is next door.

At La Foce Gardens, near Montepulciano
$$$ B&B Palazzolo La Foce lets you sleep aristocratically in a small villa just below La Foce Gardens. Its seven colorful rooms share a welcoming lounge and breakfast area with a giant fireplace, and an outdoor swimming pool with glorious Tuscan views. All the rooms bask in fine panoramas (no air-con but breezy, Strada della Vittoria 61—check in at gardens' main entrance to get specific directions to your room, villas also available, tel. 0578-69101, www. lafoce.com, info@lafoce.com, Origo family).

Montepulciano

Curving its way along a ridge, Montepulciano (mohn-teh-puhl-CHAH-noh) delights visitors with *vino*, views, and—perhaps more than any other large town in this area—a sense of being a real, bustling community rather than just a tourist depot.

Alternately under Sienese and Florentine rule, the city still retains its medieval *contrade* (districts), each with a mascot and flag. The neighborhoods compete the last Sunday of August in the Bravio delle Botti, where teams of men push large wine

casks uphill from Piazza Marzocco to Piazza Grande, all hoping to win a banner and bragging rights. The entire last week of August is a festival: Each *contrada* arranges musical entertainment and serves food at outdoor eateries, along with generous tastings of the local *vino*.

The city is a collage of architectural styles, but the elegant San Biagio Church, just outside the city walls at the base of the hill, is

HEART OF TUSCANY

its best Renaissance building. Most visitors ignore the architecture and focus more on the city's other creative accomplishment, the tasty Vino Nobile di Montepulciano red wine.

Montepulciano is a great starting and ending point for my scenic loop drive through the Heart of Tuscany, described later in this chapter.

Orientation to Montepulciano

Commercial action in Montepulciano centers in the lower town, mostly along Via di Gracciano nel Corso (nicknamed "Corso"). This stretch begins at the town gate called Porta al Prato (near the TI, bus station, and some parking) and winds slowly up, up, up through town—narrated by my self-guided walk. Strolling here, you'll find eateries, gift shops, and tourist traps. The back streets are worth exploring. The main square, at the top of town (up a steep switchback lane from the Corso), is Piazza Grande. Standing proudly above all the touristy sales energy, the square has a noble, Florentine feel.

TOURIST INFORMATION

The helpful TI is just outside the Porta al Prato city gate, in the small P1 parking lot (Mon-Sat 9:00-13:00 & 15:00-19:00, Sun 9:00-13:00, daily until 20:00 in July-Aug, sells bus and train tickets, Piazza Don Minzoni, tel. 0578-757-341, www. prolocomontepulciano.it).

The office on the main square that looks like a TI is actually the privately run Valdichiana Living agency. They provide wine-road maps, wine tours in the city, minibus winery tours farther afield, and cooking classes and other culinary experiences (Mon-Fri 10:00-13:30 & 14:30-18:00, shorter Sat hours, Sun 10:00-13:00, Piazza Grande 7, tel. 0578-717-484, www.valdichianaliving.it).

ARRIVAL IN MONTEPULCIANO

Whether you arrive by car or bus, ease your climb to the top of town by riding up on the shuttle bus. For details, see "Helpful Hints," later.

By Car: Well-signed pay-and-display parking lots ring the city center (marked with blue lines). Some free spaces are mixed in (marked with white lines)—look around before you park, and keep an eye out for time limits.

To start your visit by following my self-guided walk (up the length of the Corso to the main square), park at the north end of town, near the Porta al Prato gate. Around here, the handiest lots are P1 (in front of the TI, with some free spaces) and the unnumbered lot just above, directly in front of the stone gate. If these are full, try lots P2 or P4, or lot P5 near the bus station.

For quicker access to the main square up top, use one of the parking lots at the top end of town: Approaching Montepulciano, follow signs for *centro storico, duomo,* and *Piazza Grande,* and use the Fortezza or San Donato lots (flanking the fortress).

Avoid the "ZTL" no-traffic zone (signs marked with a red circle). If you're sleeping in town, your hotelier can give you a permit to park within the walls; be sure to get very specific instructions before you arrive.

By Bus: Buses leave passengers at the bus station on Piazza Nenni, downhill from the Porta al Prato gate. From the station, cross the street and head inside the modern orange-brick structure burrowed into the hillside, where there's an elevator. Ride to level 1, walk straight down the corridor (following signs for *centro storico*), and ride a second elevator (to a different level 1 and the Poggiofanti Gardens); walk to the end of this park and hook left to find the Porta al Prato gate.

HELPFUL HINTS

Market Day: It's on Thursday morning (8:00-13:00), near the bus station.

Services: There's no official **baggage storage,** but the TI might let you leave bags with them if they have space. Public **WCs** are located at the TI, to the left of Palazzo Comunale, and at the Sant'Agostino Church.

Shuttle Bus to the Top of Town: To avoid the hike up through town to Piazza Grande, hop on the orange shuttle bus. It departs about every 15 minutes from the parking lot near the bus station and from the lane leading to the Porta al Prato gate, just above the TI (€1.20, buy tickets at bars, tobacco shops, or the TI).

Laundry: An elegant self-service launderette is at the top of town at Via del Paolino 2, just around the corner from the recommended Camere Bellavista (daily 8:00-22:00, tel. 0578-717-544).

Taxis: Two taxi drivers operate in Montepulciano. Call 330-732-723 for short trips within town (€10 for rides up or down hill); to reach other towns, call 348-733-5343.

Montepulciano Walk

This two-part self-guided walk traces the spine of the town from its main entrance up to its hilltop seat of power. Part 1 begins at the big gate at the bottom of town, Porta al Prato (near the TI and several parking lots); Part 2 focuses on the square at the very top of

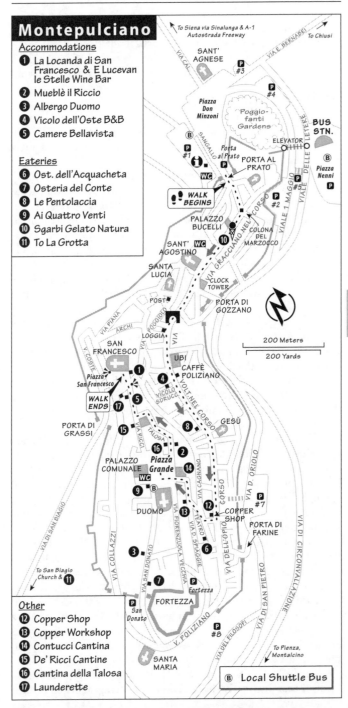

Montepulciano

Accommodations

1. La Locanda di San Francesco & E Lucevan le Stelle Wine Bar
2. Mueblè il Riccio
3. Albergo Duomo
4. Vicolo dell'Oste B&B
5. Camere Bellavista

Eateries

6. Ost. dell'Acquacheta
7. Osteria del Conte
8. Le Pentolaccia
9. Ai Quattro Venti
10. Sgarbi Gelato Natura
11. To La Grotta

Other

12. Copper Shop
13. Copper Workshop
14. Contucci Cantina
15. De' Ricci Cantine
16. Cantina della Talosa
17. Launderette

Ⓑ Local Shuttle Bus

HEART OF TUSCANY

town and the nearby streets. Part 1 is steeply uphill; to skip straight to the more level part of town (and Part 2), ride the shuttle bus up, or park at one of the lots near the Fortezza. (When you're done there, you can still do Part 1—backwards—on the way back down.)

PART 1: UP THE CORSO

This guided stroll takes you up through Montepulciano's commercial (and touristy) gamut from the bottom of town to the top. While the street is lined mostly with gift shops, you'll pass a few relics of an earlier age.

Begin in front of the imposing Porta al Prato, one of the many stout city gates that once fortified this highly strategic town. Facing the gate, find the sign for the Porta di Bacco *"passaggio segreto"* on the left. While Montepulciano did have secret passages tunneled through the rock beneath it (handy during times of siege), this particular passage—right next to the city's front door—was probably no *segreto*...though it works great for selling salami.

Walk directly through the **Porta al Prato,** looking up to see the slot where the portcullis (heavily fortified gate) could slide down to seal things off. Notice that there are two gates, enabling defenders to trap would-be invaders in a no-man's-land where they could be doused with hot tar. Besides having a drop-down portcullis, each gate also had a hinged door—effectively putting four barriers between the town and its enemies.

Pass through the gate and head a block uphill to reach the **Colonna del Marzocco.** This column, topped with a lion holding the Medici shield, is a reminder that Montepulciano existed under the auspices of Florence—but only for part of its history.

The column is also the starting point for Montepulciano's masochistic tradition, the **Bravio delle Botti,** held on the last Sunday of August, in which each local *contrada* (neighborhood) selects its two stoutest young men to roll a 180-pound barrel up the hill through town. If the vertical climb through town wears you out, be glad you're only toting a daypack. Do you see colorful flags lining the street? If so, you'll notice you're in the Gracciano *contrada*, symbolized by the green, black, and yellow lion. Notice how the flags change with the neighborhood as you continue through town.

A few steps up, on the right (at #91, with stylized lion heads), is one of the many fine noble palaces that front Montepulciano's main strip. The town is fortunate to be graced with so many bold and noble *palazzi*—Florentine nobility favored Montepulciano as a breezy and relaxed place for a secondary residence. The higher you go in Montepulciano, the closer you are to the town center...and the fancier the mansions.

Farther up on the right, at #73 (Palazzo Bucelli), take a moment to examine the **Etruscan and Roman fragments** embedded

in the wall, left here by a 19th-century antiques dealer. You can quickly distinguish which pieces came from the Romans and those belonging to the earlier Etruscans by their alphabets: The "backwards" Etruscan letters (they read from right to left) resemble Greek. Many of the fragments show a circle flanked by a pair of inward-facing semicircular designs. This symbol represents the libation cup used for drinking at an Etruscan banquet.

At the top of the block on the right is the **Church of Sant'Agostino.** Its late-Gothic facade features a terra-cotta sculpture group by the architect Michelozzo, a favorite of the Medicis in Florence. The interior is a clean, serene, white-and-beige space.

Hike up a few more steps, then take a breather to look back and see the **clock tower** in the middle of the street. The bell ringer at the top takes the form of the character Pulcinella, one of the wild and carefree revelers familiar from Italy's commedia dell'arte theatrical tradition.

Continuing up, at the *alimentari* on the right (at #23), notice the classic old sign advertising milk, butter, margarine, and olive and canola oil. Keep on going (imagine pushing a barrel now), and bear right with the street under another sturdy **gateway**—indicating that this city grew in concentric circles. Passing through the gate, you'll run into a loggia (with the Florentine Medici seal—a shield with balls).

Facing the loggia, veer left and keep on going. As you huff and puff, notice (on your right, and later on both sides) the steep, narrow, often-covered lanes called *vicolo* ("little street"). You're getting a peek at the higgledy-piggledy medieval Montepulciano. Only when the rationality of Renaissance aesthetics took hold was the main street realigned, becoming symmetrical and pretty. Beneath its fancy suit, though, Montepulciano remains a rugged Gothic city.

Again, notice the fine and ever-bulkier palaces. On the left, a tiny courtyard makes it easier to appreciate the grandiosity of the next palace, now home to **UBI Banca.** By the way, the stone scrolls under the window are a design element called a "kneeling window"—created by Michelangelo and a popular decorative element in High Renaissance and Mannerist architecture. You'll see kneeling windows all over town.

Just after is a fine spot for a coffee break (on the left, at #27): **Caffè Poliziano,** the town's most venerable watering hole (from 1868). Step inside to soak in the genteel atmosphere, with a busy espresso machine, loaner newspapers on long sticks, and a little terrace with spectacular views.

A bit farther up, on the right, notice the precipitous **Vicolo dello Sdrucciolo**—literally "slippery lane." Any *vicolo* on the right can be used as a steep shortcut to the upper part of town, while those on the left generally lead to fine vistas. Many of these side lanes are spanned by brick arches, allowing centuries-old buildings to lean on each other for support rather than toppling over—a fitting metaphor for the tight-knit communities that vitalize small Italian towns.

Continuing up, notice more kneeling windows. The next church on the left, the Jesuit **Church of Gesù,** is worth a look. Its interior is elliptical in shape and full of 3-D illusions (the side chapels and the cupola are all painted on flat surfaces). Soon the street levels out—enjoy this nice, lazy, easy stretch, with interesting shops and artisan workshops (such as the mosaics studio at #14, on the right). A few short blocks farther, across from #64, a lane leads to a charming terrace with a commanding view of the Tuscan countryside.

The **Mazzetti** copper shop (#64) is crammed full of decorative and practical items. The production of hand-hammered copper vessels like these is a dying art; in this shop, you can see works by Cesare, who makes them in his workshop just up the street.

Continuing steeply uphill will take you to the main square. At the bend just before the square, Cesare's buddy Adamo loves to introduce travelers to Montepulciano's fine wines at the **Contucci Cantina** (described later). Visit Cesare and Adamo now, or head up to the square for Part 2 of this walk.

Either way, Montepulciano's main square is just ahead. You made it!

PART 2: PIAZZA GRANDE AND NEARBY

This pleasant, lively piazza is surrounded by a grab bag of architectural sights. The medieval **Palazzo Comunale,** or town hall, resembles Florence's Palazzo Vecchio—yet another reminder that

Florence dominated Montepulciano in the 15th and 16th centuries. The crenellations along the roof were never intended to hide soldiers—they just symbolize power. The big, square central tower makes it clear that the city is keeping an eye out in all directions.

Take a moment to survey the square, where the town's four great powers stare each other down. Face

HEART OF TUSCANY

the Palazzo Comunale, and keep turning to the right. You'll see the one-time building of the courts, behind the well (Palazzo del Capitano); the noble Palazzo Tarugi, a Renaissance-arcaded confection (with a public loggia at ground level and a private loggia—now enclosed—directly above); and the aristocratic Palazzo Contucci, with its 16th-century Renaissance facade. (The Contucci family still lives in their palace, producing and selling their own wine.) Continuing your spin, you see the unfinished Duomo looking glumly on, wishing the city hadn't run out of money for its facade.

A cistern system fed by rainwater draining from the roofs of surrounding palaces supplied the fine **well** in the corner. Check out its 19th-century pulleys, the grilles to keep animals from contaminating the water supply, and its decorative top: the Medici coat of arms flanked by lions (representing Florence) dwarfing griffins (representing Montepulciano).

Climbing the town hall's **tower** rewards you with a windblown but commanding panorama from the terrace below the clock. Go into the Palazzo Comunale, head up the stairs to your left, and pay on the second floor. You can pay to go just as far as the terrace, at the base of the tower (€2.50, 71 stairs, or ride the elevator halfway up); or pay more to go all the way to the top, twisting up extremely narrow brick steps past the antiquated bell-ringing mechanism (€5, 76 additional stairs). If you don't mind the claustrophobic climb, it's worth paying extra to reach the very top, from where you can see all the way to Pienza (look just to the right of San Biagio Church; tower open daily May-Oct 10:00-18:00, closed in winter). The street to the left as you face the tower leads to the **Fortezza.**

To the Church of San Francesco and Views: From the main square, a short, mostly level walk leads to a fine viewpoint. You could head 200 yards straight down the wide street to the right as you face the tower. But for a more interesting look at Montepulciano behind its pretty Renaissance facades, go down **Via Talosa,** the narrow lane between the two palaces in the corner of the square. Pause at the recommended Mueblè il Riccio B&B (with a fine courtyard—peek inside) and look high up across the street to see how centuries of structures have been stitched together, sometimes gracelessly. Across the street is the recommended Cantina della Talosa wine cellar—imagine the wine caves below your feet.

Follow this lane as it bends left, and eventually you'll pop out just below the main square, a few doors from the recommended De' Ricci Cantine wine cellar. Turn right and head down toward the church. Just before #21 (on the left), look for a red-and-gold **shield** over a door with the name *Talosa*. This marks the home of one of Montepulciano's *contrade*, or neighborhoods; birth and death an-

The Beauty of Tuscany's Geology (and Vice Versa)

While tourists have romanticized notions of the "Tuscan" landscape, there is a surprisingly wide variety of landforms in the region. Never having been crushed by a glacier, Tuscany is anything but flat. Its hills and mountains are made up of different substances, each suited to very different types of cultivation.

The Chianti region (between Florence and Siena) is rough and rocky, with an inhospitable soil that challenges grape vines to survive while coaxing them to produce excellent wine grapes.

South of Siena, the soil switches from rock to clay, silt, and sand. The region called the Crete Senesi is the perfectly described "Sienese Clay Hills." Looking out from a breezy viewpoint, you can easily visualize how these clay hills were once at the bottom of the sea floor. The soil here is perfect for truffles and for vast fields of wheat, sun-yellow rapeseed (for canola oil), and periodically fava beans (to add nitrogen to the soil). In the spring and summer, the Crete Senesi is blanketed with brightly colorful crops and flowers in spring and summer, but by the fall, after the harvest, it's brown, dusty, and desolate. Within the Crete Senesi, you can distinguish two types of hills shaped by erosion: smooth, rounded *biancane* and pointy, jagged *calanchi*.

nouncements for the *contrada* are posted on the board next to the door.

Across the street and a few steps farther (on the right), you hit a **viewpoint.** From here, it's easy to appreciate Montepulciano's highly strategic position. The ancient town sitting on this high ridge was surrounded by powerful forces—everything you see in this direction was part of the Papal States, ruled from Rome. In the distance is Lake Trasimeno, once a notorious swampland that made it even harder to invade this town.

Continue a few steps downhill, then uphill, into the big parking lot in front of the **Church of San Francesco.** Head out to the overlook for a totally different view: the rolling hills that belonged to Siena. And keep in mind that Montepulciano itself belonged to Florence. For the first half of the 16th century, those three formidable powers—Florence, Siena, and Rome (the papacy)—vied to control this small area. You can also see Montepulciano's most impressive church, San Biagio—well-worth a visit for drivers or hikers.

From here, you can head back up to the main square, or drop into one of my recommended cantinas to spelunk their wine cellars.

The area around Montepulciano and Montalcino is more varied, with rocky protuberances that break up the undulating clay hills and provide a suitable home for wine grapes. Even farther south is the Val d'Orcia. This valley of the Orcia River is similar to the Crete Senesi, but has fewer rocks and jagged *calanchi*. Montepulciano sits in a unique position between the Val d'Orcia and the much flatter Val di Chiana (through which Italy's main north-south expressway runs).

You'll see many hot springs in this part of Tuscany, as well as town names with the word Terme (for "spa" or "hot spring") or Bagno ("bath"). These generally occur where clay meets rock: Water moving through the clay encounters a barrier and gets trapped. A byproduct of these mineral springs is the limestone called travertine, explaining the quarries you may see around spa towns.

Sights and Experiences in Montepulciano

For me, Montepulciano's best "experiences" are personal: dropping in on Adamo, the winemaker at Contucci Cantina, and Cesare, the coppersmith at Ramaio Cesare. Both will greet you with a torrent of cheerful Italian; just smile and nod, pick up what you can from gestures, and appreciate this rare opportunity to meet a true local character.

▲▲Contucci Cantina

Montepulciano's most popular attraction isn't made of stone—it's the famous wine, Vino Nobile. This robust red can be tasted in any of the cantinas lining Via Ricci and Via di Gracciano nel Corso, but the cantina in the basement of Palazzo Contucci is both historic and fun. Skip the palace's formal wine-tasting showroom facing the square, and instead head down the lane on the right to the actual cellars, where you'll meet lively Adamo (ah-DAH-moh), who has been making wine here since 1961 and welcomes tourists into the cellar. While at the palace, you may meet Andrea or Ginevra Contucci, who love to share their family's products with the public. Adamo and the Contuccis usually have a half-dozen bottles open, and at busy times, other members of their staff are likely to speak English.

After sipping a little wine with Adamo, explore the palace basement, with its 13th-century vaults. Originally part of the town's wall, these chambers have been filled since the 1500s with huge barrels of wine.

Cost and Hours: Free drop-in tasting, free cellar tour upon request, daily 10:00-18:30, shorter hours off-season, Piazza Grande 13, tel. 0578-757-006, www.contucci.it.

▲Ramaio Cesare

Cesare the coppersmith is an institution in Montepulciano, carrying on his father's and grandfather's trade by hammering into existence an immense selection of copper objects in his cavernous workshop. Though his English is limited, Cesare (CHEH-zah-ray) is happy to show you photos of his work—including the copper top of the Duomo in Siena and the piece he designed and personally delivered to Pope Benedict. Peruse his tools: a giant Road Runner-style anvil, wooden hammers, and stencils dating from 1857 that have been passed down from his grandfather and father. Next door, he has assembled a fine museum with items he and his relatives have made, as well as pieces from his personal collection. Cesare's justifiable pride in his vocation evokes the hardworking, highly skilled craft guilds that once dominated small-town Italy.

Cost and Hours: Demonstration and museum are free, Cesare is generally in his workshop Mon-Sat 9:00-12:30 & 14:30-18:30, closed Sun, 50 yards steeply downhill from the Contucci Cantina at Via del Teatro 4, tel. 0578-758-753, www.rameria.com. Cesare's delightful shop is on the main drag, a block below, at Corso #64— look for *Rameria Mazzetti*, open long hours daily.

Duomo

This church's unfinished facade—rough stonework left waiting for the final marble veneer—is not that unusual. Many Tuscan churches were built just to the point where they had a functional interior, and then, for various practical reasons, the facades were left unfinished. But step inside, where, amid the fairly austere interior, you'll be rewarded with some fine art. A beautiful blue-and-white, glazed terra-cotta *Altar of the Lilies* by Andrea della Robbia is behind the baptismal font (on the left as you enter). The high altar, with a top like a pine forest, features a luminous, late-Gothic Assumption triptych by the Sienese artist Taddeo di Bartolo. Showing Mary in her dreamy eternal sleep as she ascends to be crowned by Jesus, it illustrates how Siena clung to the Gothic aesthetic—elaborate gold leaf and lacy pointed arches—to show heavenly grandeur.

Cost and Hours: Free, daily 8:30-18:30.

▲De' Ricci Cantine

The most impressive wine cellars in Montepulciano sit below the Palazzo Ricci, just a few steps off the main square (toward the Church of San Francesco). Enter through the unassuming door and find your way down, down, down a spiral staircase—with rounded steps designed to go easy on fragile noble feet, and lined with rings held in place by tiny, finely crafted wrought-iron goat heads. You'll wind up in the dramatic cellars, with gigantic barrels under even more gigantic vaults—several stories high. As you go deeper into the cellars, natural stone seems to take over the brick. At the deepest point, you can peer into the atmospheric Etruscan cave, where a warren of corridors spins off from a filled-in well. Finally you wind up in the shop, where you're welcome to taste a few wines (with some local cheese). Don't miss their delightful dessert wine, vin santo.

Cost and Hours: First three tastings-free, two additional premium tastes-€5, €12-35 bottles, affordable shipping, daily 10:30-18:30, enter Palazzo Ricci at Via Ricci 11—look for signs for *Cantine de' Ricci,* tel. 0578-757-166, www.cantinadericci.it, Enrico.

Cantina della Talosa

This historic cellar, which goes down and down to an Etruscan tomb at the bottom, ages a well-respected wine. With a passion and love of their craft, Andrea and Cristian Pepi give enthusiastic tours and tastings. While you can drop by for a free sample, it's also possible to call ahead to book a complete tour and tasting (€20, including five wines to taste and light food).

Cost and Hours: Free tasting, daily March-Oct 10:30-19:00, shorter hours off-season, a block off Piazza Grande at Via Talosa 8, tel. 0578-757-929, www.talosa.it.

ON THE OUTSKIRTS

▲San Biagio Church (Chiesa de San Biagio)

The church is just west of town, at the base of Montepulciano's hill, down a picturesque cypress-lined driveway. Often called the "Temple of San Biagio" because of its Greek-cross style, this church—designed by Antonio da Sangallo the Elder and built of locally quarried travertine—feels like Renaissance perfection. If the church is empty, experiment worshipfully with the marvelous acoustics. Consider a picnic or snooze on the grass in back, with fine vistas over the Chiana Valley. The recommended La Grotta restaurant is across the street from the church.

Cost and Hours: €3.50, includes 20-minute audioguide; daily 10:00-18:00, longer hours in summer, shorter hours in winter.

Sleeping in Montepulciano

$$$$ La Locanda di San Francesco is overpriced but luxurious, with four stylish view rooms over a classy wine bar on a quiet square at Montepulciano's summit (closed Nov-Easter, air-con, free parking nearby, Piazza San Francesco 5, tel. 0578-758-725, www.locandasanfrancesco.it, info@locandasanfrancesco.it, Luca).

$$ Mueblè il Riccio ("The Hedgehog") is medieval-elegant, with 10 modern and spotless rooms, an awesome roof terrace, and friendly owners. Five are newer "superior" rooms with grand views across the Tuscan valleys (family rooms, breakfast extra, air-con, limited free parking—request when you reserve, a block below the main square at Via Talosa 21, tel. 0578-757-713, www.ilriccio.net, info@ilriccio.net, Gió and Ivana speak English). Charming Gió and his son Iacopo give tours of the countryside (€50/hour) in one of their classic Italian cars.

$$ Albergo Duomo is big, modern, and nondescript, with 13 simple but dignified rooms (with small bathrooms) and a comfortable lounge downstairs. With a handy location just a few steps from the main square, it's at the very top of town, with free private parking nearby (RS%—use code "Steves," family rooms, elevator, air-con in some rooms—extra charge, Via di San Donato 14, tel. 0578-757-473, www.albergoduomo.it, albergoduomo@libero.it, Simone).

$$ Vicolo dell'Oste B&B, just off the main drag halfway up through town, has five family-friendly modern rooms. Some are like tiny apartments (RS%, includes breakfast at nearby café, on Via dell'Oste 1—an alley leading right off the main drag just after Caffè Poliziano and opposite the *farmacia* at #47, tel. 0578-758-393, www.vicolodelloste.it, info@vicolodelloste.it, Luisa and Giuseppe).

$ Camere Bellavista has 10 tidy rooms. True to its name, the rooms have fine views—though some are better than others. Room 6 has a view terrace worth reserving; there's also one economy room without a view (cash only, no breakfast, lots of stairs with no elevator, reception not always staffed—call before arriving or ring bell, Via Ricci 25, mobile 347-823-2314, www.camerebellavista.it, info@camerebellavista.it, Gabriella and Alessio speak just enough English).

Eating in Montepulciano

Unless otherwise noted, these places are all open for lunch (about 12:30-14:30) and again for dinner (about 19:30-22:00).

$$$ Osteria dell'Acquacheta is a carnivore's dream come true, beloved among locals for its beef steaks. Its long, narrow

room is jammed with shared tables and tight, family-style seating, with an open fire in back and a big hunk of red beef lying on the counter like a corpse on a gurney. Giulio and his wife, Chiara, run a fun-loving but tight ship—posing with slabs of red meat yet embracing decades of trattoria tradition (you'll get one glass to use alternately for wine and water). Steaks are sold by weight (€32/kilo). Typically, two people split a 1.6-kilo steak (that's 3.5 pounds; the smallest they'll cook is 1.2 kilos). They also serve hearty pastas and salads and a fine house wine (or bring your own wine for a tiny corkage fee, reservations required; seatings generally at 12:30, 14:30, 19:30, and 21:30 only; closed Tue and unpredictably on other days; Via del Teatro 22, tel. 0578-717-086, www.acquacheta.eu).

$$ Osteria del Conte, an attractive but humble family-run bistro, offers cooking like your Italian mom's. While the interior is very simple, they also have outdoor tables on a stony street at the top of the historic center (closed Mon, Via San Donato 19, tel. 0578-756-062).

$$ Le Pentolaccia is a small, family-run restaurant about two-thirds of the way up the main drag. With both indoor and outdoor seating, they make tasty traditional Tuscan dishes as well as daily fish specials. Cristiana serves, and husband-and-wife team Jacobo and Alessia stir up a storm in the kitchen (closed Thu, Corso 86, tel. 0578-757-582).

$$ Ai Quattro Venti is right on Piazza Grande, with a simple dining room and outdoor tables on the square. It offers reasonable portions of unfussy Tuscan food in an unpretentious setting. Try their own organic olive oil and wine (closed Thu, next to City Hall on Piazza Grande, tel. 0578-717-231, Chiara).

Wine Bar/Bistro: With a terrace on a tranquil square in front of the Church of San Francesco, **$ E Lucevan le Stelle** (part of La Locanda di San Francesco) is a fine place to nurse a glass of local wine (also pastas, salads, and soups; daily 12:00-24:00, closed Nov-Easter, Piazza San Francesco 5, tel. 0578-758-725, Luca).

Gelato: For the best gelato in town, look for **Sgarbi Gelato Natura,** near the bottom of the main drag. Owner Nicola makes his gelato fresh every morning, using locally sourced ingredients from producers he knows personally. The gelato is ready around 13:00—and when it's gone, it's gone (daily 11:00-20:00, Corso 50; also runs Buon Gusto in Pienza).

Just Outside Montepulciano: Facing San Biagio Church (at the base of Montepulciano's hill, and described earlier), **$$$ La Grotta** has an excellent reputation for elevated Tuscan cuisine in a sophisticated, dressy setting. Reservations are recommended (Thu-Tue 12:30-14:15 & 19:30-22:00, closed Wed, Via di San Biagio 15, tel. 0578-757-479, www.lagrottamontepulciano.it).

Near Montepulciano: Skim this chapter for recommendations, and consider combining dinner with a scenic joyride. Good choices include **Ristorante Daria** in Monticchiello (page 124) and **The Isabella Experience**'s dinners near Castelmuzio (page 110).

Montepulciano Connections

Get bus schedules at the TI or the bus station on Piazza Pietro Nenni, which seems to double as the town hangout, with a lively bar and locals chatting inside. In fact, there's no real ticket window—buy your tickets at the bar. Check www.tiemmespa.it for schedules.

By Bus to: Florence (1/day departs in the wee hours, 2/week additional departures a bit later in the morning, 2 hours, LFI bus, www.lfi.it; or take a bus to Chiusi to catch a train—see below), **Siena** (6-7/day, none on Sun, 1.5 hours, also possible to change here for Florence express bus), **Pienza** (8/day, 30 minutes), **Montalcino** (3-4/day, none Sun, change in Torrenieri, 1 hour; or consider a taxi—see below).

By Train: Trains are impractical here; the Montepulciano train station, five miles from town and connected by a 15-minute bus ride, has only milk-run trains (but could be useful for reaching Siena on a Sunday, when buses are scarce—get details at the TI). More convenient, consider riding the hourly bus 50 minutes to the town of **Chiusi,** which is on the main Florence-Rome rail line.

Taxi Alternatives: As the **Montalcino** bus connection is infrequent and complicated, consider hiring a taxi (about €70; see contact info under "Helpful Hints," earlier).

Pienza

Set on a crest and surrounded by green, rolling hills, the small town of Pienza packs a lot of Renaissance punch. In the 1400s, locally born Pope Pius II of the Piccolomini family decided to remodel his birthplace into a city fit
for a pope, in the style that
was all the rage: Renais-
sance. Propelled by papal
clout, the town of Corsignano was transformed—in
only five years' time—into
a jewel of Renaissance architecture. It was renamed
Pienza, after Pope Pius.

Pienza's architectural focal point is its main square, Piazza Pio II, surrounded by the Duomo and the pope's family residence, Palazzo Piccolomini. While Piazza Pio II is Pienza's pride and joy, the entire town—a mix of old stonework, potted plants, and grand views—is fun to explore, especially with a camera or sketchpad in hand. You can walk every lane in the tiny town in well under an hour. Pienza is situated on a relatively flat plateau rather than the steep pinnacle of more dramatic towns like Montepulciano and Montalcino. (This is a plus for visitors with limited mobility, who find basically level Pienza easy to explore.)

Tourists flood Pienza on weekends and in peak season, and authentic local shops are outnumbered by boutiques selling gifty packages of pecorino cheese and local wine. Restaurants here tend to be more expensive and less reliable than alternatives in the nearby countryside. For these reasons, Pienza is made to order as a stretch-your-legs break to enjoy the townscape and panoramas, but it's not ideal for lingering overnight (though some excellent options exist just outside town; see "Countryside Accommodations," earlier). For the best experience, visit late in the day, after the day-trippers have dispersed.

Nearly every shop sells the town's specialty: pecorino, a pungent sheep's cheese (you'll smell it before you see it) that's sometimes infused with other ingredients, such as truffles or cayenne pepper. Look on menus for warm pecorino *(al forno* or *alla griglia)*, often topped with honey and pine nuts or pears and served with bread. Along with a glass of local wine, this just might lead you to a new understanding of *la dolce vita.*

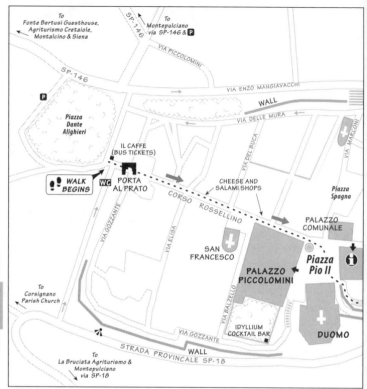

HEART OF TUSCANY

Orientation to Pienza

Tourist Information: The TI is 10 yards up the street from Piazza Pio II, inside the skippable Diocesan Museum (Wed-Mon 10:30-18:30 except Sat-Sun 10:00-16:00 off-season, closed Tue year-round, Corso il Rossellino 30, tel. 0578-749-905). Ignore the *Informaturista* kiosk just outside the gate—it's a private travel agency.

Arrival in Pienza: If **driving,** read signs carefully—some parking spots are reserved for locals, others require the use of a cardboard clock, and others are pay-and-display. Parking is tight, so if you don't see anything quickly, head for the large pay lot at Piazza del Mercato near Largo Roma outside the old town: As you approach town and reach the "ZTL" cul-de-sac (marked with a red circle) in front of the town gate, head up the left side of town and look for the parking turnoff on the left (closed Fri morning during market). **Buses** drop you just a couple of blocks from the town's main entrance.

Helpful Hints: On Friday mornings, a **market** fills Piazza del

To
Piazza
del Mercato
Parking

100 Meters

100 Yards

SP-18

P

Largo
Roma

P

BUON
GUSTO
GELATERIA

"NEW HOUSES"

VIA CASA NUOVE

VIA PIA

VIA DOGALI

VIA DELL'APPARITA

VIA DELLA VOLPE

SAN
CARLO

SP-18

WALK
ENDS

LA BANDITA
TOWNHOUSE
CAFFÉ

VIA SAN CARLO

PORCHETTA
SHOP

CORSO

VIA FORTUNA

VIA SANT'ANDREA

ROSSELLINO

VIA BUIA

TRATTORIA
LATTE DI LUNA

BISHOP'S
PALACE
& DIOCESAN
MUSEUM

VIA DELL'AMORE

VIA

PORTA
AL CIGLIO

VIEW TERRACE

WALL

P

SP-18

PORTA
AL SANTO

Note: No cars allowed
in town center

HEART OF TUSCANY

Mercato, the main parking lot just outside the town walls. A public **WC,** marked *gabinetti pubblici,* is on the right as you face the town gate from outside on Piazza Dante Alighieri (down the lane next to the faux TI).

Sights in Pienza

I've connected Pienza's main sights with walking directions, which can serve as a handy little orientation to the town. You could do this stroll in 30 minutes, but entering some of the sights could extend your visit to a few hours.

• *Begin in the little park just in front of the town (near the main roundabout and bus stop), called Piazza Dante Alighieri. Facing the town, go through the big, ornamental gateway on the right (which was destroyed in World War II, and rebuilt in 1955) and head up the main street...*

Corso il Rossellino

This main drag—named for Bernardo Rossellino (1409-1464), the Renaissance architect who redesigned Pienza according to Pius' orders—is jammed with touristy boutiques. While you won't find great values, these shops are (like Pienza) cute and convenient.

As you stroll this street, step into one of the many **cheese-and-salami shops.** Take a deep whiff and survey the racks of pecorino cheese, made from sheep's milk. There are three broad categories of pecorino: *fresco* (young, soft, and mild), *medio* (medium), and *stagionato* (hard, crumbly, and pungent). Consider stocking up at one of these shops for a pricey but memorable picnic; some shops may be willing to give you a free sample. *Finocchiona* is salami with fennel seeds. This was first popularized by wine traders, because fennel seeds make wine taste better. To this day, Italians use the word *infinocchiare* ("fennel-ize") to mean "to trick."

Farther along, watch for the **Church of San Francesco** on the right. It's the only important building in town that dates from before the Pius II extreme makeover. Its humble facade, simple nave, wood-beamed ceiling, bits of 14th-century frescoes, and tranquil adjacent cloister have a charm that's particularly peaceful in the 21st century. But this gloomy medieval style was exactly what Pius wanted to get away from.

• *Continuing one more block, you'll pop out at Pienza's showcase square...*

▲Piazza Pio II

Pienza's small main piazza gets high marks from architecture highbrows for its elegance and artistic unity. One day, Pope Pius II (who was born here) was traveling nearby with Leon Battista Alberti, one of the great architectural pioneers of the Renaissance. Proud to show off his hometown, Pius brought Alberti here...but, seeing it through the eyes of his esteemed companion, he was filled with embarrassment rather than pride at its primitive architectural style. Pius decided this just wouldn't do, and commissioned Alberti's student Bernardo Rossellino to remake the town into a Renaissance masterpiece.

Rossellino designed the piazza and surrounding buildings to form an "outdoor room." Everything is perfectly planned and plotted. Do a clockwise spin to check out the buildings that face the square, starting with the **Duomo** (which we'll enter soon). High up on the facade is one of many examples you'll spot around town of the Piccolomini family crest: five half-moons, advertising the number of crusades that his family funded.

To the right of the Duomo is the **Piccolomini family palace,** now a tourable museum. Notice that the grid lines in the square's pavement continue all the way up the sides of this building, creat-

Pope Pius II

Pope Pius II (Enea Silvio Bartolomeo Piccolomini, 1405-1464) was born into one of the most powerful families in Siena. He had an illustrious career as a diplomat, traveled far and wide (fathering two illegitimate children, in Switzerland and Scotland), and gained a reputation for his erotic writings (*The Tale of Two Lovers*). Upon donning the frock, Piccolomini went from ordination to the papacy in just 11 years—a stunning pace spurred, no doubt, by his esteemed lineage. Owing to his educated and worldly upbringing, upon ascending to the papacy Piccolomini chose a name that was not religious, but literary: the ancient poet Virgil first used the term "pious" to describe his hero, Aeneus. One of the most enlightened popes of his time, Pius embraced the burgeoning Renaissance and set out to remake his hometown in pure Renaissance style. Pius was also the first prominent figure known to have suggested the notion of a united Europe, with a common heritage and shared goals (at that time, facing off against the invading Ottomans).

ing a Renaissance cube. Upon closer inspection, you can see that the windows at the far end of the building are a bit narrower—creating an optical illusion that the palace is longer than it actually is.

Looking farther right, you'll see **City Hall** (Palazzo Comunale), with a Renaissance facade and a fine loggia (to match the square) but a 13th-century bell tower that's shorter than the church's tower. That's unusual here in civic-minded Tuscany, where municipal towers usually trumpet the importance of town over Church.

Looking up the lane to the left of City Hall, notice the cantilevered upper floors of the characteristic old houses—a reminder that, while Pienza appears Renaissance on the surface, much of that sheen was added later to fit Pius' vision. Turning right again, see the **Bishop's Palace,** also called the Borgia Palace (now housing the TI and the skippable Diocesan Museum). Pius envisioned his remade hometown as a sort of "summer Vatican," where an entourage of VIPs would spend time—and each one needed their own palace. The Borgia clan, who built this palace, produced one of the most controversial popes of that age, Alexander VI, who ascended to the papacy a few decades after Pius II.

Finally, between the Bishop's Palace and the Duomo, a lane leads to the best **view terrace** in town.

• *Before going there, take the time to tour whichever of the square's sights interest you:*

Duomo

The cathedral's classic, symmetrical Renaissance facade (1462) dominates Piazza Pio II. The interior, bathed in light, is an illuminating encapsulation of Pius II's architectural philosophy (free, generally daily 7:00-13:00 & 14:30-19:00). Pius envisioned this church as an antidote to dark, claustrophobic medieval churches, like the Church of San Francesco we saw earlier. Instead, this was to be a "house of glass," representing the cultural enlightenment that came with the Renaissance. As you walk to the end of the church, notice the cracks in the apse walls and floor, and get seasick behind the main altar. The church's cliff-hanging position bathes the interior in light, but the building also feels as though it could break in half if you jumped up and down.

▲Palazzo Piccolomini

This palace, the home of Pius II and the Piccolomini family (until 1962), is not quite the interesting slice of 15th-century aristocratic life that it could be (I'd like to know more about the pope's toilet). But this is still the best small-town palace experience I've found in Tuscany. (It famously starred as the Capulets' home in Franco Zeffirelli's 1968 Academy Award-winning *Romeo and Juliet*.) You can peek inside the door for free to check out the well-preserved courtyard. In Renaissance times, most buildings were covered with elaborate paintings like those you'll see here.

Cost and Hours: €7, includes dry audioguide, Wed-Mon 10:00-18:30, until 16:00 off-season, closed Tue, Piazza Pio II 2, tel. 0578-748-392, www.palazzopiccolominipienza.it.

• *When you're done sightseeing, head up the little lane to the left of the church facade. This takes you out to a grand pedestrian-only...*

View Terrace

Stroll this panoramic promenade to the end, taking in views over the Tuscan countryside and, in the distance, Monte Amiata, the largest mountain in southern Tuscany. Retrace your steps and exit the viewpoint down the first alley, Via del'Amore—the original Lover's Lane—which leads back to the main drag, Corso il Rossellino.

• *Turn right and stroll along this street one block, then turn left up Via Sant'Andrea. Soon you'll run into Via delle Case Nuove, a charming row of homes with staggered doorways. These "new houses" (as the street's name means) were built by the pope to house the poor. Just to the left (as you face these houses) is Pienza's "destination" gelateria, the recommended Buon Gusto.*

JUST OUTSIDE PIENZA
Corsignano Parish Church (Pieve di Corsignano)
This classic Romanesque parish church *(pieve)*, hugging the slope just below Pienza, is a reminder of a much earlier, rougher, simpler time (before Pope Pius II). This was one of the medieval pilgrimage stops on the Via Francigena.

The round, eighth-century watchtower guards the squat, 11th-century church, whose unusual exterior iconography is from an age when the pagan roots of early Christianity were vivid and unmistakable—especially here, deep in the countryside. The church is decorated not with saints and angels, but with geometric and flowery motifs as well as mysterious creatures. Inside, near the entrance on the right, look for the font that was used to baptize the infant who would grow up to be Pope Pius II.

Getting There: On foot from Pienza, it's a steep 10-minute downhill walk (as you exit Pienza into the main park, look to your left for *pieve di Corsignano* signs). Drivers loop around the far end of town (as described on my Heart of Tuscany drive, later); just before the road bends sharply left and twists downhill, watch for the *pieve di Corsignano* signs on the right (free parking).

Eating in and near Pienza

IN PIENZA
$$$ La Bandita Townhouse Caffè offers a break from Tuscan rusticity, focusing instead on tempting modern Italian cuisine (such as spring pea soup or spicy Chianina beef tartare). Diners watch the chef work in his open kitchen (dinner nightly 19:30-22:00, lunch Tue-Sun 12:30-15:00, indoor/outdoor seating, Corso il Rossellino 111, easier to enter around the corner on Via Sant'Andrea, tel. 0578-749-005).

$$ Trattoria Latte di Luna, with outdoor tables filling a delightful little square, is the more traditional choice. While the food can be hit-or-miss, locals swear by their specialty, roast suckling pig *(maialino da latte arrosto)*. Run by friendly Roberto with Delfina in the kitchen, the dining room features an ancient well and sits on top of Etruscan tunnels (Wed-Mon 12:10-15:30 & 19:10-22:00, closed Tue, at the far end of town at Via San Carlo 2, tel. 0578-748-606).

Quick Lunch: For something cheap, characteristic, and fast, just grab a tasty **$** *porchetta* **sandwich** at the little no-name shop 30 yards off the main square (at Corso il Rossellino 81) and munch it under the loggia or at the viewpoint (daily 8:00-20:00).

Top-Quality Gelato: Small batches and quality ingredients are on the menu at **Buon Gusto.** Nicola creates fun original fla-

HEART OF TUSCANY

vors, which can include carrot-ginger, creamy basil, or kiwi-spinach. The gelato is typically ready by around 13:30—just in time for after lunch. They also do fresh-pressed juices and smoothies (daily 11:00-20:00, until 22:00 in summer, closed off-season, Via delle Case Nuove 26, mobile 335-704-9165). Nicola also runs Sgarbi Gelato Natura in Montepulciano.

Cocktails with Nibbles: Pienza isn't much for nightlife, but for a cocktail in a somewhat local-feeling setting, drop in at **Idyllium**—a hip cocktail bar serving creative herb-infused drinks, light food, and outdoor seating facing grand Tuscan splendor (daily 11:00-late, from the main square, go down the little lane to the right of the church to Via Gozzante 67, tel. 0578-748-176).

NEAR PIENZA

Despite having more than its share of tourists, Pienza suffers from a lack of quality restaurants. These options are all within about a 15-minute drive and offer a more memorable meal than places in town. To locate Castelmuzio, see the "Heart of Tuscany" map on page 84.

Just Outside Castelmuzio: For an excellent meal and a memorable activity, consider dinner at the fine **$$$$** restaurant at **La Moscadella,** run by The Isabella Experience (recommended in "Countryside Accommodations," earlier in this chapter). A limited number of tables are available to nonguests who book ahead. One evening there may be a truffle hunt through the woods followed by a truffle dinner; the next, an olive oil tasting session may be followed by a meal with olive oil pairings. Expect to pay around €60 per person, including the premeal experience, a four-course meal, *aperitivo,* and wine; the truffle hunt/meal is €120/person (reservations required, usually offered Fri-Tue, veggie alternatives available, tel. 0577-665-516, info@theisabellaexperience.com).

In Castelmuzio: To escape Pienza's tourist crowds, drive about 15 minutes to the remote village of Castelmuzio. The hamlet's lone restaurant, **$$ Locanda di Casalmustia,** is a cozy and typically uncrowded spot serving good local cuisine. Choose between sitting out on the stony lane or in a cute fresco-ceilinged dining room. While not quite a destination restaurant, it's a good excuse to explore an untrampled hill town and enjoy sweeping views of the countryside (Tue-Sun 8:00-22:00, closed Mon, in the heart of the town at Piazza della Pieve 3, tel. 0577-665-166).

In Monticchiello: In the opposite direction, but about the same distance away is the excellent **Ristorante Daria** (see "Eating in Monticchiello," later in this chapter; for location see the "Heart of Tuscany" drive map on page 121).

Pienza Connections

Bus tickets are sold at the bar/café (marked *Il Caffè*, closed Tue) just outside Pienza's town gate (or pay a little extra and buy tickets from the driver). Buses leave from a few blocks up the street, directly in front of the town entrance. Montepulciano is the nearest transportation hub.

From Pienza by Bus to: Siena (6/day, none on Sun, 1.5 hours), **Montepulciano** (8/day, 30 minutes), **Montalcino** (3-4/day, none Sun, change in Torrenieri, 60 minutes). Bus info: www.tiemmespa.it.

Montalcino

On a hill overlooking vineyards and valleys, Montalcino is famous for its delicious and pricey Brunello di Montalcino red wines. It's a pleasant, low-impact town crawling with wine-loving tourists and a smattering of classy shops, but little sightseeing. Everyone touring this area seems to be relaxed and in an easy groove...as if enjoying a little wine buzz.

While today it's all about the wine, Montalcino (mohn-tahl-CHEE-noh) has an incredibly long history—human settlement here dates back some 200,000 years. That's because Montalcino has a unique setting, with protective caves and a freshwater spring high atop a rocky pinnacle—a highly desirable position for Neolithic humans. For much of its long history, Montalcino was a veritable fortress, perched high overlooking the valley below and its Via Francigena pilgrim route.

Flash forward to the Middle Ages, when Montalcino was considered Siena's biggest ally. Originally aligned with Florence, the town switched sides after the Sienese beat up Florence in the Battle of Montaperti in 1260. The Sienese persuaded the Montalcinesi to join their side by forcing them to collect corpses and sleep one night in the bloody, Florentine-strewn battlefield. Later, the Montalcinesi took in Sienese refugees. To this day, in gratitude for their support, the Sienese invite the Montalcinesi to lead the parade that kicks off Siena's Palio celebrations.

Montalcino prospered under Siena, but like its ally, it waned after the Medici family took control of the region. The village became a humble place. Then, in the late 19th century, the Biondi Santi family created a fine, dark red wine, calling it "the brunette" (Brunello). Today's affluence is due to the town's much-sought-after wine. (For more on this wine, see the "Wines in the Region" sidebar later in this chapter). Montalcino provides a handy springboard for exploring the surrounding wine region.

HEART OF TUSCANY

Orientation to Montalcino

Sitting atop a hill amidst a sea of vineyards, Montalcino is surrounded by walls and dominated by the Fortezza (a.k.a. "La Rocca"). From here, roads lead down into the two main squares: Piazza Garibaldi and Piazza del Popolo.

Tourist Information: The helpful TI, just off Piazza Garibaldi in City Hall, sells bus tickets; can call ahead to book a visit at a countryside winery (small fee); and has information on taxis to nearby towns, abbeys, and monasteries (daily 10:00-13:00 & 14:00-17:50, tel. 0577-849-331, www.prolocomontalcino.com).

Arrival in Montalcino: For a short visit here by **car,** drivers should head to the pay lot in Piazzale Fortezza. Skirt around the fortress,

take the first right (just past a little park), and follow signs to *parking* and *Fortezza* (€1.60/hour, free 20:00-8:00). Or, if you don't mind a short climb, park for free below the fortress: At the roundabout with the ugly statue, take the small downhill lane into the big lower parking lot (blue lines mean that you have to pay, but the lower-level unmarked spots are always free). If these lots are full, follow the town's western wall toward the Madonna del Soccorso church and a long pay lot.

The **bus** stop is on Piazza Cavour, a little park about 300 yards from the town center. From here, simply follow the main drag, Via Mazzini, straight up into town. While Montalcino has no official baggage storage, a few shops are willing to hold on to one or two bags on a short-term basis; ask at the TI.

Helpful Hints: Friday is **market** day (7:00-13:00) on Viale della Libertà, near the Fortezza.

Sights in Montalcino

Piazza del Popolo

All roads in tiny Montalcino lead to the main square, Piazza del Popolo ("People's Square").

City Hall was the fortified seat of government. It's decorated with the coats of arms of judges who, in the interest of fairness, were from outside of town. Like Siena, Montalcino was a republic in the Middle Ages. When Florentines took Siena in 1555, Siena's ruling class retreated here and held out for four more years. The Medici coat of arms (with the six balls, or pills) dominates the others. The one-handed **clock** was the norm until 200 years ago.

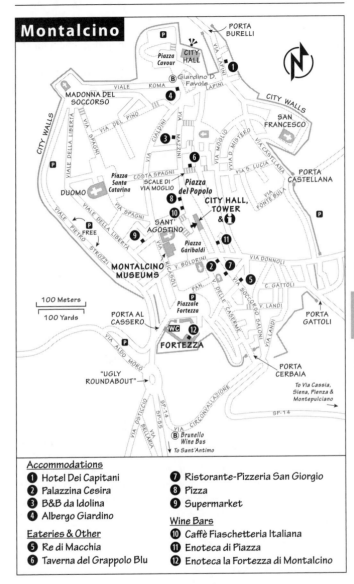

Montalcino

Accommodations

1. Hotel Dei Capitani
2. Palazzina Cesira
3. B&B da Idolina
4. Albergo Giardino

Eateries & Other

5. Re di Macchia
6. Taverna del Grappolo Blu
7. Ristorante-Pizzeria San Giorgio
8. Pizza
9. Supermarket

Wine Bars

10. Caffè Fiaschetteria Italiana
11. Enoteca di Piazza
12. Enoteca la Fortezza di Montalcino

For five centuries, the large arcaded **loggia** (on your left as you face the clock tower) hosted the town market.

For some wine-centric whimsy, go up around the right side of the City Hall and find a series of **plaques** (each designed by a different artist), which show off the annual rating of the Brunello harvest from two to five stars—important, as wine is the lifeblood of the local economy. And, of course, it's fun to simply observe the *passeggiata*—these days mostly a parade of tourists here for the wine.

Back on the square, notice the grand café (on the right as you face the clock tower). Since 1888, **Caffè Fiaschetteria Italiana** has been *the* elegant place to enjoy a drink. Its founder, inspired by Caffè Florian in Venice, brought fine coffee to this humble town of woodcutters.

Montalcino Museums (Musei di Montalcino)

While technically two museums in one (archaeology and medieval and modern art), and surprisingly big and modern for this little town, Montalcino's lone museum ranks only as a decent bad-weather activity. The cellar is filled with interesting artifacts dating back as far as—gulp—200,000 BC. The ground, first, and second floors hold the medieval and modern art collections, with an emphasis on Gothic sacred art (with works from Montalcino's heyday, the 13th to 16th century). The ground floor is best, with a large collection of crucifixes and the museum's highlights, a glazed terra-cotta altarpiece and a statue of St. Sebastian, both by Andrea della Robbia.

Cost and Hours: €4.50, €6 combo-ticket with Fortezza, Tue-Sun 10:00-13:00 & 14:00-17:30, closed Mon, Via Ricasoli 31, to the right of Sant'Agostino Church, tel. 0577-846-014.

Fortezza

This 14th-century fort, built under Sienese rule, is now little more than an empty shell (with a popular wine bar—see below). It was built to defend against catapults and arrows, but the cannon was invented shortly thereafter. You can still see pockmarks from cannonballs fired here in 1553 on the outer wall (facing away from the town), but the fort withstood the attack. You're welcome to enter the big, open courtyard (with WCs out the far end), or just enjoy a picnic in the park surrounding the fort, but if you want to climb the ramparts for a panoramic view, you'll have to pay.

Cost and Hours: €4, €6 combo-ticket with Montalcino Museums, enter though wine bar, daily 9:00-20:00, off-season 10:00-18:00.

Wine Bars in Town

If you won't make it to the wineries outside Montalcino, simply visit a wine bar in town, where you can comfortably taste a variety of vintages before stumbling safely back to your hotel. This is also a great strategy for Sundays, when many countryside wineries are closed.

Caffè Fiaschetteria Italiana, a classic café/wine bar, was founded by Ferruccio Biondi Santi, the creator of the famous Brunello wine. The wine library in the back of the café boasts many local choices. A meeting place since 1888, this grand café also serves light lunches. But if you're not seeking venerable ambience and sidewalk seating, you can taste wine more affordably elsewhere (Brunellos by the glass, light snacks and plates; same prices inside, outside, or in back room; daily 7:30-23:00, Piazza del Popolo 6, tel. 0577-849-043).

Enoteca di Piazza—part of a chain of wine shops with mechanical dispensers—is a fun way to efficiently taste a variety of different wines in a forgettable setting. Here's how it works: A "drink card" (like a debit card) keeps track of the samples you take, for which you'll pay from €1 to €9 apiece. They stock 100 different wines, including some whites— rare in this town. This is a  good spot to assemble a box of wines from different local producers to ship home. Their small restaurant lets you enjoy your drink card with local dishes (daily 9:00-20:00, near Piazza del Popolo at Via Matteotti 43, tel. 0577-848-104, www.enotecadipiazza.com).

Enoteca la Fortezza di Montalcino offers a chance to taste top-end wines by the glass, each with an English explanation. While the prices are a bit higher than other *enoteche* in town, the medieval setting inside Montalcino's fort is popular with tourists. Spoil yourself with Brunello in the cozy *enoteca* or at an outdoor table in the fortress courtyard (tastings start at €15 for 3 wines and go up from there; pricey full meals and sampler plates of cheeses, *salumi*, honeys, and olive oil available; daily 9:00-20:00, until 18:00 Nov-March, inside the Fortezza, tel. 0577-849-211).

Wineries near Montalcino

The countryside around Montalcino is littered with wineries, some of which offer tastings. As Brunello is the poshest of Italian wines, these wineries feel a bit upscale, and most require an advance reservation. It's a simple process (just call and arrange a time), and they'll delight in showing you around. Tours generally last 45-60 minutes, cost €10-15 per person, and conclude with a tasting of three or four wines. The Montalcino TI can give you a list of more than 150 regional wineries and will call ahead for you. Or check with the vintners' consortium (tel. 0577-848-246, www.consorziobrunellodimontalcino.it). Many wineries are closed on

Wines in the Region

This region has two well-respected red wines, each centered on a specific town: Montepulciano is known for its Vino Nobile, while Montalcino is famous for its Brunello. In each wine, the predominant grape is a clone of sangiovese (Tuscany's main red wine grape).

Vino Nobile di Montepulciano ("noble wine of Montepulciano") is a high-quality, dry ruby red, made mostly with the Prugnolo Gentile variety of sangiovese (70 percent), plus other varieties including Mammolo (30 percent). Aged two years (or three for a *riserva*)—one year of which must be in oak casks—it pairs well with meat, especially roasted lamb with rosemary, rabbit or boar ragù over pasta, grilled portobello mushrooms, and local cheeses like pecorino. Several large wineries produce and age their Vino Nobile in the sprawling cellars beneath the town of

Montepulciano. Three of these are fun and easy to tour (see "Sights and Experiences in Montepulciano" on page 97). The oldest red wine in Tuscany, Vino Nobile has been produced since the late 1500s.

Sunday, so check before heading out. For locations of the wineries listed below, see the "Heart of Tuscany" map, near the beginning of the chapter.

If you lack a car (or don't want to drive), you can take a tour on the **Brunello Wine Bus,** which laces together visits to four wineries, with a lunch break in the middle, either on your own in Montalcino or at a farmhouse for an extra fee (€140; tours run March-Nov Tue and Thu only; departs at 10:00, returns at 19:00; tours leave from their office, or they will pick you up within 3 miles—5 km—of Montalcino; half-day tours available Tue and Thu-Sat for €75; Via Circonvallazione 3, tel. 0577-846-021, www.winetravelsforyou.com, info@winetravelsforyou.com).

If you're paying for a wine tasting, you aren't obligated to buy. But if a winery is doing a small tasting just for you, they're hoping you'll buy a bottle or two.

South of Montalcino
Tornesi
This charmingly low-key, family-run winery is a short drive outside of Montalcino, perched on a grand view terrace overlooking the famous Biondi Santi winery (where Brunello was invented).

Brunello di Montalcino ("the little brown one of Montalcino"—named for the color of the grapes before harvest) is even more highly regarded and ranks among Italy's finest and most expensive wines. Made from 100 percent Sangiovese Grosso (a.k.a. Brunello) grapes, it's smooth, dry, and aged for a minimum of two years in wood casks, plus an additional four months in the bottle. *Riserva* wines are aged an additional year. Brunello is designed to cellar for 10 years or longer—but who can wait? It pairs well with the local cuisine, but the perfect match is the fine Chianina beef.

Today, there are around 240 mostly small producers of Brunello in the Montalcino region; I've recommended just a few, which I find fun and accessible. A simpler option is to sample a few different wines at one of the good wine bars in Montalcino (see page 114).

You'll also see Rosso di Montalcino (a younger version of Brunello), which is aged for one year. This "poor man's Brunello" is very good, at half the price.

Maurizio, Elisa, and Valentina offer tours and tastings in this scenic setting. They enjoy explaining how their logo—the cuckoo *(kukula)* bird—was inspired by their chatty grandfather (reserve ahead, €13 for 3 tastes plus tour, €20 includes tasting and lunch, €20-40 bottles, closed Sun, mobile 349-093-2167, www.brunellotornesi.it). Leaving Montalcino, at the main roundabout, go uphill toward *Grosetto*, then watch for the brown *Benducce* sign on the left (just before the road bends right). Tornesi is a short drive down this gravel road, on the left.

Mastrojanni

Perched high above the Romanesque Sant'Antimo Abbey, overlooking sprawling vineyards, this winery (owned by the Illy coffee company) is big and glitzy—yet doesn't feel as corporate or soulless as some of the bigger players (€17-36 bottles, reserve ahead, Podere Loreto e San Pio, tel. 0577-835-681, www.mastrojanni.com). To reach it, head up into the town of Castelnuovo dell'Abate (just above Sant'Antimo Abbey), bear left at the Bassomondo restaurant, and continue up along the gravel road (enjoying vineyard and abbey views).

Ciacci Piccolomini d'Aragona

This well-respected, family-run vineyard has a classy tasting room/*enoteca* and an outdoor view terrace. If you're just dropping in, belly up to the wine bar for two or three free tastes. Or reserve ahead for a more formal tasting of top-quality wines for €10-25, which includes a tour of the cellar (April-Oct Mon-Fri 9:00-19:00, Sat 10:30-18:30, closed Sun; down a back lane near Sant'Antimo Abbey—head toward Castelnuovo dell'Abate but go right before entering that town, following signs toward *Sant'Angelo in Colle*, tel. 0577-835-616, www.ciaccipiccolomini.com, visite@ciaccipiccolomini.com).

Castello Banfi-Poggio alle Mura

Much bigger and glossier than the other recommended wineries, Banfi is one of the largest producers in the area. Despite its size, the estate is charming, set in a castle located in a picturesque corner southwest of Sant'Antimo. This is a good option for Sundays, when other places are closed, or for a spontaneous drop-in tasting at the winery's *enoteca* (tastings start at €12, daily 10:00-19:30, until 18:00 Nov-March, tours available on request, tel. 055-877-500, www.castellobanfiilborgo.com, enoteca@banfi.it). You'll find Banfi about 20 minutes south of Montalcino; follow SP-14 to Borgo Santa Rita and cut back north, following signs to *Poggio alle Mura*.

North of Montalcino

Altesino

Elegant and stately, Altesino owns perhaps the most stunning location of all, just off the back road connecting Montalcino north to Buonconvento. You'll twist up on cypress-lined gravel lanes to this perch, which looks out over an expanse of vineyards with Montalcino hovering on the horizon (€15 for tour and basic tasting, daily, reserve ahead, Loc. Altesino 54, tel. 0577-806-208, www.altesino.it, info@altesino.it). You'll find the turnoff for Altesino along the back road (SP-45) between Montalcino and Buonconvento.

Santa Giulia

On the outskirts of Torrenieri, this is a quintessential family-run winery, with an emphasis on quality over quantity (only 20,000 bottles a year). They also produce excellent olive oil, prosciutto, and salami. Less picturesque and much more rustic than the other wineries listed here, a tour at Santa Giulia is a Back Door experience. Call to find a time that fits their schedule; around lunchtime, you can arrange a "Zero Kilometer" tasting, with farm-fresh cold cuts, cheese, and bruschetta for €20; add pasta and dessert for €15 more (€20 for 3 tastes and tour, 2-person minimum, €15-32 bottles, Loc. Santa Giulia 48, closed Sun, tel. 0577-834-270, www.

santagiuliamontalcino.it, info@santagiuliamontalcino.it). From Torrenieri's main intersection, follow the brown *Via Francigena* signs. After crossing the train tracks and a bridge, watch on the left to follow signs for *Sasso di Sole,* then *Sta. Giulia;* you'll take gravel roads through farm fields to the winery.

Sleeping in Montalcino

$$$ Hotel Dei Capitani, at the end of town near the bus station, has plush public spaces, an inviting summertime pool, and a cliff-side terrace offering plenty of reasons for lounging. About half the 29 rooms come with vast Tuscan views and are worth paying a bit extra for (request a view room when you reserve); the nonview rooms are bigger but face a somewhat noisy street (RS%, air-con, elevator, limited free parking—first come, first served, Via Lapini 6, tel. 0577-847-227, www.deicapitani.it, info@deicapitani.it).

$$ Palazzina Cesira (cheh-SHEE-rah), right in the heart of the old town, is a gem, renting five spacious and tastefully deco-rated rooms in a fine 13th-century residence with a palatial lounge and a pleasant garden. You'll enjoy a refined and tranquil ambience, a nice breakfast (with eggs), and the chance to get to know Lucilla and her American husband Roberto, who are generous with local advice (2-night minimum, air-con, free off-street parking, Via Soccorso Saloni 2, tel. 0577-846-055, www.montalcinoitaly.com, info@montalcinoitaly.com).

$ B&B da Idolina has four good rooms above a wine shop on the main street (includes basic breakfast in shared kitchen, check-in 15:00-19:00—call if arriving later, parking available, Via Mazzini 65, check in at the wine shop next door, tel. 0577-849-212, www. idolina1946.com, fulvia.soda@gmail.com, Fulvia).

$ Albergo Giardino, a great value, has nine big rooms done in a modern-minimalist style, no public spaces, and a convenient location near the bus stop (RS%, no breakfast, Piazza Cavour 4, tel. 0577-848-257, mobile 320-404-4655, www.albergoilgiardino. it, info@albergoilgiardino.it, Roberto and dad Mario).

Eating in Montalcino

$$$ Re di Macchia is an invitingly intimate restaurant where An-tonio serves up the big, hearty portions of Tuscan fare that Roberta cooks. Look for their seasonal menu and a fine Montalcino wine list (Fri-Wed 12:00-14:00 & 19:00-21:00, closed Thu, reservations strongly recommended, Via Soccorso Saloni 21, tel. 0577-846-116).

$$ Taverna del Grappolo Blu, tucked in a cellar down a pic-turesque staircase off the main drag, is serious about its wine, game, homemade pasta, and vegetarian options (reservations smart, daily

12:00-15:00 & 19:00-22:00, a few steps off Via Mazzini at Scale di Via Moglio 1, tel. 0577-847-150, www.grappoloblu.it, Luciano).

$$ Ristorante-Pizzeria San Giorgio is a homey trattoria/pizzeria with traditional decor and reasonable prices. It's great for families and a reliable choice for a simple meal (daily 12:00-15:00 & 19:00-22:30, closed Tue off-season, Via Soccorso Saloni 10, tel. 0577-848-507, Mara).

Quick Bite: The **$** *pizza al taglio* shop, right on Piazza del Popolo at #11, has both pizza slices and sandwiches that they can heat up for you—ask for *scalda* (daily 10:30-21:30).

Picnic: Gather ingredients at the **Co-op supermarket** on Via Sant'Agostino (Mon-Sat 8:30-13:00 & 16:00-20:00, closed Sun, just off Via Ricasoli in front of Sant'Agostino Church), then enjoy your feast up at the Madonna del Soccorso Church, with vast territorial views.

Montalcino Connections

Montalcino is well connected to Siena; other bus connections are inconvenient but generally workable. Montalcino's bus stop is on Piazza Cavour, within the town walls. Bus tickets are sold at the bar on Piazza Cavour, at the TI, and at some tobacco shops, but not on board. Check schedules at the TI, at the bus station, or online (at www.tiemmespa.it). The nearest train station is a 30-minute bus ride away, in Buonconvento.

From Montalcino by Bus: For long-distance journeys, you'll always start out on bus #114, which goes to **Siena** (6/day Mon-Sat, 4/day Sun, 1.5 hours). En route, this bus goes through Torrenieri (change for **Pienza** or **Montepulciano,** 3-4/day, none on Sun); from Torrenieri it's 25 minutes to Pienza, 45 minutes to Montepulciano, then **Buonconvento** (where you can catch a train to **Florence**). You can also reach Florence by riding the bus to Siena, then taking the train from there. Since the Montepulciano bus connection is sporadic, consider hiring a taxi (about €70 one-way).

Heart of Tuscany Drive

VAL D'ORCIA LOOP

If you have just one day to connect the ultimate Tuscan towns and views, this is the loop I'd stitch together with a driving tour. In addition to larger towns (Montepulciano, Pienza) and smaller ones (Bagno Vignoni, Rocca d'Orcia), this loop drive, worth ▲▲▲, gives you a good look at the area called the Val d'Orcia (val DOR-chah), boasting some of the best scenery in Italy. Most of this jour-

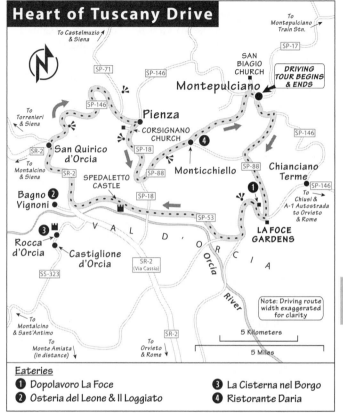

Heart of Tuscany Drive

To Montepulciano
Train Stn.

To Castelmuzio
& Siena

SP-17

SAN
BIAGIO
CHURCH

**DRIVING
TOUR BEGINS
& ENDS**

SP-71   SP-146

Montepulciano

Pienza

To
Torrenieri
& Siena

SP-146

CORSIGNANO
CHURCH

SP-146

San Quirico
d'Orcia

SP-18

❹

SR-2

To
Montalcino
& Siena

SR-2

SPEDALETTO
CASTLE

SP-88

Monticchiello

SP-88

Chianciano
Terme

SP-146

To
Chiusi &
A-1 Autostrada
to Orvieto
& Rome

Bagno ❷
Vignoni ●

SP-18

SP-53

❶

V   A   L

D   O

**LA FOCE
GARDENS**

❸

R   C   I   A

Rocca
d'Orcia ●

Castiglione
d'Orcia

SS-323

SR-2
(Via Cassia)

Orcia

River

Note: Driving route
width exaggerated
for clarity

To
Montalcino
& Sant'Antimo

To
Monte Amiata
(in distance)

SR-2

To
Orvieto
& Rome

5 Kilometers

5 Miles

Eateries
❶ Dopolavoro La Foce
❷ Osteria del Leone & Il Loggiato
❸ La Cisterna nel Borgo
❹ Ristorante Daria

HEART OF TUSCANY

ney is through velvety, gentle, rolling hillsides generously draped with vivid-green crops in the springtime, and a parched moonscape in the late summer and fall. This almost otherworldly smoothness constitutes many travelers' notions of Tuscan perfection.

Planning Your Drive: If you're in a rush and don't linger in any of the towns, you could do this drive in a couple of hours. To hit the sights, explore the towns, and linger over a meal or a glass of wine, spread it out over an entire day. (You could even splice in a side trip to a Brunello winery for a tasting.) I've started and ended the clockwise loop in Montepulciano, but you could just as easily start and end in Pienza. If gardens are your thing, do this loop when La Foce Gardens are open.

From Montepulciano to Bagno Vignoni (via La Foce)

Before leaving Montepulciano, consider dropping by the showpiece Renaissance **San Biagio Church,** which sits at the base of the town (watch for its long, level, tree-lined driveway exactly where you leave Montepulciano on the road toward Pienza—see "Sights and Experiences in Montepulciano," earlier in this chapter).

To begin our loop, drive south, at first following signs to *Chianciano Terme* and *Chiusi*. Just 1 kilometer south of Montepulciano, watch on the right for the turnoff to *Castelluccio* and *Monticchiello*. Turn off here and zip along a pastoral back road for 5 kilometers. Pass the turnoff for Monticchiello on your right, and carry on straight ahead, as the road continues uphill and becomes gravel. Grinding your way up, watch on your right for the jagged Tuscan cliffs called *calanchi*. You'll pop out at the T-intersection in front of the entrance to **La Foce Gardens** (from this intersection, parking and reception are 50 yards to the left—look for *Loc. La Foce;* learn more about the gardens later in this chapter).

From La Foce, head downhill tracking signs toward *Siena* and *Roma*. After a few hundred yards, watch on the left for the big gravel parking lot of the recommended **Dopolavoro La Foce** restaurant (across the street). From this lot, you have a fine view of one of the iconic cypress-lined driveways of Tuscany.

Continue downhill along this road for about 5 kilometers, through pristine farm fields, until you reach a major intersection, where you'll turn right toward *Pienza* and *Siena* (on SP-53). Immersed in spectacular scenery, you'll twist between giant cypresses for about 10 kilometers. This road parallels the region's namesake **Orcia River** ("Val d'Orcia" means "Orcia River Valley").

Take a moment to simply appreciate your surroundings. The famous Chianti region to the north (right) and the Brunello region to the west (straight ahead) are each a short drive away; in those places, the rocky soil is perfect for grapes. But here, instead of rocks, you're surrounded by clay hills—once the floor of a prehistoric sea—that are ideal for cereal crops. Grains alternate every few years with a crop of fava beans, which help reintroduce nitrogen to the soil. It seems that every grassy hilltop is capped with a family farmhouse. Partway along this road, you'll pass a turnoff (on the right) offering a speedy shortcut to Pienza, just 8 stunning kilometers away. But there's so much more to see; I'd rather carry on with our loop.

The tower looming on the hill ahead of you is Rocca d'Orcia's Tentennano Castle (described later). Nearing the end of the road, you'll pass (on the left) the front door of an old farmhouse with oddly formidable crenellated towers, like a little castle in the field. This is **Spedaletto Castle,** built during the 12th century as a hospice for pilgrims walking the Via Francigena to Rome. Today it serves a similar purpose, as an *agriturismo* called La Grancia ("The Granary"), housing wayfarers like you.

When you reach a T-intersection with the main SR-2 highway,

turn left (toward *Roma*), then immediately take the exit for **Bagno Vignoni.** To explore this fascinating medieval spa town—with its main square filled with a thermal-spring-fed pool—see "Heart of Tuscany Sights," in the next section. To see the empty fortress at **Rocca d'Orcia,** stay on the SR-2 highway just 1 kilometer past Bagno Vignoni, then watch for the next turnoff.

From Bagno Vignoni to Pienza (with Detours to Brunello Wineries and Tuscan Views)

From Bagno Vignoni, head north on SR-2 (toward *San Quirico d'Orcia* and *Siena*). After just 4 kilometers, in San Quirico d'Orcia, turn off onto the SP-146 road to Pienza, also marked for *Chiusi, Chianciano Terme,* and *Montepulciano.*

But before heading down that road, consider a few potential detours: First, if you won't have time to delve deeply into Brunello wine country, now is a good time to side-trip to your choice of **Brunello wineries;** those I've recommended on page 115 are all within about a 20- to 25-minute drive of San Quirico. Read the descriptions, take your pick, and ideally call ahead to reserve a tour and tasting. Another option is to zip into the town of **Montalcino** itself—an easy and well-signed 15-minute drive from San Quirico—and taste some local vintages at a wine bar there.

Back on the SP-146 road from San Quirico to Pienza, you enjoy one of the region's most postcard-worthy stretches—with grand panoramas in both directions, including two more quintessential Tuscan scenes: the **Chapel of Madonna di Vitaleta** (after 2 kilometers, on the right); and a classic **farmhouse with trees,** just before Pienza (about 9 kilometers after San Quirico, on the left).

Finally, you'll pull into **Pienza,** where you can park and tour the town using the information earlier in this chapter.

From Pienza to Montepulciano (via Monticchiello)

If you're in a hurry or losing sunlight, just hop back on the main SP-146 road for the 12-kilometer straight shot back to Montepulciano (enjoying some pullouts on the left with fine views of the town). But I prefer this longer, even more dramatic route, via the fortified village of Monticchiello.

From the traffic circle at the entry to Pienza's town center, instead of heading for Montepulciano, follow the road that runs along the left side of town (marked *Amiata* and *Monticchiello*—as you face Pienza, you'll continue straight when the main road bends left). This road loops around behind and below the far end of the village, where you can consider a brief detour to see Pienza's oldest church: Turn off on the right at the brown sign for *Pieve di*

Corsigiano and drive a few hundred yards to **Corsignano Parish Church** (described on page 109).

Continuing on the main road past that turnoff, you'll drop steeply down into the valley, feeling as if you're sinking into a lavish painting. Dead ahead is **Monte Amiata,** the tallest mountain in Tuscany. This looming behemoth blocks bad weather, creating a mild microclimate that makes the Val d'Orcia a particularly pleasant place to farm...or to vacation. Meanwhile, don't forget to savor the similarly stellar views of Pienza in your rearview mirror. After 5 kilometers, look on the left for the turnoff to Monticchiello (brown sign). From here, carry on for 4 kilometers—watching on the left for fine vistas of Pienza and for another classic twisty cypress-lined road—to the pleasant town of **Monticchiello.** This town, with an excellent recommended restaurant (Daria) and a compact, fortified townscape worth exploring, is a good place to stretch your legs; see more in the next section.

From Monticchiello, there are two routes back to Montepulciano: For the shorter route (6 kilometers), partly on gravel roads, drive all the way to the base of the Monticchiello old town, then turn right. For the longer route (10 kilometers), which stays on paved roads but circles back the way our loop started, turn off for Montepulciano at the main intersection, in the flat part of town that's lower down.

HEART OF TUSCANY SIGHTS

Below are the main sights you'll pass on my Heart of Tuscany driving route. Two of the main stops—the towns of Montepulciano and Pienza—are covered earlier in this chapter.

▲La Foce Gardens

One of the finest gardens in Tuscany, La Foce (lah FOH-cheh) caps a hill with geometrical Italian gardens and rugged English gardens that flow seamlessly into the Tuscan countryside. The gardens were a labor of love for Iris Origo, an English-born, Italian-bred aristocrat who left her mark on this area and wrote evocatively about her time here. The gardens—which are worth a pilgrimage for garden lovers—can be visited only with a  guided tour, and only three days a week (Wed, Sat, Sun) and some holidays.

Cost and Hours: €10; 45-minute tours offered April-Oct Wed at 15:00, 16:00, 17:00, and 18:00, Sat-Sun and holidays at

11:30, 15:00, and 16:30—but can be closed for private events, so check online in advance; private tours available, no tours in winter, ticket office opens 15 minutes before tour time, tel. 0578-69101, www.lafoce.com.

Getting There: La Foce sits in the hills above the busy town of Chianciano Terme. You can avoid SP-146 from Montepulciano through Chianciano (heavy traffic, poor signage) by following a more scenic route through the countryside (described at the start of my Heart of Tuscany Drive).

Eating and Sleeping near La Foce: Near the gardens, the Origo family runs a memorably charming roadside restaurant, **$$ Dopolavoro La Foce** ("After Work"). Once the quitting-time hangout for local farmers, today its interior is country-chic. The menu offers basic sandwiches or pasta and meat (featuring elegant hamburgers). The garden terrace out back is a chirpy delight, and the parking lot across the busy road offers one of the best vantage points on that perfect Tuscan road (Tue-Sun 9:00-22:00, closed Mon and Nov-March, Strada della Vittoria 90, tel. 0578-754-025, run with flair by Asia). Also nearby is their remote, restful B&B (described on page 88).

▲Bagno Vignoni

Thanks to the unique geology of this part of Tuscany (see sidebar, page 96), several natural hot springs bubble up between the

wineries and hill towns. And the town of Bagno Vignoni (BAHN-yoh veen-YOH-nee)— with a quirky history, a pleasant-to-stroll street plan punctuated with steamy canals, and various places to take a dip—is the most accessible and enjoyable to explore. If you'd like to recuperate from your sightseeing and wine tasting by soaking in the thermal baths, bring your swimsuit.

Getting There: Bagno Vignoni is well signed, just off the main SR-2 highway linking Siena to Rome (5 kilometers south of San Quirico d'Orcia). Park in the pay lot (coins only) by the big roundabout and walk into town, taking the left fork (in front of Hotel Le Terme).

Bagno Vignoni Town Walk: Emerging into the main square, walk under the covered loggia and look out over the aptly named **Piazza delle Sorgenti** ("Square of the Sources"), filled with a vast pool. Natural spring water bubbles up at the far end at temperatures around 125 degrees Fahrenheit. Known since Roman times, these hot springs were harnessed for their medicinal properties in the Middle Ages.

You're not allowed to wade or swim in this main pool today, but an easy stroll through town shows you other facets of these healing waters. Facing the pool, turn left, walk to the end of the loggia, then turn left again down Via delle Sorgenti. Listen for the water that gushes under your feet, as it leaves the pool and heads for its big plunge over the cliff. You'll emerge at an open zone with the cliff-capping **ruins** of medieval mills and cisterns that once made full use of Bagno Vignoni's main resource. Here you'll have a chance to dip your toes or fingers into streams of now-tepid water. At the canals' end, the water plunges down into the gorge carved by the Orcia River.

Taking the Waters: The modern **Piscina Val di Sole** bath complex, inside Hotel Posta Marcucci, is simple but sophisticated. It's a serene spot to soak (in water ranging from 80 to 105 degrees Fahrenheit) while taking in soaring views of Rocca d'Orcia across the valley (€20-27, €5 towel rental with €10 deposit, Fri-Wed 9:30-18:00, Wed and Sat also 21:00-24:00, closed Thu, tel. 0577-887-112, www.postamarcucci.it).

Eating in Bagno Vignoni: The town's class act is **$$$ Osteria del Leone,** on the cheery little *piazzetta* just behind the loggia, with charming tables out on the square. Inside it's dull and modern, with a fine interior garden (closed Mon, Via dei Mulini 3, tel. 0577-887-300, www.osteriadelleone.it). For something a bit more affordable and casual, drop by the nearby **$$ Il Loggiato,** with stony indoor seating or outdoor tables (closed Thu, Via delle Sorgenti 36, tel. 0577-888-973).

Rocca d'Orcia

The fortress looming over Rocca d'Orcia (ROH-kah DOR-chah) perches high above the main SR-2 highway. Likely inhabited and fortified since Etruscan times, this strategic hilltop was a seat of great regional power in the 12th century. During this time, Rocca d'Orcia was one of a chain of forts that watched over pilgrims walking the Via Francigena to Rome.

Today the **Rocca di Tentennano** fortress—an empty shell of a castle with modern steel stairs and a grand 360-degree panorama at its top—looks stark and abandoned. It seems to dare you to pay €3 to take the very steep hike up from the parking lots below (May-Sept daily 10:30-13:30 & 16:30-18:30; shorter hours off-season, mobile 392-003-3028 or 333-986-0788).

Eating in Rocca d'Orcia: On Rocca's main square, **$$ La Cisterna nel Borgo** faces the town's namesake cistern. Marta and Fede serve up deliciously executed dishes in a classic setting (Mon-

Fri 12:00-14:00 & 19:00-22:00, Sat-Sun 19:00-22:00 only, Borgo Mestro 37, tel. 0577-887-280).

▲Monticchiello

This 200-person fortified village clings to the high ground in the countryside just south of Pienza and Montepulciano. While not quite "undiscovered," Monticchiello is relatively untrampled, and feels like a real place where you can get in touch with authentic Tuscan village life.

Eating in Monticchiello: At the warm and classy **$$$ Ristorante Daria,** owner Daria pleases diners with seasonal, traditional Tuscan dishes presented with flair in a modern setting. It's in the heart of the stony hill town amid sumptuous scenery. Reservations are wise (Thu-Tue 12:15-14:30 & 19:15-22:00, closed Wed, Via San Luigi 3, tel. 0578-755-170, www.ristorantedaria.it). Arriving in Monticchiello, walk through the town's gate, head about 50 yards straight up the hill, and bear right.

ASSISI

Assisi is famous for its hometown boy, St. Francis, who made very, very good. While Francis the saint is interesting, Francesco Bernardone the man is even more so, and mementos of his days in Assisi are everywhere—where he was baptized, a shirt he wore, a hill he prayed on, and a church where a vision changed his life.

Around the year 1200, this simple friar from Assisi countered the decadence of Church government and society in general with a powerful message of nonmaterialism and a "slow down and smell God's roses" lifestyle. Like Jesus, Francis taught by example, living without worldly goods and aiming to love all creation. A huge monastic order grew out of his teachings, which were gradually embraced (some would say co-opted) by the Church. Christianity's most popular saint and its purest example of simplicity is now glorified in beautiful churches, along with his female counterpart, St. Clare. In 1939, Italy made Francis one of its patron saints; in 2013, the newly elected pope took his name.

Francis' message of love, simplicity, and sensitivity to the environment has a broad and timeless appeal. But every pilgrimage site inevitably gets commercialized, and Francis' legacy is now Assisi's basic industry. In summer, this Umbrian town bursts with flash-in-the-pan Francis fans and Franciscan knickknacks. Those able to see past the glow-in-the-dark rosaries and bobble-head friars can have a "travel on purpose" experience. Even a block or two off the congested main drag, you'll find pockets of serenity that, it's easy to imagine, must have made Francis feel at peace.

PLANNING YOUR TIME

Assisi is worth a day and a night. Its walled old town has a half-day of sightseeing and another half-day of wonder. The essential sight is the Basilica of St. Francis. For a good visit, take my self-guided Assisi Walk, going from the top of town to the basilica at the bottom, and my Basilica of St. Francis Tour. With more time, wander the back streets and linger on the main square, Piazza del Comune.

Most visitors are day-trippers. While the town's a zoo by day, it's a delight at night. Assisi after dark is closer to a place Francis could call home. But for most visitors, two nights is more than you really need.

Orientation to Assisi

Crowned by a ruined castle, Assisi spills downhill to its famous Basilica of St. Francis. The town is beautifully preserved and rich in history. A 5.5-magnitude earthquake in 1997 did more damage to the tourist industry than to the town's buildings. Fortunately, tourists—whether art lovers, pilgrims, or both—have returned, drawn by Assisi's special allure.

The city stretches across a ridge that rises from a flat plain. The Basilica of St. Francis sits at the low end of town; Piazza Matteotti (bus stop and parking lot) is at the high end; and the main square, Piazza del Comune, lies in between. The main drag (called Via San Francesco for most of its course) runs from Piazza del Comune to the basilica. Capping the hill above the town is the ruined castle, called the Rocca Maggiore, and rising above that is Mount Subasio. The town is smaller than its fame might lead you to think: Walking uphill from the basilica to Piazza Matteotti takes 30 minutes, while the downhill journey takes about 15 minutes. Some Francis sights lie outside the city walls, in the flat area beneath the ridge (the modern part of town, called Santa Maria degli Angeli) and in the hills above.

ASSISI

TOURIST INFORMATION

The TI is in the center of the old town on Piazza del Comune (daily 9:00-19:00, tel. 075-813-8680, www.visit-assisi.it). From April to October, there's also a branch (with shorter hours) down in the valley, across the street from the big piazza in front of the Basilica of Santa Maria degli Angeli.

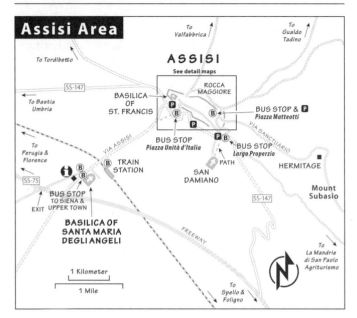

ASSISI

ARRIVAL IN ASSISI

By Train: The train station is about two miles below Assisi, in Santa Maria degli Angeli. There is no official baggage storage, but the bar on the main floor will hold bags for a small charge (look for *ristorante* sign on the platform). There's no baggage storage in the old town.

Gray-and-blue Busitalia city **buses** (line #C) connect the station with the hilltop old town, stopping just outside the wall at three convenient places. Buses usually leave twice hourly from the bus stop immediately to your left as you exit the station (daily 5:30-23:00, schedule posted at stop, 15-minute ride; buy tickets at the newsstand inside the train station for €1.30, or on board the bus for €2—exact change only, validate ticket at yellow box as you board). The bus may be awaiting the arrival of your train. If so, don't dawdle or you may miss it.

Be sure you're on a bus going toward the center (ask *"Centro?"*—it should be marked *Matteotti/S. Francesco*). On the way up into town, the bus makes three stops: **Piazza Unità d'Italia** (near Porta San Pietro, below the Basilica of St. Francis), **Largo Properzio** (just outside Porta Nuova), and finally up top at **Piazza Matteotti**. The middle stop, Largo Properzio, is best for hotels in the center—just walk through the gateway and take the straight, mostly level street (past the Basilica of St. Clare) about 10 minutes to the main square.

Returning from the old town to the train station, buses reverse the route, leaving Piazza Matteotti twice hourly, driving down through town to the train station (then proceeding one more stop to the Basilica of Santa Maria degli Angeli).

Taxis from the train station to the old town cost about €15, with extra charges for luggage, night service, additional people (four is customary)...and sometimes just for being a tourist. When departing the old town, you'll find taxi stands at Piazza Giovanni Paolo II, the Basilica of St. Francis, the Basilica of St. Clare, and Piazza del Comune (or have your hotel call for you, tel. 075-813-100). Expect to pay a minimum of €10 for any ride.

By Bus: Buses from Siena generally arrive at the stop next to the Basilica of Santa Maria degli Angeli, near the train station (see earlier for directions from the station into town). Most other inter-city buses arrive at the base of the old town.

By Car: Drivers coming in for the day can follow the signs to several handy parking lots *(parcheggi)*. Piazza Matteotti's wonderful underground parking garage is at the top of the town and comes with bits of ancient Rome in the walls. Another big lot, Parcheggio Giovanni Paolo II, is at the bottom end of town, 200 yards below the Basilica of St. Francis (next to the Piazza Unità d'Italia bus stop). At Parcheggio Porta Nuova, at the south end of town, an escalator delivers you to Porta Nuova near St. Clare's. The lots vary in price (about €1.50/hour, most €20/day). For day-trippers, the best plan is to park at Piazza Matteotti, follow my self-guided town walk, tour the Basilica of St. Francis, and then either catch a bus back to Piazza Matteotti or simply wander back up through town to your car.

HELPFUL HINTS

Best Shopping: Tacky knickknacks line the streets leading to the Basilica of St. Francis. For better shops (with local handicrafts), head to Via San Rufino and Corso Mazzini (both just off Piazza del Comune; some shops described on page 141). A Saturday-morning market fills Via Borgo San Pietro (along the bottom edge of town).

Festivals: Assisi hosts several annual festivals commemorating St. Francis and life in the Middle Ages. The springtime medieval **Festa di Calendimaggio** features costume parades, concerts, and competitions among Assisi's rival neighborhoods (www.calendimaggiodiassisi.it). The **Settimana Francescana** commemorates the beginning of the end of Francis' life, when he made his way for the last time to the Porziuncola Chapel (Sept 28). This week-long celebration culminates on October 4 in the **Festa di San Francesco,** which marks his death with religious processions, special church services, and an arts, crafts, and folklore fair.

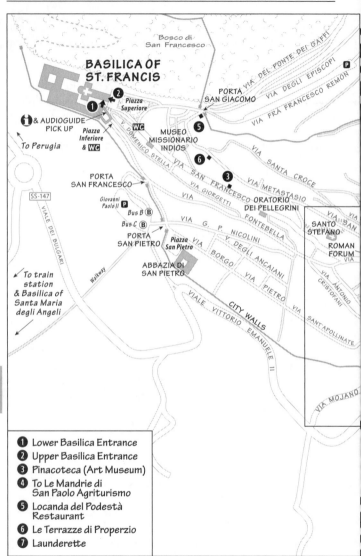

BASILICA OF ST. FRANCIS

Bosco di San Francesco

VIA DEL PONTE DEI GAFFI

VIA DEGLI EPISCOPI

PORTA SAN GIACOMO

VIA FRÀ FRANCESCO REMÓN

● **2** Piazza Superiore

❶

ℹ & AUDIOGUIDE PICK UP

Piazza Inferiore & **WC**

To Perugia

WC

V. DOMENICO STELLA

MUSEO MISSIONARIO INDIOS

5

6

VIA SANTA CROCE

VIA SAN FRANCESCO

3

VIA METASTASIO

PORTA SAN FRANCESCO

VIA

VIA GIORGETTI

ORATORIO DEI PELLEGRINI

SS-147

Giovanni Paolo II

Bus B ⑧

Bus C ⑧

PORTA SAN PIETRO

VIA G. P. NICOLINI

FONTEBELLA

VIA

VIALE DEI BULGARI

VIA

VIA SAN...

SANTO STEFANO

ROMAN FORUM

VIA

To train station & Basilica of Santa Maria degli Angeli

Walkway

Piazza San Pietro

ABBAZIA DI SAN PIETRO

VIA BORGO

V. DEGLI ANCAIANI

VIA PIETRO

VIALE VITTORIO EMANUELE II

CITY WALLS

VIA ANTONIO CRISTOFANI

VIA SANT'APOLLINATE

VIA MOJANO

❶ Lower Basilica Entrance
❷ Upper Basilica Entrance
❸ Pinacoteca (Art Museum)
❹ To Le Mandrie di San Paolo Agriturismo
❺ Locanda del Podestà Restaurant
❻ Le Terrazze di Properzio
❼ Launderette

ASSISI

Laundry: If they're not too busy, **3 Elle Blu' Lavanderia** can do same-day laundry for you at a reasonable price (Mon-Fri 9:00-18:00, Sat until 13:00, closed Sun, Via Borgo Aretino 6a, tel. 075-816-084).

Travel Agencies: You can purchase train, bus, and plane tickets at **Agenzia Viaggi Stoppini,** centrally located between Piazza del Comune and the Basilica of St. Clare. Manager Fabrizio is patient with tourists' needs (Mon-Fri 9:00-12:30 & 15:30-19:00, Sat 9:00-12:30, closed Sun, also offers day trips

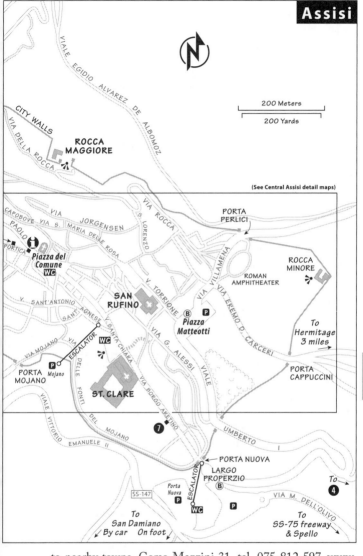

to nearby towns, Corso Mazzini 31, tel. 075-812-597, www. viaggistoppiniassisi.it).

Local Guides: Giuseppe Karabotis is a good licensed guide (€130/3 hours, €260/6 hours, mobile 328-867-0567, iokarabot@libero.it). **Daniela Moretti** is a hardworking young guide from Perugia who knows Assisi and all of Umbria (€120/half-day, €240/day, mobile 335-829-9984, www. danyguide.com, danyguide@hotmail.com). If they're busy, they can recommend other guides.

GETTING AROUND ASSISI

Most visitors need only their feet to get everywhere in Assisi, except to the lower town—with the train station and Basilica of Santa Maria degli Angeli—which can be reached on Busitalia line #C (see directions earlier, under "Arrival in Assisi").

Within the old town, minibuses #A and #B run every 20-40 minutes, linking the lower end (near the Basilica of St. Francis) with the middle (Piazza del Comune) and the top (Piazza Matteotti). While it's only a 15-minute stroll from the upper end to the lower, the climb back up can have you looking for a lift. Hop on a bus marked *Piazza Matteotti* if you're exhausted after your Basilica of St. Francis visit and need a sweat-free five-minute return to the top of the old town. Before boarding, confirm the destination (catch the bus below the basilica, just outside the Porta San Francesco).

You can buy a bus ticket (good on any city bus) at a newsstand or tobacco shop for €1.30, or get a ticket from the driver for €2 (exact change only). After you've stamped your ticket on board, it's valid for 90 minutes.

Assisi Walk

There's much more to Assisi than just St. Francis and what the blitz tour groups see. This self-guided walk, worth ▲▲, covers the town from top to bottom, starting near Piazza Matteotti. To reach the piazza, ride the bus from the train station (or from Piazza Giovanni Paolo II) to the last stop; drive up (and park in the underground lot); or hike 10 minutes uphill from Piazza del Comune.

🎧 Download my free Assisi Town Walk audio tour.

• *Start 50 yards beyond Piazza Matteotti (down the small lane between two stone houses, away from city center—see map).*

❶ Roman Amphitheater (Anfiteatro Romano)

A lane named Via Anfiteatro Romano skirts the cozy neighborhood built around the site of a long-gone Roman amphitheater—a reminder that Assisi was once an important Roman town. Circle to the right along the curved lane that marks the amphitheater's footprint. Imagine how colorful the town laundry basin (on the right) must have been in previous generations, when the women of Assisi gathered here to do their wash. Just beyond, above another small rectangular basin, are the coats of arms of Assisi's leading families. A few steps farther, leave the amphitheater, hiking up the stairs on the right to the top of the hill, for an overhead view of the ancient oval. The Roman stones have long been absorbed into the medieval architecture. It was Roman tradition to locate the amphitheater outside of town, which this used to be. While the amphitheater dates from the first century AD, the buildings filling it today were built in the 13th and 14th centuries. Notice the town's carefully maintained complexion: When redoing a roof, locals will mix old and new tiles.

• *Continue on, enjoying the grand view of the fortress in the distance. Take the gravel lane that branches off to the right, leading down to a city gate (on the right). Step through the gate for an...*

➋ Umbrian View

Outside of Assisi's Porta Perlici stretches a commanding view. Umbria, called the "green heart of Italy," is the country's geographical center and only landlocked region. Enjoy the various shades of green: silver green on the valley floor (olives), emerald green (grapevines), and deep green on the hillsides (evergreen oak trees). The valleys are dotted by small family farms, many of which rent rooms as *agriturismi*. Also notice Rocca Maggiore ("big fortress"), which provided townsfolk a refuge in times of attack. In the opposite direction, Rocca Minore ("little fortress")—which you saw a moment ago—gives the town's young lovers a little privacy. A quarry under the Rocca Maggiore was a handy source for Assisi's characteristic pink limestone.

• *Go back through the gate and follow Via Porta Perlici—it's immediately on your right—downhill into town (toward Hotel la Rocca). Enjoy the higgledy-piggledy architecture (this neighborhood has some of the most photogenic back lanes in town). Fifty yards down, to the left of the arched gate, find the wall containing an **aqueduct** that dates from Roman times. It still brings water from a mountain spring into the city (push the brass tap for a taste). After another 50 yards, turn left through a medieval town gate (with Hotel la Rocca on your right). Just after the hotel, you'll pass a second gate dating from Roman times. Follow Via Porta Perlici a few atmospheric blocks downhill until you hit a fine square facing a big church.*

➌ Cathedral of San Rufino
(Cattedrale San Rufino)

Trick question: Who's Assisi's patron saint? While Francis is one of Italy's patron saints, Rufino (the town's first bishop, martyred and buried here in the third century) is Assisi's. This cathedral (seat of the local bishop)—worth ▲▲—is 11th-century Romanesque with a Neoclassical interior, and dedicated to Rufino. Although it has what is considered to be one of the best and purest Romanesque facades in all of Umbria, the big triangular top (just a decorative wall) was added in Gothic times.

Cost and Hours: Cathedral—free, daily 7:00-19:00, Nov-mid-March closed Mon-Fri 12:30-14:30, tel. 075-812-283;

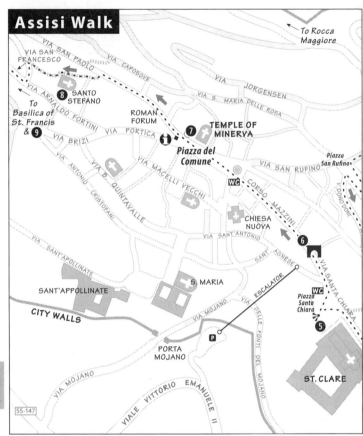

Assisi Walk

To Rocca Maggiore

VIA SAN PAOLO

VIA SAN FRANCESCO

VIA CAPOBOVE

VIA JORGENSEN

VIA S. MARIA DELLE ROSA

VIA ARNALDO FORTINI

❽ SANTO STEFANO

To Basilica of St. Francis & ❾

VIA BRIZI

ROMAN FORUM

VIA PORTICA

❼ TEMPLE OF MINERVA

ℹ️

Piazza del Comune

VIA SAN RUFINO

Piazza San Rufino

VIA ANTONIO - CRISTOFANI

VIA B. QUINTAVALLE

VIA MACELLI VECCHI

WC

CORSO MAZZINI

VICO DONO DONI

VIA SANT'APOLLINATE

CHIESA NUOVA

VIA SANT'ANTONIO

❻

VIA SANT'AGNESE

SANT'APPOLLINATE

S. MARIA

VIA ESCALATOR

VIA MOJANO

CITY WALLS

VIA SANTA CHIARA

WC

Piazza Santa Chiara

❺

VIA DELLE FONTI DEL MOJANO

P

PORTA MOJANO

VIA MOJANO

VIALE VITTORIO EMANUELE II

ST. CLARE

SS-147

ASSISI

museum—€3.50, Thu-Tue 10:00-13:00 & 15:00-18:00, closed Wed, shorter hours off-season and Sun, www.assisimuseodiocesano.it.

Visiting the Church: Before going in, study the facade—a jungle of beasts emphasizing how the church was a refuge and sanctuary in a scary world. Notice the lions at the base of the facade, flanking each door. One is eating a Christian martyr, reminding worshippers of the courage of early Christians. Here, as in other medieval Assisi churches, worshippers absorbed pre-Christian themes and symbols into their world.

Enter the church. While the front of the church is an unremarkable mix of 17th- and 18th-century Baroque and Neoclassical,

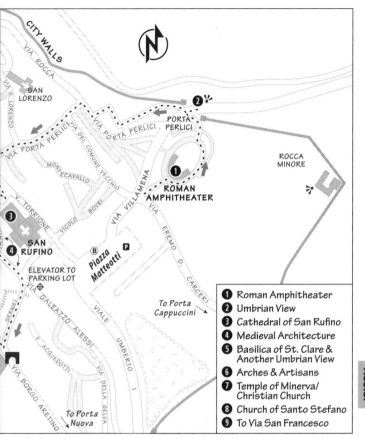

CITY WALLS

VIA S. LORENZO

SAN LORENZO

VIA ROCCA

VIA PORTA PERLICI

VIA DEL COMUNE VECCHIO

VIA PORTA PERLICI

MONTECAVALLO

PORTA PERLICI

❷

ROCCA MINORE

❶
ROMAN AMPHITHEATER

VIA VILLAMENA

VIA EREMO D. CARCERI

V. TORRIONE

VICOLO BOVEI

❸

SAN RUFINO

❹

⑧
Piazza Matteotti

P

ELEVATOR TO PARKING LOT

V. SERMEI

VIA GALEAZZO ALESSI

VIALE UMBERTO

To Porta Cappuccini

VIA DELLA SELVA

F. ACQUEDOTTI

VIA BORGO ARETINO

To Porta Nuova

❶ Roman Amphitheater
❷ Umbrian View
❸ Cathedral of San Rufino
❹ Medieval Architecture
❺ Basilica of St. Clare & Another Umbrian View
❻ Arches & Artisans
❼ Temple of Minerva/ Christian Church
❽ Church of Santo Stefano
❾ To Via San Francesco

ASSISI

the rear (near where you enter) has several points of interest. Notice the two fine statues at the bases of the first pillars: *St. Francis* and *St. Clare* (by Giovanni Dupré, 1888).

In the church's back-right corner is an old baptismal font (surrounded by a semicircular black iron grate). In about 1181, a baby boy was baptized in this font. His parents were upwardly mobile Francophiles who called him Francesco ("Frenchy"). In 1194, a nobleman baptized his daughter Clare here. Eighteen years later, their paths crossed in this same church, when Clare attended a class and became mesmerized by the teacher—Francis. Traditionally, the children of Assisi are still baptized here.

In the nave, the striking glass panels in the floor reveal foundations preserved from the ninth-century church that once stood here. You're walking on history. After the 1997 earthquake, structural inspectors checked the church from ceiling to floor. When they looked under the paving stones, they discovered graves (until Napoleon decreed otherwise, it was common practice to bury peo-

St. Francis of Assisi (1181-1226)

In 1202, young Francesco Bernardone donned armor and rode out to battle the Perugians (residents of Umbria's capital city). The battle went badly, and Francis was captured and imprisoned for a year. He returned a changed man. He avoided friends and his father's lucrative business and spent more and more time outside the city walls fasting, praying, and searching for something.

In 1206, a vision changed his life, culminating in a dramatic confrontation. He stripped naked before the town leaders, threw his clothes at his father—turning his back on the comfortable material life—and declared his loyalty to God alone.

Idealistic young men flocked to Francis, and they wandered Italy like troubadours, spreading the joy of the Gospel to rich and poor. Francis became a cult figure, attracting huge crowds. They'd never seen anything like it—sermons preached outdoors, in the local language (not Church Latin), making God accessible to all. Francis' new order of monks was also extremely unmaterialistic, extolling poverty and simplicity. Despite their radicalism, the order eventually gained the pope's approval and spread through the world. Francis, who died in Assisi at the age of 44, left a legacy of humanism, equality, and love of nature that would eventually flower in the Renaissance.

In Francis' Sandal Steps

1. Baptized in Assisi's **Cathedral of San Rufino.**
2. Raised in the family home just off Piazza del Comune (now the **Chiesa Nuova**).
3. Heard call to "rebuild church" in **San Damiano.** (The crucifix of the church is now in the **Basilica of St. Clare.**)
4. Settled and established his order of monks at the **Porziuncola Chapel** (inside today's Basilica of Santa Maria degli Angeli).
5. Met Clare. (Her tomb and possessions are at the **Basilica of St. Clare.**)
6. Received the pope's blessing for his order (1223 document in the reliquary chapel at the **Basilica of St. Francis**).
7. Had many visions and was associated with miracles during his life (depicted in **Giotto's frescoes** in the Basilica of St. Francis' upper level).
8. Died at the **Porziuncola,** his body later interred beneath the **Basilica of St. Francis.**

ple in churches). Underneath that level, they found Roman foundations and some animal bones (suggesting the possibility of animal sacrifice). There might have been a Roman temple here; churches were often built upon temple ruins. Stand at the back of the church facing the altar, and look left to the Roman cistern that collected rainwater (just beyond the great stone archway, next to where you entered). Take the three steps down (to trigger the light) and marvel at the fine stonework and Roman engineering. In the Middle Ages, this was the town's emergency water source when under attack.

Diocesan Museum: Underneath the church, incorporated into the Roman ruins and columns, are the foundations of an earlier Church of San Rufino, now the crypt and a fine little museum. When it's open, you can go below to see the saint's sarcophagus (third century) and the cathedral's art from centuries past (down the stairs, near the baptismal font, well-described in English).

• *Leaving the church, walk to the end of the square and take a sharp left (at the pizza-by-the-slice joint, on Via Dono Doni). After 20 yards, take a right and go all the way down the stairway to see some...*

❹ Medieval Architecture

At the bottom of the stairs, notice the pink limestone pavement, part of the surviving medieval town. The arches built over doorways indicate that the buildings date from the 12th through the 14th century, when Assisi was booming. Italian cities such as Assisi—thriving on the north-south trade between northern Europe and Rome—were in the process of inventing free-market capitalism, dabbling in democratic self-rule, and creating the modern urban lifestyle. The vaults you see that turn lanes into tunnels are reminders of medieval urban expansion—creating more living space (mostly 15th century). While the population grew, people wanted to live within the town's protective walls. Medieval Assisi had several times the population density of modern Assisi.

Notice the blooming balconies; Assisi holds a flower competition each June.

• *From the bottom of the stairs, head to the left and continue downhill. When you arrive at a street, turn left, going slightly uphill for a long block, then take the low road (right) at the Y, and head down Via Sermei. Continue down to the big church. Walk right, under the three massive buttresses, to Piazza Santa Chiara and the front of the church.*

❺ Basilica of St. Clare (Basilica di Santa Chiara)

Dedicated to the founder of the Order of the Poor Clares, this Umbrian Gothic church—worth ▲▲—is simple, in keeping with the nuns' dedication to a life of contemplation. In Clare's lifetime, the order was located in the humble Church of San Damiano, in the valley below, but after Clare's death, they needed a bigger and more glorious building. The church was built in 1265, and the huge buttresses were added in the next century.

Cost and Hours: Free, daily 6:30-12:00 & 14:00-19:00, until 18:00 in winter, crypt opens Mon-Fri at 9:00, tel. 075-812-282.

Visiting the Basilica: The interior's fine frescoes were white-washed in Baroque times. The battered remains of one on the left show how the fresco surface was hacked up so whitewash would stick. Imagine all the pristine frescoes hiding behind the whitewash (here and all over Europe).

On the right is the door to the Chapel of the Crucifix of San Damiano, with the simple wooden crucifix that changed Francis' life. In 1206, an emaciated, soul-searching, stark-raving Francis knelt before this crucifix of a living Christ (then located in the Church of San Damiano) and asked for guidance. According to legend, the crucifix spoke: "Go and rebuild my Church, which you can see has fallen into ruin." Francis followed the call.

Stairs lead from the nave down to the tomb of St. Clare. Her tomb—discovered in about 1850—is at the far right end of the richly ornamented neo-Gothic crypt (the image is fiberglass; her actual bones lie underneath). As you circulate with the crowd of pilgrims, notice the paintings on the walls depicting spiritual lessons from Clare's life and death. At the opposite end of the crypt (back between the stairs, in a large glassed-in area, well-described on the wall) are important relics: the saint's robes, hair (in a silver box), and an enormous tunic she made—along with relics of St. Francis (including a bloodstained stocking he wore after receiving the stigmata). The attached cloistered community of the Poor Clares has flourished for 700 years.

• *Leave the church and belly up to the viewpoint at the edge of the square for...*

Another Umbrian View: On the left is the convent of St. Clare (global headquarters of all the Poor Clares). Below you lies the olive grove of the Poor Clares, which has been there since the 13th century. In the distance is a grand Umbrian view. Assisi overlooks the richest and biggest valley in otherwise hilly and mountainous Umbria. Across the valley to the far right (and over the Tiber River), the rival town Perugia, where Francis was imprisoned, sits on its own hill.

The lower town, called Santa Maria degli Angeli, grew up

St. Clare (1194-1253)

The 18-year-old rich girl of Assisi fell in love with Francis' message, and made secret arrangements to meet him. The night

of Palm Sunday, 1212, she slipped out of her father's mansion in town and escaped to the valley below. A procession of friars with torches met her and took her to (what is today) the Basilica of Santa Maria degli Angeli. There, Francis cut her hair, clothed her in a simple brown tunic, and welcomed her into a life of voluntary poverty. Clare's father begged, ordered, and physically threatened her to return, but she would not budge.

Clare was joined by other women who banded together as the Poor Clares. She spent the next 40 years of her life within the confines of the convent of San Damiano: barefoot, vegetarian, and largely silent. Her regimen of prayer, meditation, and simple manual labor—especially knitting—impressed commoners and popes, leading to her canonization almost immediately after her death. St. Clare is often depicted carrying a monstrance (a little temple holding the Eucharist wafer).

ASSISI

with the coming of the railway in the 19th century. In the haze, the church with the grayish-blue dome is the Basilica of Santa Maria degli Angeli (described later), the cradle of the Franciscan order. A popular pilgrimage site today, it marks the place where St. Francis lived, worked, and died.

By the way, many Spanish-speaking Franciscans settled in California. Three of their missions grew into major cities: Los Angeles (named after this church), San Francisco (named after St. Francis), and Santa Clara (named after St. Clare).

• *From the church square, step out into Via Santa Chiara.*

❻ Arches and Artisans

Look left and right to find three old town gates, which illustrate how the city has grown (in concentric circles) since antiquity. First, look to the left, uphill on Via Santa Chiara, the high road. This first arch marks the site of the original Roman wall. In Roman days, this was the extent of Assisi. Now look right, beyond the church. This old gate over the road dates from 1265, as the town expanded during the boom years and the city wall was pushed outward. Farther on, you can just make out the crenellations of the third gate:

the Porta Nuova. Built in 1316, this "New Gate" marks the final expansion of Assisi, before its centuries of slow decline.

Walk uphill along Via Santa Chiara (which becomes Corso Mazzini) to the city's main square. As you pass under the arch you enter what was Roman Assisi—the city that Francis knew. The street is lined with interesting shops selling traditional embroidery, religious souvenirs, and gifty edibles. The shops on Corso Mazzini, on the stretch between the gate and Piazza del Comune, show off many local crafts. As you browse, watch for the following shops:

Galleria d'Arte Perna (on the left, #20b) sells the medieval fantasy townscapes of Paolo Grimaldi, a local painter who runs this shop with his brother, Alessandro.

A helpful travel agency is across the street and a few steps up (at #31, Agenzia Viaggi Stoppini; see "Helpful Hints," earlier).

Next, the aptly named Assisi Olive Wood (on the left at #14E) sells olive-wood carvings, as does d'Olivo, across the street at #23. It's said that St. Francis made the first Nativity scene to help humanize and, therefore, teach the Christmas message. That's why you'll see so many crèches in Assisi. (Even today, nearby villages are enthusiastic about their "living" manger scenes, and Italians everywhere enjoy setting up elaborate crèches in churches for Christmas.)

At #14A (also on the left) is a bakery, Bar Sensi, selling the traditional raisin-and-apple strudel called *rocciata* (roh-CHAH-tah, big enough to share).

Farther along on the left (on the corner at #2A) is Antichita il Duomo, selling religious art, manger scenes, Christmas ornaments, and Crucifixion figurines. Across the street at #5A is Galleria del Corso, selling finely embroidered linens and baby clothes.

And on the square (at #34, on the right), the recommended La Bottega dei Sapori is worth a visit for edible and drinkable souvenirs.

You've walked up what was, in ancient times, the main drag into town. Ahead of you, the six fluted Corinthian columns of the Temple of Minerva marked the forum (today's Piazza del Comune). Sit at the fountain on the piazza for a few minutes of people-watching—don't you just love Italy? Within a few hundred yards of this square, on either side, were the medieval walls. Imagine the commotion of 5,000 people confined within these walls. No wonder St. Francis needed an escape for some peace and quiet.

Today, while the municipality of Assisi has a population of 25,000, only 3,500 people live in the old town: Many who left damaged homes after the 1997 earthquake decided to stay in the modern city below. This is one reason for the old town's plethora of tourist shops (and few services for residents like supermarkets or hardware stores).

• *Now, head over to the temple on the square.*

❼ Temple of Minerva/Christian Church

Assisi has always been a spiritual center. The Romans went to great lengths to make this first-century BC Temple of Minerva a centerpiece of their city. Notice the columns that cut into the stairway. It was a tight fit here on the hilltop. In ancient times, the stairs went down—about twice as far as they do now—to the main drag, which has gradually been filled in over time. The Church of Santa Maria sopra ("over") Minerva was added in the 9th century. The bell tower is from the 13th century.

Pop inside the temple/church (free, daily 7:15-19:30, in winter closes at sunset and midday). Today's interior is 17th-century Baroque. Walk to the front. Flanking the altar to the back are the original Roman temple floor stones. You can even see the drains for the bloody sacrifices that took place here. Behind the statues of Peter and Paul, the original Roman embankment peeks through.

As you exit the church, look to the right, next to the door of the bell tower. The shapes set into the wall are the medieval city standards for the market that used to take place here. The large shapes are building materials, bricks, and roof tiles. The metal bars were the official measuring sticks for goods sold by length, a measurement that could change from city to city.

• *Across the square next to #11, step into the 16th-century frescoed vaults of the...*

Loggia of the Palazzo del Comune: Notice the Italian flair for fine design. Even this little loggia features decorative art (in the Grotesque style—named for the fanciful paintings of bizarre creatures found on unfinished lower-level walls at Nero's Golden House in Rome). This scene was indisputably painted after 1492. How do they know? Because it features turkeys—first seen in Europe after Columbus returned from the Americas with his ship full of exotic souvenirs. The turkeys painted here may have been that bird's European debut.

• *From the main square, hike left past the temple up the high road, Via San Paolo. After 150 yards (across from #24), a sign on the left directs you down a stepped lane to the...*

❽ Church of Santo Stefano
(Chiesa di Santo Stefano)

Surrounded by cypress, fig, and walnut trees, Santo Stefano—which used to be outside the town walls in the days of St. Francis—is a delightful bit of offbeat Assisi (free, daily 8:30-20:00, shorter hours off-season). Legend has it that Santo Stefano's bells miraculously rang on October 3, 1226, the day St. Francis died. Step inside. This is the typical rural Italian Romanesque church—no architect, just built by simple stonemasons who put together the most basic design. Hundreds of years later, it still stands.

• *The lane zigzags down to Via San Francesco. When you reach the narrow lane, go left (downhill). Then, emerging at the wider street, turn right and walk under the arch toward the Basilica of St. Francis. To trace the rest of our route, see the "Assisi" map on page 133.*

❾ Via San Francesco

This main drag leads from the town to the basilica holding the body of St. Francis. Francis was a big deal even in his own day. He was made a saint in 1228—the same year that the basilica's foundations were laid—and his body was moved here by 1230. Assisi was a big-time pilgrimage center, and this street was its booming hub. The arch marks the end of what was Assisi in St. Francis' day. Notice the fine medieval balcony immediately past the arch (on the left).

About 30 yards farther down (on the left), find the **fountain** where medieval pilgrims might have cooled themselves. The hospice next door was built in 1237 to house pilgrims. Notice the three surviving faces of its fresco: Jesus, Francis, and Clare.

Farther down on the left, across from #12A, is the **Oratorio dei Pellegrini,** dating from the 1450s. A brotherhood ran a hostel here for travelers passing through to pay homage to St. Francis. The chapel offers a richly frescoed 14th-century space designed to inspire pilgrims—perfect for any traveler to pause and contemplate the saint's message (Mon-Fri 9:00-12:00 & 16:00-18:00, Sat afternoon only, closed Sun).

From here, the road continues a few more short blocks downhill to the Basilica of St. Francis. Just before the basilica is a three-floor museum about Capuchin missionaries' work in the Amazon region since 1909 (**Museo Missionario Indios,** on the left at #19, closed Mon). Depending on your feelings about missionaries in the developing world, this may be of interest—with exhibits on ethnography, flora and fauna, and Franciscan theology.

• *Continuing on, you'll reach Assisi's main sight, the Basilica of St. Francis. For the start of my self-guided tour, walk downhill to the basilica's lower courtyard.*

Basilica of St. Francis Tour

The Basilica of St. Francis (Basilica di San Francesco), worth ▲▲▲, is one of the artistic and religious highlights of Europe.

It stands where, in 1226, St. Francis was buried (with the outcasts he had stood by) outside of his town on the "Hill of the Damned"—now called the "Hill of Paradise." The basilica is frescoed from top to bottom with scenes by the leading artists of the day: Cimabue, Giotto, Simone Martini, and Pietro Lorenzetti. A 13th-century historian wrote, "No more exquisite monument to the Lord has been built."

From a distance, you see the huge arcades "supporting" the basilica. These were 15th-century quarters for the monks. The arcades that line the square and lead to the church housed medieval pilgrims.

ORIENTATION

Cost and Hours: The complex is free to enter, with different hours for various parts. The **lower basilica** and **tomb** are open to tourists daily 6:00-17:30, Nov-March until 16:30—but in practice, the space remains open for worship (and discreet sightseers) more than an hour later. Within the lower basilica, the **reliquary chapel** opens at 9:00 but is often closed Sat-Sun (and occasionally at other times for religious services). The **upper basilica** is open daily 8:30-18:50, Nov-March until 18:00. And the skippable **treasury/museum** is open Mon-Tue and Thu-Sat 9:30-18:00, Sun 11:00-17:00, closed Wed, shorter hours off-season, closed Jan-Feb.

Dress Code: Modest dress is required to enter the church—no above-the-knee skirts or shorts and no sleeveless tops for men, women, or children.

Information: Tel. 075-819-0170, www.sanfrancescoassisi.org. Call or check the website to find out about upcoming events at the basilica. A handy information office is in the arcade of the lower courtyard—on the right as you face the church (Mon-Sat 9:00-18:00, closed Sun, shorter hours off-season).

Tours: Videoguides loaded with a one-hour tour are available at the information office under the arcade in the courtyard of the lower basilica (€6, €10/2 people).

   ∩ Download my free Basilica of St. Francis audio tour.

ASSISI

Bookstore: The church bookshop is in the inner courtyard behind the upper and lower basilica. It sells an excellent guidebook, *The Basilica of Saint Francis: A Spiritual Pilgrimage* (€3, by Goulet, McInally, and Wood); I used this book, and a tour with Brother Michael, as sources for this self-guided tour.

Church Services: To worship in the basilica, consider joining the Franciscan brothers for Mass in *Italiano* (Mon-Sat at 7:15, 11:00, and 18:00—or 17:00 off-season; Sun at 7:30, 9:00, 10:30, 12:00, 17:00, and 18:30), or experience a Mass sung by the basilica choir many Sundays at 10:30. On Sundays in summer (Easter-Oct), there's an English Mass in the upper basilica at 9:00. Additional English and sung Masses don't follow a set schedule. Call the basilica to find out when English-speaking pilgrimage groups or choirs have reserved Masses, and attend with them (tel. 075-819-0170).

OVERVIEW

The Basilica of St. Francis, a theological work of genius, can be difficult for the 21st-century tourist/pilgrim to appreciate.

Since the basilica is the reason that most people visit Assisi, and the message of St. Francis has even the least devout sightseers blessing the town Vespas, I've designed this self-guided tour with an emphasis on the place's theology (rather than art history).

A disclaimer before we start: Just as Francis used many biblical legends to help teach the Christian message, legends from the life of Francis were told in later ages to teach the same message. Are they true? In general, probably not. Are they in keeping with Francis' message? Yes. Do I share legends here as if they are historic? Sure.

The church has three parts: the upper basilica, the lower basilica, and the saint's tomb (below the lower basilica). We'll tour the complex from the bottom up. To get oriented, head down the ramp from the grassy lawn and stand in the big plaza that stretches in front of the lower entrance. While empty today, centuries ago this main piazza was cluttered with pilgrim services and the medieval equivalent of souvenir shops. As you face the church, the information office is under the arcade to your right, and the WCs are just behind that. (Go before you enter, as there aren't any WCs inside the basilica.)

➋ SELF-GUIDED TOUR

Enter through the grand doorway of the lower basilica. Just inside, decorating the top of the first arch, look up and see St. Francis, who greets you with a Latin inscription. Sounding a bit like John Wayne, he says the equivalent of, "Slow down and be joyful, pilgrim. You've reached the Hill of Paradise. And, if you're observant and thoughtful, this church will knock your spiritual socks off."

• *Start with the tomb. To get there, turn left into the nave. Midway down, follow the signs and go right, to the tomb downstairs.*

The Tomb

The saint's remains are above the altar in the stone box with the iron ties. In medieval times, pilgrims came to Assisi because St. Francis was buried here. Holy relics were the "ruby slippers" of medieval Europe. Relics gave you power—they answered your prayers and won your wars—and ultimately helped you get back to your eternal Kansas. Assisi made no bones about promoting the saint's relics, but hid his tomb for obvious reasons of security. His body was buried secretly while the basilica was under construction, and over the next 600 years, the exact location was forgotten. When the tomb was to be opened to the public in 1818, it took more than a month to find his actual remains.

Francis' four closest friends and first followers are memorialized in the corners of the room. Opposite the altar, up four steps between the entrance and exit, notice the small copper box behind the metal grille. This contains the remains of Francis' rich Roman patron, Jacopa dei Settesoli. She traveled to see him on his deathbed but was turned away because she was female. Francis waived the rule and welcomed "Brother Jacopa" to his side. These five tombs—in the Franciscan spirit of being with your friends—were added in the 19th century.

The candles you see are the only real candles in the church (others are electric). Pilgrims pay a coin, pick up a candle, and place it in the small box on the side. The friars will light it later.

• *Climb back up to the lower nave.*

Lower Basilica

Appropriately Franciscan—subdued and Romanesque—this nave is frescoed with parallel scenes from the lives of Christ (right) and Francis (left), connected by a ceiling of stars. The Passion of Christ and the Compassion of Francis lead to the altar built over Francis' tomb. After the church was built and decorated, side chapels were erected to provide mausoleums for the rich families that patronized the work of the order. Unfortunately, in the process, huge arches were cut out of some frescoed scenes, but others survive.

In the fresco directly above the entry to the tomb, Christ is

ASSISI

Basilica of St. Francis—Lower Level

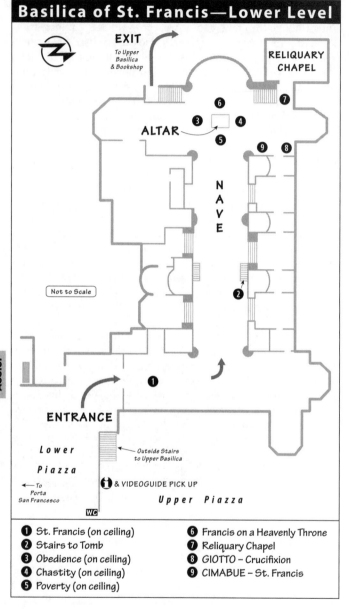

EXIT
To Upper Basilica & Bookshop

RELIQUARY CHAPEL

6

3 **4**

ALTAR

5

9 **8**

7

N
A
V
E

Not to Scale

2

1

ENTRANCE

Lower Piazza

Outside Stairs to Upper Basilica

← To Porta San Francesco

& VIDEOGUIDE PICK UP

Upper Piazza

WC

1 St. Francis (on ceiling)
2 Stairs to Tomb
3 Obedience (on ceiling)
4 Chastity (on ceiling)
5 Poverty (on ceiling)

6 Francis on a Heavenly Throne
7 Reliquary Chapel
8 GIOTTO – Crucifixion
9 CIMABUE – St. Francis

ASSISI

being taken down from the cross (just the bottom half of his body can be seen, on the left), and it looks like the story is over. Defeat. But in the opposite fresco (above the tomb's exit), we see Francis preaching to the birds, reminding the faithful that the message of the Gospel survives.

These stories directed the attention of the medieval pilgrim to the altar, where he could meet God through the sacraments. The church was thought of as a community of believers sailing toward God. The prayers coming out of the nave (*navis*, or ship) fill the triangular sections of the ceiling—called *vele*, or sails—with spiritual wind. With a priest for a navigator and the altar for a helm, faith propels the ship.

Walk around the altar, stand behind it (toes to the bottom step, facing the entrance), and look up. The three scenes above you represent the creed of the Franciscans: Directly above the tomb of St. Francis, to the right, *Obedience* (Francis appears twice, wearing a rope harness and kneeling in front of Lady Obedience); to the left, *Chastity* (in her tower of purity held up by two angels); and straight ahead, *Poverty.* Here Jesus blesses the marriage as Francis slips a ring on Lady Poverty. In the foreground, two "self-sufficient" yet pint-size merchants (the new rich of a thriving northern Italy) are throwing sticks and stones at the bride. But Poverty, in her patched wedding dress, is fertile and strong, and even bare brambles blossom into a rosebush crown.

St. Francis called money the "devil's dung." The jeweled belt of a rich person was all about material wealth. A bag of coins hung from it, as did a weapon to protect that wealth. The simple rope Franciscan monks use to tie their tunics has three knots that symbolize—and serve as constant reminders of—their vows of obedience, chastity, and poverty.

Now turn around and put your heels to the altar and—bending back like a drum major—look up for a peek at the reward for a life of obedience, chastity, and poverty: **Francis on a heavenly throne** in a rich, golden robe. He traded a life of earthly simplicity for glory in heaven.

• *Turn to the right and march to the corner, where steps lead down into the...*

Reliquary Chapel

This chapel is filled with fascinating relics (which a €0.50 flier explains in detailed English; often closed Sat-Sun). Step in and circle the room clockwise. You'll see the silver chalice and plate that Francis used for the bread and wine of the Eucharist (in a small, dark, windowed case set into the wall, marked *Calice e Patena*). Francis believed that his personal possessions should be simple, but the items used for worship should be made of the finest materials.

The Franciscan Message

Francis' message caused a stir. Not only did he follow Christ's teachings, he also followed Christ's lifestyle, living as a poor, wandering preacher. He traded a life of power and riches for one of obedience, poverty, and chastity. He was never ordained as a priest, but his influence on Christianity was monumental.

The Franciscan realm (Brother Sun, Sister Moon, and so on) is a space where God, man, and the natural world frolic harmoniously. Francis treated every creature—animal, peasant, pope—with equal respect. He and his "brothers" (*fratelli,* or friars) slept in fields, begged for food, and exuded the joy of nonmaterialism. Franciscan friars were known as the "Jugglers of God," modeling themselves on French troubadours who roved the countryside singing, telling stories, and cracking jokes.

In an Italy torn by rival political factions, Francis promoted peace and the restoration of order. (He set an example by reconstructing the crumbled San Damiano chapel.) While the Church was waging bloody Crusades, Francis pushed ecumenism and understanding. And the Franciscan message had an impact. In 1288, just 62 years after Francis died, a Franciscan became pope (Nicholas IV). Francis' message also led to Church reforms that

Next, the Veli di Lino is a cloth Jacopa wiped her friend's brow with on his deathbed. In the corner display case is a small section of the itchy haircloth *(cilizio)*—not sheep's wool, but cloth made from scratchy horse or goat hair—worn by Francis as penance (the cloth he chose was the opposite of the fine fabric his father sold). In the next corner are the tunic and slippers that Francis donned during his last days. Next, find a prayer (in a fancy silver stand) that St. Francis wrote for Brother Leo and signed with a T-shaped character—his tau cross. The last letter in the Hebrew alphabet, tav ("tau" in Greek) is symbolic of faithfulness to the end, and Francis adopted it for his signature. Next is a papal document (1223) legitimizing the Franciscan order and assuring his followers that they were not risking a (deadly) heresy charge. Finally, just past the altar, see the tunic that was lovingly patched and stitched by followers of the five-foot, four-inch-tall St. Francis.

Before leaving the chapel, notice the modern paintings done recently by local artists. Over the entrance, Francis is shown being many believe delayed the Protestant Reformation by a century.

The richly decorated Assisi basilica seems to contradict the teachings of the poor monk it honors, but it was built as an act of religious and civic pride to remember the hometown saint. It was also designed—and still functions—as a pilgrimage center and a splendid classroom. Though monks in robes may not give off an "easy-to-approach" vibe, the Franciscans of today are still God's jugglers (and many of them speak English).

Here is Francis' message, in his own words:

The Canticle of the Sun

Good Lord, all your creations bring praise to you!

Praise for Brother Sun, who brings the day. His radiance reminds us of you!

Praise for Sister Moon and the stars, precious and beautiful.

Praise for Brother Wind, and for clouds and storms and rain that sustain us.

Praise for Sister Water. She is useful and humble, precious and pure.

Praise for Brother Fire who cheers us at night.

Praise for our sister, Mother Earth, who feeds us and rules us.

Praise for all those who forgive because you have forgiven them.

Praise for our sister, Bodily Death, from whose embrace none can escape.

Praise and bless the Lord, and give thanks, and, with humility, serve him.

ASSISI

born in a stable like Jesus (by Capitini). Scenes from the life of Clare and Padre Pio (a Capuchin priest, very popular in Italy, who was sainted in 2002) were painted by Stefanelli and Antonio.

• *Return up the stairs, stepping into the...*

Lower Basilica's Transept

The decoration of this church brought together the greatest Sienese (Lorenzetti and Simone Martini) and Florentine (Cimabue and Giotto) artists of the day.

Look around at the painted scenes. In 1300, this was radical art—believable homespun scenes, landscapes, trees, real people. Directly opposite the reliquary chapel, study **Giotto's painting of the Crucifixion,** with the eight sparrow-like angels. For the first time, holy people are expressing emotion: One angel turns her head sadly at the sight of Jesus, and another scratches her hands down her cheeks, drawing blood. Mary (lower left), previously in control, has fainted in despair. The Franciscans, with their goal of bringing

God to the people, found a natural partner in Europe's first naturalist (and therefore modern) painter, Giotto.

To grasp Giotto's artistic leap, compare his work with the painting to the right, by Cimabue. It's Gothic, without the 3-D architecture, natural backdrop, and slice-of-life reality of Giotto's work. **Cimabue's St. Francis** (far right) shows the saint with the stigmata—Christ's marks of the Crucifixion. Contemporaries described Francis as being short, with a graceful build, dark hair, and sparse beard. (This is considered the most accurate portrait of Francis—done according to the description of one who knew him.) The sunroof haircut (tonsure) was standard  for monks of the day. According to legend, the brown robe and rope belt were inventions of necessity. When Francis stripped naked and ran away from Assisi, he grabbed the first clothes he could, a rough wool peasant's tunic and a piece of rope, which became the uniform of the Franciscan order.

To the left, at eye level under the sparrow-like angels, are paintings of **saints** and their exquisite halos (by Simone Martini or his school). To the right of the door at the same level, see five of Francis' closest **followers**—clearly just simple folk.

Francis' friend, **"Sister Bodily Death,"** was really not all that terrible. In fact, Francis would like to introduce you to her now (above and to the right of the door leading into the reliquary chapel). Go ahead, block the light from the door with this book and meet her. Before his death, Francis added a line to *The Canticle of the Sun:* "Praise for our sister, Bodily Death, from whose embrace none can escape."

• *Now, cross the transept to the other side of the altar (enjoying some of the oldest surviving bits of the inlaid local-limestone flooring—c. 13th century) and find the staircase going up. Immediately above the stairs is* **Lorenzetti's Francis Receiving the Stigmata.** *(Francis is considered the first person ever to earn the marks of the cross through his great faith and love of the Church.) Make your way up the stairs to the...*

Courtyard

The courtyard overlooks the 15th-century cloister, the heart of this monastic complex. Pope Sixtus IV (of Sistine Chapel fame) had it built as a secure retreat for himself. Balanced and peaceful by design, the courtyard also functioned as a cistern to collect rainwater, supplying enough for 200 monks (today, there are about 40). The Franciscan order emphasizes teaching. This place functioned as a kind of theological center of higher learning, which rotated monks in for a six-month stint, then sent them back home more prepared and better inspired to preach effectively. That explains the complex narrative of the frescoes wallpapering the walls and halls here.

The **treasury** *(Museo del Tesoro)* to the left of the bookstore features ornately decorated chalices, reliquaries, vestments, and altarpieces.

• *From the courtyard, climb the stairs (next to the bookshop) to the...*

Upper Basilica

Built later than its counterpart below, the brighter upper basilica is considered the first Gothic church in Italy (started in 1228). You've

followed the intended pilgrims' route, entering the lower church and finishing here. Notice how the pulpit (embedded in the corner pillar) can be seen and heard from every spot in the packed church. The spirit of the order was to fill the church and preach. See also the design in the round window in the west end (high above the entry). The tiny centerpiece reads "IHS" (the first three letters of Jesus' name in Greek). And, as you can see, this trippy kaleidoscope seems to declare that all light radiates from Jesus.

The windows here are treasures from the 13th and 14th centuries. Those behind the altar are among the oldest and most precious in Italy. Imagine illiterate medieval peasants entranced by these windows, so full of meaning that they were nicknamed "Bibles of the Poor."

But for art lovers, the basilica's draw is that Giotto and his assistants practically wallpapered it circa 1297-1300. Or perhaps the job was subcontracted to other artists—scholars debate it. Whatever the case, the anatomy, architectural depth, and drama of these frescoes helped to kick off the Renaissance. The gallery of frescoes shows 28 scenes from the life of St. Francis. The events are a mix of documented history and folk legend.

• *Take a walk through Francis' life, via these glorious illustrations. As you stand in front of the altar, facing the front of the church, begin with the first fresco on the right. From here, you'll work clockwise (moving to the right) along the north wall. Follow along with the help of the num-*

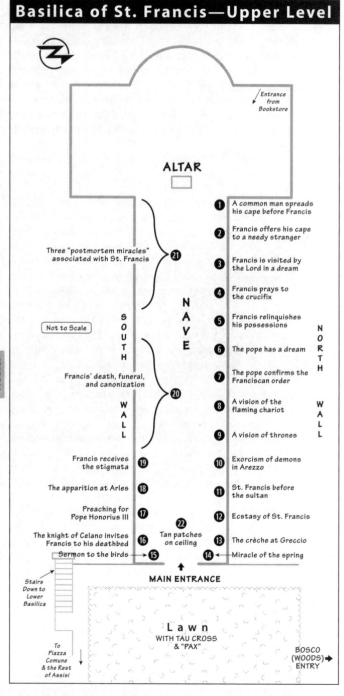

Basilica of St. Francis—Upper Level

Entrance from Bookstore

ALTAR

1 A common man spreads his cape before Francis

2 Francis offers his cape to a needy stranger

3 Francis is visited by the Lord in a dream

4 Francis prays to the crucifix

5 Francis relinquishes his possessions

6 The pope has a dream

7 The pope confirms the Franciscan order

8 A vision of the flaming chariot

9 A vision of thrones

10 Exorcism of demons in Arezzo

11 St. Francis before the sultan

12 Ecstasy of St. Francis

13 The crèche at Greccio

14 Miracle of the spring

15 Sermon to the birds

16 The knight of Celano invites Francis to his deathbed

17 Preaching for Pope Honorius III

18 The apparition at Arles

19 Francis receives the stigmata

20 Francis' death, funeral, and canonization

21 Three "postmortem miracles" associated with St. Francis

22 Tan patches on ceiling

Three "postmortem miracles" associated with St. Francis 21

Francis' death, funeral, and canonization 20

Not to Scale

SOUTH WALL

NAVE

NORTH WALL

MAIN ENTRANCE

Stairs Down to Lower Basilica

To Piazza Comune & the Rest of Assisi

Lawn WITH TAU CROSS & "PAX"

BOSCO (WOODS) ENTRY

ASSISI

bered map key. The subtitles in the faded black strip below the frescoes describe each scene in clear Latin—and affirm my interpretation.

❶ **A common man spreads his cape before Francis** in front of the Temple of Minerva on Piazza del Comune. Before his conversion, young Francis was the model of Assisian manhood—handsome, intelligent, and well-dressed, befitting the son of a wealthy cloth dealer. Above all, he was liked by everyone, a natural charmer who led his fellow teens in nights of wine, women, and song. Medieval pilgrims understood the deeper meaning of this scene: The "eye" of God (symbolized by the rose window in the Temple of Minerva) looks over the young Francis, a dandy "imprisoned" in his own selfishness (the Temple—with barred windows—was once a prison).

❷ **Francis offers his cape to a needy stranger.** Francis was always generous of spirit. He became more so after being captured in battle and held for a year as a prisoner of war, then suffering from illness. Charity was a Franciscan forte.

❸ **Francis is visited by the Lord in a dream.** Still unsure of his calling, Francis rode off to the Crusades. One night, he dreams of a palace filled with armor marked with crosses. Christ tells him to leave the army—to become what you might consider the first "conscientious objector"—and go home to wait for a nonmilitary assignment in a new kind of knighthood. He returned to Assisi and, though reviled as a coward, would end up fighting for spiritual wealth, not earthly power and riches.

❹ **Francis prays to the crucifix** in the Church of San Damiano. After months of living in a cave, fasting, and meditating, Francis kneels in the run-down church and prays. The crucifix speaks, telling him: "Go and rebuild my Church, which you can see has fallen into ruin." Francis hurried home and sold his father's cloth to pay for God's work. His furious father dragged him before the bishop.

❺ **Francis relinquishes his possessions.** In front of the bishop and the whole town, Francis strips naked and gives his dad his clothes, credit cards, and a time-share on Capri. Francis raises his hand and says, "Until now, I called you father. From now on, my only father is my Father in Heaven." Notice God's hand blessing the action from above. Francis then ran off into the hills, naked and singing. In this version, Francis is covered by the bishop, symbolizing his transition from a man of the world to a man of the Church. Notice the disbelief and concern on the bishop's advisors' faces; subtle expressions like these wouldn't have made it into other medieval frescoes of the day.

❻ **The pope has a dream.** Francis headed to Rome, seeking the pope's blessing on his fledgling movement. Initially rebuffing

ASSISI

Francis, the pope then dreams of a simple, barefooted man propping up his teetering Church, and then...

❼ **The pope confirms the Franciscan order,** handing Francis and his gang the 1223 document now displayed in the reliquary chapel.

Francis' life was peppered with visions and miracles, shown in three panels in a row: ❽ **vision of the flaming chariot,** ❾ **vision of thrones,** and ❿ **exorcism of demons in Arezzo.**

• *Next see...*

⓫ **St. Francis before the sultan.** Francis' wandering ministry took him to Egypt during the Crusades (1219). He walked unarmed into the Muslim army camp. They captured him, but the sultan was impressed with Francis' manner and let him go, reportedly whispering, "I'd convert to your faith, but they'd kill us both." Here the sultan gestures from his throne.

⓬ **Ecstasy of St. Francis.** This oft-painted scene shows the mystic communing with Christ.

⓭ **The crèche at Greccio.** A creative teacher, Francis invents the tradition of manger scenes.

• *Around the corner, see the...*

⓮ **Miracle of the spring.** Shown here getting water out of a rock to quench a stranger's thirst, Francis felt closest to God when in the hills around Assisi, seeing the Creator in the creation.

• *Cross over to the far side of the entrance door.*

⓯ **Sermon to the birds.** In his best-known miracle, Francis is surrounded by birds as they listen to him teach. Francis embraces all levels of creation. One interpretation of this scene is that the birds, which are of different species, represent the diverse flock of humanity and nature, all created and beloved by God and worthy of one another's love.

This image of well-fed birds is an appropriate one to take with you. It's designed to remind pilgrims that, like the birds, God gave us life, plenty of food, feathers, wings, and a world to fly around in. Francis, patron saint of the environment and animals, taught his followers to see God in nature and to count their blessings. A monk here reminded me that even a student backpacker today eats as well as the wealthiest nobleman in the days of Francis.

• *Continue to the south wall for the rest of the panels.*

Despite the hierarchical society of his day, Francis was welcomed by all classes, shown in these three panels: ⓰ **the knight of Celano invites Francis to his deathbed;** ⓱ **preaching for Pope Honorius III,** who listens intently; and ⓲ **the apparition at Arles,** which illustrates how Francis could be in two places at once (something only Jesus and saints can pull off). The proponents of Francis, who believed he was destined for sainthood, show him performing the necessary miracles.

❶ Francis receives the stigmata. It's September 17, 1224, and Francis is fasting and praying on nearby Mount Alverna when a six-winged angel (called a seraph) appears with holy laser-like powers to burn in the marks of the Crucifixion, the stigmata. For the strength of his faith, Francis is given the marks of his master, the "battle scars of love." These five wounds suffered by Christ (nails in palms and feet, lance in side) marked Francis' body for the rest of his life.

The next panels deal with **❷ Francis' death, funeral, and canonization.** The last panels show **❸ miracles** associated with the saint after his death, proving that he's in heaven and bolstering his eligibility for sainthood.

Francis died thanking God and singing his *Canticle of the Sun,* in which he refers to the sun as his brother and the moon as his sister. Francis also called his body "Brother Ass" (because of the heavy burdens he asked it to carry)—and conceded on his deathbed that he'd been a bit tough on Brother Ass. Ravaged by an asceticism extreme enough to earn him the stigmata, Francis died in 1226.

Before leaving through the front entrance, look up at the ceiling and the walls near the rose window to see **❹ large tan patches.** In 1997, when a 5.5-magnitude quake hit Assisi, it shattered the upper basilica's frescoes into 300,000 fragments. An aftershock then shook the ceiling frescoes down, killing two monks and two art scholars who were standing here. Later, the fragments were meticulously picked up and pieced back together.

Outside, on the lawn, the Latin word *pax* (peace) and the Franciscan tau cross are sculpted from shrubbery. For a drink or snack, the Bar San Francesco (facing the upper basilica) is handy. For *pax,* take the high lane back to town, up to the castle, or into the countryside.

More Sights in Assisi

IN THE OLD TOWN
These sights are in the upper town, near the main square or basilica.

▲Roman Forum (Foro Romano)
For a look at Assisi's Roman roots, check out the Roman Forum from the town of "Asisum"—beneath today's Piazza del Comune. You'll enter through a nondescript doorway (just a few steps off the main square) into a room filled with carved stone capitals, tombstones, sarcophagi, and sculpture fragments. From there, you'll follow tunnels back under the square itself, seeing various landmarks that once lined the streets of Asisum: a tribunal for speeches, a fountain, columns, the original Roman road, and much more, all displayed in situ (where it was discovered). A helpful five-minute

ASSISI

video (subtitled in English) helps resurrect the rubble.

Cost and Hours: €5, €9 combo-ticket with the next two sights, daily 10:00-18:00, June-Sept until 19:00, enter at Via Portica 2, tel. 075-815-5077.

Pinacoteca

This small, unexciting museum attractively displays its 13th- to 17th-century art (mainly frescoes). There's a damaged Giotto Madonna and a rare secular fresco (to the right of the Giotto art), but it's mainly a peaceful walk through a pastel world—best for art lovers.

Cost and Hours: €3, €9 combo-ticket includes Forum and Rocca Maggiore, April-Oct daily 10:00-18:00, closed Nov-March except by appointment, on the main drag between Piazza del Comune and Basilica of St. Francis at Via San Francesco 12—look for banner above entryway, tel. 075-867-4341.

▲Rocca Maggiore

The "big castle" offers a few restored medieval rooms, a good look at a 14th-century fortification, and a fine view of Assisi and the Umbrian countryside. If you're pinching your euros, skip it—the view is just as good from outside the castle.

Cost and Hours: €6, €9 combo-ticket includes Forum and Pinacoteca, daily June-Aug 9:00-20:00, Sept from 10:00, April-May and Oct 10:00-18:30, shorter hours off-season, last entry 45 minutes before closing, Via della Rocca, tel. 075-815-5077.

IN THE LOWER TOWN
▲▲Basilica of Santa Maria degli Angeli
(Basilica of St. Mary of the Angels)

This huge basilica, towering above the buildings of Santa Maria degli Angeli—the modern part of Assisi in the flat valley below the hill town—marks the spot where Francis lived, worked, and died. It's a grandiose church built around a humble chapel—reflecting the monumental impact of this simple saint on his town and the world.

Cost and Hours: Free, Mon-Sat 6:15-12:40 & 14:30-19:30, Sun from 6:45, tel. 075-805-11.

Dress Code: Modest dress is required (no shorts or tank tops).

Visitor Services: A little TI is across the street from the souvenir stands, under the arches (generally Tue-Sun 10:00-12:30 & 15:30-18:00, closed Mon, tel. 075-804-4554). As you face the church, there are big pay WCs behind the bushes on your right.

Getting There: Whether you're traveling by car or by train, it's most practical to visit this sight on the way into or out of town. From Assisi's train station, it's a five-minute walk (exit station left, after 50 yards take the underground pedestrian walkway—*sotto-passaggio*—on your left, then walk straight ahead, passing several handy eateries). There's ample, well-marked parking next to the train station, and some free (time-limited) spaces tucked behind the basilica.

From the old town, you can reach the basilica on the same Busitalia (line #C) that runs down to the train station (stay on one more stop to reach the basilica; confirm with driver). In the opposite direction, buses from the basilica up to the old town run twice hourly. Leaving the church, the stop is on your right, by the side of the building. For more bus details, see "Getting Around Assisi," earlier.

Visiting the Basilica: This grand church was built in the 16th century around the tiny but historic **Porziuncola Chapel** (now directly under the dome) after the chapel became too small to accommodate the many pilgrims wanting to pay homage to St. Francis. Some local monks had given Francis this *porziuncola*, or "small portion," after his conversion—a little land with a fixer-upper chapel. Francis lived here after he founded the Franciscan order, and this was where he consecrated St. Clare as a Bride of Christ. What would humble Francis think of the huge church—Christianity's 10th largest—built over his tiny chapel?

Behind the Porziuncola Chapel on the right, find the **Cappella del Transito,** which marks the site of Francis' death on October 3, 1226. Only 44 years old, Francis died as he'd lived—simply, in a small hut located here. On his last night on earth, he invited some friars to join him in a Last Supper-style breaking of bread. Then he undressed, lay down on the bare ground, and began to recite Psalm

141: "Lord, I cry unto thee." He spoke the last line, "Let the wicked fall into their own traps, while I escape"...and he passed on.

From the right transept, follow *Roseto* signs to the rose garden. You'll walk down a passage with gardens on either side (viewable through the windows)—on the left, a tranquil park with a statue of Francis petting a sheep, and on the right, the **rose garden.** Francis, fighting a temptation that he never named, once threw himself onto the roses. As the story goes, the thorns immediately dropped off. Thornless roses have grown here ever since.

Exiting the passage, turn right to find the **Rose Chapel** (Cappella delle Rose), built over the place where Francis lived.

The next hallway has exhibits that change occasionally, but you'll likely see a giant **Nativity scene**—a reminder to pilgrims that Francis first established the tradition of manger scenes as a teaching aid. The bookshop has some works in English and an "old pharmacy" selling herbal cures.

Porziuncola Museum: Continuing on, you'll pass this small museum featuring early depictions of St. Francis by 13th-century artists, a model of Assisi during Francis' lifetime, and religious art and objects from the basilica. On the museum's upper floor are some monks' cells, which provide intriguing insight into the spartan lifestyles of the pious and tonsured (€3, ask for English brochure, Thu-Tue 9:00-13:00 & 14:30-17:00, closed Wed, tel. 075-805-1419, www.porziuncola.org).

ON THE OUTSKIRTS
Church of San Damiano (Chiesa di San Damiano)

Located on the slope steeply below the Basilica of St. Clare, this modest church and convent was where Francis received his call and where Clare spent her days as mother superior of the Poor Clares. As you enter, signs point you through a series of simple rooms—including the dining hall where Clare ate with her flock and the room where she died—to a peaceful, flowery courtyard. Drivers can zip right there (watch for the turnoff on the road up to Piazza Matteotti), while walkers descend pleasantly from Assisi for 15 minutes through an olive grove.

In 1206, Francis was inside when he heard the wooden crucifix order him to rebuild the church. (The crucifix in San Damiano is a copy; the original is now displayed in the Basilica of St. Clare.) Francis initially interpreted these miraculous words as a call to rebuild crumbling San Damiano. He sold his father's cloth for money to fix the church. (The church we see today, however, was rebuilt later by others.) Eventually, Francis realized his charge was to revitalize the Christian Church at large.

As he approached the end of his life, Francis came to San Damiano to visit his old friend Clare. She set him up in a simple reed hut in the olive grove, where he was inspired to write his poem *The Canticle of the Sun* (see page 151).

Cost and Hours: Free, daily, convent open 10:00-12:00 & 14:00-18:00, until 16:30 in winter, church opens at 6:15; start walking from the Porta Nuova parking lot at the south end of Assisi and follow the signs; tel. 075-812-273, www.assisiofm.it.

Commune with Nature

For a picnic with the same birdsong and views that inspired St. Francis, leave the tourists behind and **hike to the Rocca Minore** (small private castle, not tourable) above Piazza Matteotti.

For a more organized nature experience, try the 160-acre **San Francesco Woods** (Bosco di San Francesco), where you can follow three routes through forest, monastery ruins, and a land-art installation (€5 suggested donation, picnic area; daily 10:00-19:00, Oct-March until 16:00 and closed Mon Sept-June, last entry one hour before closing, off the piazza in front of the upper basilica, tel. 075-813-157).

▲Hermitage (Eremo delle Carceri)

If you want to follow further in St. Francis' footsteps, take a trip up the rugged slopes of nearby Mount Subasio to the humble, peaceful hermitage where Francis and his followers retreated for solitude. Today the spot is marked by a 14th-century friary that's still occupied by Franciscan monks. You'll twist through the head-thumping doorframes and steep stairways of the medieval structure, the highlight of which is the tiny, dank cave where Francis would retire for private prayer. Emerging at the far side, near a stone bridge, you'll see a tree (held together with braces) dating from Francis' time. This is said to be where Francis preached to the birds. From here, rustic paths lead to open-air "chapels" in the surrounding forest. Be a Franciscan for a little while. Sit peacefully and listen. Pick out the different sounds of nature: wind blowing through the trees, chirping birds, gravel crunching underfoot. And listen for the spaces *between* the sounds. That's where Francis found God.

Cost and Hours: Free, daily 8:30-19:00, until 18:00 in winter, tel. 075-812-301.

Getting There: Drive, take a taxi, or hike—there is no public transportation. Drivers can follow signs out of Assisi toward Mount Subasio, then park on the switchback just above the entrance. For hikers starting from Assisi's Porta Cappuccino gate, it's a stiff 3-mile, 1.5-hour hike with an elevation gain of about 1,000 feet. You'll walk along a narrow, paved road (with no shoulders) enjoying brisk air and sporadic views. A souvenir kiosk at the entrance sells drinks and sandwiches, and there are WCs just uphill from the friary.

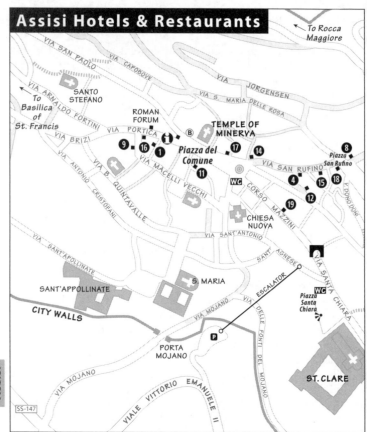

Sleeping in Assisi

Assisi accommodates large numbers of pilgrims on religious holidays (see page 221). Finding a room at any other time should be easy. My price rankings are based on rates in spring (April-mid-June) and fall (mid-Aug-Oct). Few hotels are air-conditioned.

HOTELS AND ROOMS

$$ Hotel Umbra, a peaceful villa in the middle of town, has 24 spacious, antique-furnished rooms with great view terraces. It's a bit old-fashioned, but well-run, well-maintained, friendly, and beautifully located. Stepping into the breakfast room is like entering a time warp (RS%, family rooms, air-con, elevator, garden, and view sun terrace, most rooms have views, closed Dec-March, just off Piazza del Comune under the arch at Via degli Archi 6, tel.

Accommodations

1. Hotel Umbra
2. Hotel Ideale
3. Hotel Belvedere
4. Hotel Pallotta
5. Hotel San Rufino
6. Hotel il Duomo
7. Hotel la Rocca
8. Camere Carli
9. Camere Annalisa Martini
10. St. Anthony's Guest House

Eateries & Other

11. Trattoria Pallotta
12. Osteria Piazzetta dell'Erba
13. Trattoria da Erminio
14. Trattoria degli Umbri
15. Hostaria Terra Chiama
16. Pizzeria il Menestrello
17. La Bottega dei Sapori
18. Pizza al Taglio da Andrea
19. Agenzia Viaggi Stoppini (Train & Bus Tickets)

ASSISI

075-812-240, www.hotelumbra.it, info@hotelumbra.it, Laudenzi family).

$$ Hotel Ideale, on a ridge overlooking the valley, offers 13 bright and airy rooms (all with views and balconies), a tranquil garden setting, and free (but tight) private parking. As it's just off the main road into town, it's a handy pick for timid drivers—but it means a longer walk to the sights (RS%, two apartments with kitchens available, air-con, Piazza Matteotti 1, tel. 075-813-570, www.hotelideale.it, info@hotelideale.it, sisters Lara and Ilaria).

$ Hotel Belvedere, along the road into town from Porta Nuova, has 12 dated rooms—eight with sweeping views (breakfast extra, elevator, large communal view terrace, 2 blocks past Basilica of St. Clare at Via Borgo Aretino 13, tel. 075-812-460, www. assisihotelbelvedere.com, hotelbelvedereassisi@yahoo.it, thoughtful Enrico speaks fluent New Jerseyan).

$ Hotel Pallotta offers seven tight rooms and a beautiful top-floor lounge with rooftop views. The conscientious hosts provide guests with loads of extra niceties including a loaner Assisi guide-book, 24-hour laundry service, and free hot drinks and cake at tea-time (RS%, a steep block up from Piazza del Comune at Via San Rufino 6, mobile 338-740-7574, www.pallottaassisi.it, pallotta@pallottaassisi.it; Stefano and Jenni).

$ Hotels on Via Porta Perlici: This steep and characteristic lane, stretching uphill from the Church of San Rufino, is home to three interchangeable hotels with the same owners (Carlo and Christian). Inexpensive and straightforward, these are nicely lo-cated at the top of town (all have air-con, elevators, and pay park-ing nearby). In order from the bottom to the top, there's **Hotel San Rufino** (11 rooms, breakfast extra, at #7a; tel. 075-812-803, www.hotelsanrufino.it, info@hotelsanrufino.it); **Hotel il Duomo** (14 modern rooms with somewhat less character, a bit pricier but breakfast is included, at #13, tel. 075-812-742, www.hotelilduomo.it); and **Hotel la Rocca** (at the peaceful top end of town, 32 rooms in a medieval shell, breakfast extra, sunny rooftop terrace, decent restaurant upstairs, at #27, tel. 075-812-284, www.hotelarocca.it, info@hotelarocca.it).

$ Camere Carli has six spacious rooms with bizarre floor plans in a solid, minimalist place above an art gallery. The loft rooms are a great value for families (RS%, no breakfast, family rooms, lots of stairs and no elevator, free parking 150 yards away, just off Piazza San Rufino at Via Porta Perlici 1, tel. 075-812-490, mobile 339-531-1366, www.camerecarli.it, carliarte@live.it, pleasant Franco runs the pottery shop below and speaks limited English).

¢ Camere Annalisa Martini is a cheery home amid vines and roses in the town's medieval core. This is a good budget choice—Annalisa enthusiastically accommodates her guests with a picnic garden, communal refrigerator, and six homey rooms with cheerful peeling wallpaper and flea market furniture (cash only, 3 rooms share 2 bathrooms, laundry service, no breakfast; one block from Piazza del Comune—go downhill toward the Basilica of St. Francis, turn left on Via San Gregorio to #6; tel. 075-813-536, cameremartini@libero.it). Mamma Rosignoli doesn't speak Eng-lish, but Annalisa does.

SWEET DREAMS IN A CONVENT

Assisi is filled with convents, most of which rent rooms to pilgrims and travelers. While you don't need to be a pilgrim or even a Chris-tian to be welcome, it's just common sense to stay in a convent *only* if you're approaching Assisi with a contemplative mindset. Con-vents feel institutional, house many groups, and are not particu-larly cheap—but they come with all the facilities you might need to enjoy a spirit-filled visit to Assisi.

$ St. Anthony's Guest House is where the Franciscan Sisters of the Atonement offer a very warm and tranquil welcome. Their oasis of peace is just above the Basilica of St. Clare. They have 35 beds in 19 sparkling-clean rooms, some with great views—request when you reserve (family rooms available, 2-night minimum, no problem if couples want to share a bed, elevator, no air-con but fans, 23:00 curfew, closed mid-Nov-Feb, library, views, picnic garden, parking by donation; from the parking cashier in Piazza Matteotti, take the stairs down to the *"tunnel romano,"* walk around the little park, then continue down on the elevator—it's just to the left at Via Galeazzo Alessi 10; tel. 075-812-542, atoneassisi@tiscali.it).

AGRITURISMO NEAR ASSISI

$$ Le Mandrie di San Paolo ("The Herd of St. Paul") is a meticulously restored 1,000-year-old stone house renting 13 rustic but comfortable rooms on a hillside high above the valley. Soulful Alex, his brother Andrew, and their team are justifiably proud of their passion for hospitality and connection to the land. They have an olive grove, lots of animals, a beautiful swimming pool, a sauna, a fine restaurant, and spectacular views over Assisi and the valleys of Umbria (apartments and family rooms, mobile 349-821-7867, tel. 075-806-4070, www.agriturismomandriesanpaolo.it, mandrie10@gmail.com). It's about a 10-minute drive from Assisi, above the village of Viole (a.k.a. San Vitale). Just head southeast of Assisi following signs for *Viole;* when you enter town, turn left before you reach the arch and follow signs up the hill. Their recommended **$$$$** restaurant is a great choice: They produce their own olive oil, cheese, salami, and flour, and fire their ovens with their own wood.

Eating in Assisi

I've listed decent, central, good-value restaurants. Assisi's food is heavy and rustic. Locals brag about their sausage and love to grate truffles on pasta.

To bump up any meal, consider a glass or bottle of the favorite homegrown red wine, Sagrantino de Montefalco. Sagrantino is Umbria's answer to Brunello (although many wine lovers around here would say that it's vice versa). Before or after dinner, enjoy a drink on the main square facing the Roman temple...or hang out with the local teens with a takeaway beer under the temple's columns.

IN THE TOWN CENTER

$$$ Trattoria Pallotta is a local favorite with white tablecloths and a living-room ambience. It's run by a friendly and hardworking family—with Margarita in charge of the kitchen—and of-

ASSISI

fers delicious, well-presented regional specialties, such as *piccione* (squab, a.k.a. pigeon) and *coniglio* (rabbit). And they enjoy serving split courses *(bis)* featuring the two local pastas. They have various fixed-price choices, including an €18 tourist meal, a blowout €35 tasting *menu* showcasing local specialties, and a vegetarian option. Reservations are smart (Wed-Mon 12:00-14:30 & 19:00-21:30, closed Tue, a few steps off Piazza del Comune across from temple/church at Vicolo della Volta Pinta 2, tel. 075-815-5273, www. pallottaassisi.it).

$$$ Osteria Piazzetta dell'Erba is an inviting, trendy, youthful-feeling restaurant under medieval vaulted ceilings. Dishes are beautifully presented and inspired by local cuisine (Tue-Sun 12:30-14:30 & 19:30-22:30, closed Mon, seating indoors and on a peaceful square, reservations smart, just off the main piazza toward the Cathedral of San Rufino at Via S. Gabriele dell'Addolorata 15a, tel. 075-815-352, www.osterialapiazzetta.it, chef Matteo).

$$ Trattoria da Erminio has peaceful tables on a tiny square and indoor seating under a big, medieval (but air-conditioned) brick vault. Run by Federico and his family for three generations, it specializes in local meat cooked on an open-fire grill. They have good Umbrian wines—before you order, ask for a taste of their specialties (Fri-Wed 12:00-14:30 & 19:00-21:00, closed Thu; from Piazza San Rufino, go a block up Via Porta Perlici and turn right to Via Montecavallo 19a; tel. 075-812-506).

$$ Trattoria degli Umbri has a few nice tables just above the fountain overlooking Assisi's main square (the main reason to come here). They serve delightful Umbrian dishes and quality wines by the glass (Fri-Wed 12:00-15:00 & 19:00-22:00, closed Thu, Piazza del Comune 40, tel. 075-812-455).

$$ Hostaria Terra Chiama is a bright, modern little place run by Diego and his family, who serve traditional Umbrian dishes with seasonal specials (daily, lunch from 12:30, dinner from 19:00, Via San Rufino 16, tel. 075-819-9051).

$ Pizzeria il Menestrello serves huge, inexpensive Umbrian-style pizzas (wood-fired, thin, and crisp) in an elegant medieval vaulted setting that makes your beer and pizza feel like something King Arthur would eat for dinner (daily 12:00-14:30 & 19:00-22:30, Via San Gregorio 1a, tel. 075-812-746).

PICNIC ON THE MAIN SQUARE

There are a few little grocery stores *(alimentari)* near Piazza del Comune (one is a block uphill from the main square, at Via San Rufino 19), plus bakeries selling pizza by the slice.

La Bottega dei Sapori is handy for assembling a picnic of Umbrian treats: good *porchetta* sandwiches and specialty items, including truffle paste and olive oil. Sandwich chef Saverio also makes a nice *taglieri misti* (meat and cheese plate) starting at €18 for two people. They like expensive ingredients, so it can get pricey here—be sure you're clear on the cost when you order (daily 9:30-21:00, shorter hours off-season, Piazza del Comune 34, tel. 075-812-294, Fabrizio). You can eat your sandwich on any of the benches surrounding the piazza.

Pizza al Taglio da Andrea, facing the Church of San Rufino on Piazza San Rufino, has perhaps the best pizza-by-the-slice in town. Locals also like their *torta al testo,* the Umbrian flatbread sandwich (daily 8:00-21:30, Via San Rufino 26, tel. 075-815-325).

ABOVE THE BASILICA OF ST. FRANCIS

For locations, see the "Assisi" map near the beginning of this chapter.

$$ Locanda del Podestà, tucked inside a medieval gate just above the basilica, is a cozy spot with a traditional menu of tasty grilled Umbrian sausages, *gnocchi della locanda* (with gorgonzola and truffles), and tasty *scottadito* ("scorch your fingers") lamb chops (Thu-Tue 12:00-14:30 & 19:00-21:30, closed Wed and Feb, 5-minute walk uphill along Via Cardinale Merry del Val from basilica, Via San Giacomo 6C, tel. 075-816-553).

$$$ Le Terrazze di Properzio, just up the street from Podestà, is the place to go to dine with a big view on a lovely terrace. The traditional menu includes seasonal specials. While the interior has a nice atmosphere, I'd skip this restaurant unless you're seated outside—you're paying a premium for the terrace (daily 12:00-14:30 & 19:00-21:30, terrace closed in bad weather, Via Metastasio 9, tel. 075-816-868).

COUNTRYSIDE FARM-TO-TABLE DINNER

$$$$ Le Mandrie di San Paolo, in a 1,000-year-old farmhouse a 10-minute drive outside Assisi, makes many of its own ingredients and serves an exquisite dinner to guests and nonguests alike. This is a good example of a "zero-kilometer meal"—all the ingredients are sourced on the property (€30-35 four-course meal, daily 19:45-22:00, in winter on request, reservations preferred, see "Sleeping in Assisi" for location, www.agriturismomandriesanpaolo.it).

Assisi Connections

If the train station's ticket office is closed, you'll find a ticket machine on the platform. Up in Assisi's old town, you can get train information and tickets from Agenzia Viaggi Stoppini (see listing under "Helpful Hints," earlier). That's also the best place to buy bus tickets—except for the FlixBus connection to Siena, which can easily be booked online.

From Assisi by Train to: Rome (6/day direct, 2 hours, more options with a change in Foligno), **Florence** (7/day direct, 2-3 hours), **Orvieto** (roughly hourly, 2-3 hours, with transfer in Terontola or Orte), **Siena** (10/day, about 4 hours, most involve 2 changes; bus is faster). Italian train timetables change frequently—double-check details at www.trenitalia.com.

By Bus: Service to **Rome** is operated by the Sulga bus company (2/day, 3 hours, pay driver, departs from Piazza San Pietro below the Basilica of St. Francis, arrives at Rome's Tiburtina station, one departure continues on weekdays to Fiumicino airport, tel. 800-099-661, www.sulga.it). FlixBus runs buses to **Siena** (2 hours, better than the long train ride, https://global.flixbus.com). Be clear on the departure point for your bus: Sometimes it leaves from Santa Maria degli Angeli, in the valley below Assisi (you'll find the stop at the far end of the big, long park in front of the Basilica of Santa Maria degli Angeli); other departures are from Piazza Unità d'Italia, below the Basilica of St. Francis. Don't take the bus to **Florence;** the train is better.

By Plane: Perugia/Assisi Airport is about 10 miles from Assisi (code: PEG, tel. 075-592-141, www.airport.umbria.it). Bus service between Assisi and the airport is so sporadic (just a few times a day—see www.umbriamobilita.it) that most travelers wind up taking a taxi (about €30).

ASSISI

ORVIETO & CIVITA

While Tuscany is justifiably famous for its many fine hill towns, Umbria, just to the south, has some stellar offerings of its own. Assisi (covered in its own chapter) is a must for nature lovers and Franciscan pilgrims. But if you're after views, wine, and charming villages, you'll find Umbria's best in Orvieto and in Civita di Bagnoregio (which is technically just across the border in Lazio, the same region as Rome).

About a 30-minute drive apart, these hill towns—one big, one small—perch high above scenic plains. Pleasant Orvieto is best known for its colorful-inside-and-out cathedral and its fine Orvieto Classico wine. Tiny Civita di Bagnoregio is a "dead city": It's effectively one big open-air museum with a smattering of accommodations and eateries, perched precariously on a hill pinnacle that you pay to enter. Taken together, Orvieto and Civita make a perfect duet for experiencing what all the hill-town fuss is about.

PLANNING YOUR TIME

Orvieto and Civita deserve at least an overnight, although even a few hours in each is enough to sample what they have to offer. Both are also great places to slow down and relax. Stay in one and side-trip to the other (Orvieto has more restaurants and other amenities and is easier to reach, while Civita really lets you get away from it all). The two are connected by a 30-minute drive or a one-hour bus ride. Orvieto is conveniently close to Rome (about an hour away by train or expressway).

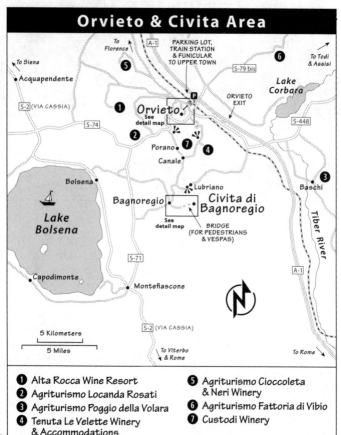

Orvieto & Civita Area

1 Alta Rocca Wine Resort
2 Agriturismo Locanda Rosati
3 Agriturismo Poggio della Volara
4 Tenuta Le Velette Winery
   & Accommodations
5 Agriturismo Cioccoleta
   & Neri Winery
6 Agriturismo Fattoria di Vibio
7 Custodi Winery

ORVIETO & CIVITA

Orvieto

Just off the freeway and the main train line, Umbria's grand hill town entices those zipping between Florence and Rome. The town sits majestically on its *tufo* throne a thousand feet above the valley floor. The city's stony streets are a delight to explore. With its brown stone cityscape, atmospheric covered alleys, and well-tended flowerpots, Orvieto is a photographer's dream. Every side street is a still life. The cathedral provides a great sightseeing experience: detailed scenes carved into its outer columns and a priceless chapel slathered in colorful art by Renaissance big shots Luca Signorelli and Fra Angelico.

Orvieto also provides perhaps the easiest introduction to Umbria—that pastoral region that all too often gets overshadowed by

Orvieto's (Very Long) History

For a little town, Orvieto has a very big history. A few centuries before Christ, Orvieto—then called Velzna—was one of a dozen major Etruscan cities. Some historians believe it may have been a religious center—a kind of Etruscan Mecca (they're still looking for archaeological proof—the town and surrounding countryside are dotted with Etruscan ruins).

Imagine the history: From 900 BC to 264 BC, the town was Etruscan Velzna. After a two-year Roman siege, it was destroyed and the ruins left abandoned for six centuries. Rome fell in AD 476, and in the chaos of that power vacuum, with invaders from the north terrorizing the peninsula, people in the valley headed back into the hills in search of safety. They rebuilt over the old Etruscan foundations, and named the settlement Urbs Vetus, meaning "old town" in Latin. Over time, Urbs Vetus became Orvieto.

Orvieto flourished as a Middle Ages regional power. During Orvieto's glory days—from the 11th to 13th century—it was a city-state of about 30,000 people (like Perugia, Assisi, and Siena) and an occasional home to the pope. Today, with only 5,000 people living in less than a square mile atop its hill, and only half of its 50 churches still active, Orvieto is again a small town.

neighboring Tuscany. Orvieto's many excellent restaurants serve up toothsome pastas, flavorful game, and pungent truffles.

Orvieto has three claims to fame: cathedral, Classico wine, and ceramics. Drinking a shot of the local white wine in a ceramic cup as you gaze up at the cathedral lets you experience Orvieto's three C's all at once. (Is the cathedral best in the afternoon, when the facade basks in golden light, or early in the morning, when it rises above the hilltop mist? You decide.) Though loaded with tourists by day, Orvieto is quiet by night, and a visit here comes with a wonderful bonus: close proximity to the unforgettable Civita di Bagnoregio.

Orientation to Orvieto

Orvieto has two distinct parts: the old-town hilltop and the dreary modern town below (called Orvieto Scalo). Whether coming by train or car, you first arrive in the nondescript lower part of town. From there you can drive or take the funicular to the medieval upper town, an atmospheric labyrinth of streets and squares where all the sightseeing action is.

ORVIETO & CIVITA

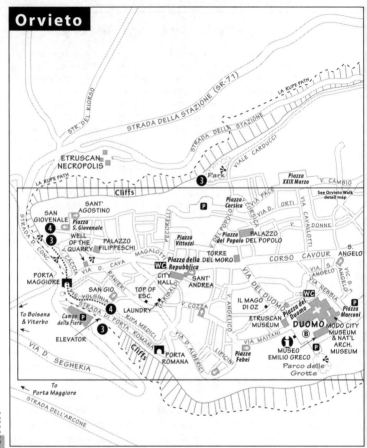

TOURIST INFORMATION

The well-organized TI is on the cathedral square at Piazza del Duomo 24 (Mon-Thu 8:15-13:50 & 16:00-19:00, Fri-Sun 9:00-19:00, tel. 0763-341-772, www.liveorvieto.com). The TI has several excellent maps: a general city map with current hours for sights, the *Anello della Rupe* map for a hike around the base of the city, and maps for longer hikes into the countryside. The ticket office next door sells combo-tickets and books reservations for Orvieto Underground Tours (tel. 0763-340-688).

Combo-Tickets: Orvieto's sights are covered by a constantly changing array of combo-tickets.

The full-meal deal is the €20 **Carta Unica** combo-ticket, which covers virtually every sight recommended here (including the underground tours) and one round-trip on the bus and funicular. This is a good value only if you plan to do everything covered.

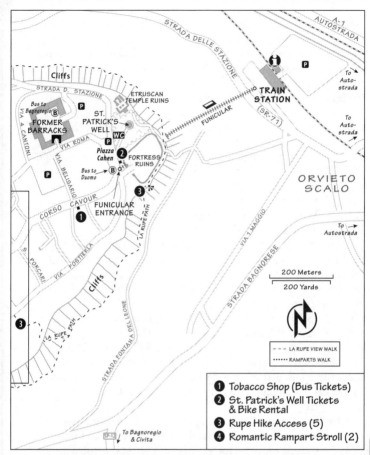

- 1 Tobacco Shop (Bus Tickets)
- 2 St. Patrick's Well Tickets & Bike Rental
- 3 Rupe Hike Access (5)
- 4 Romantic Rampart Stroll (2)

--- LA RUPE VIEW WALK

······ RAMPARTS WALK

ORVIETO & CIVITA

To use the combo-ticket for your funicular ride, buy it on arrival at the lower funicular station (also available at the bar inside the train station). It's also sold at the ticket office next to the TI on Piazza del Duomo and at most covered sights.

For a quicker, more targeted visit—just to the sights around the cathedral, but not the underground tour or the funicular—consider the €10 **La Piazza dei Musei** combo-ticket, which covers the cathedral, MoDo City Museum, Etruscan Museum, and National Archaeological Museum (sold at covered sights).

ARRIVAL IN ORVIETO

By Train: The train station is at the foot of the hill the old town sits on. There's a convenient baggage-check service below and behind the station at the bus parking lot (described later, under "Helpful Hints"). Check at the station for the train schedule to your next destination (schedule also available at the TI or online at www.trenitalia.com).

The easiest way to the top of town is by **funicular** (runs about every 10 minutes Mon-Sat 7:15-20:30, less frequent Sun from 8:00). Exiting the train station, it's across the square to the left (look for *Funicolare* sign). Tickets (€1.30) include both the funicular and the connecting bus to Piazza del Duomo. If you plan to get a Carta Unica combo-ticket (described earlier), buy it at the lower funicular station and use it to cover the funicular ride.

The funicular brings you up to Piazza Cahen, at the east end of the upper town. As you exit, to your left is a ruined fortress with a garden and a commanding view. Beyond that is a war memorial with more fine views. To your right, down a steep path, is St. Patrick's Well. Farther to the right is a park with the ruins of an Etruscan temple and another sweeping view.

Just in front of you is the small **shuttle bus** waiting to take you to Piazza del Duomo (runs roughly every 10-15 minutes, timed to arriving funiculars). The views from the ruined fortress are worth pausing for—just catch the next bus. Or you can just walk to the cathedral (head uphill on Corso Cavour; after about 10 minutes, take a left at the clock tower onto Via del Duomo). The bus drops you in Piazza del Duomo, just steps from the TI and within easy walking distance of most of my recommended sights and hotels.

If you arrive outside the funicular's operating hours, you can reach the upper part of town by **taxi** (an exorbitant €15) or **bus** to Piazza della Repubblica (roughly 2/hour until midnight; buy €1.30 ticket at bar inside station).

By Car: Driving inside the upper town of Orvieto is stressful. It's a maze of narrow lanes, several of which are marked with red "ZTL" circles (if you drive there, you could get an expensive ticket). Consider using one of two parking lots outside the old center. The free option is the big lot **below the train station** (turn right immediately after the autostrada underpass and follow *Tour Bus Parking* signs). From the parking lot, walk through the station and ride the funicular up the hill (see "By Train," earlier). The other stress-free option is the **Campo della Fiera** garage, which is tucked behind Orvieto's hill (as you approach town, follow signs with a *P*, a little bullseye, and elevator and escalator icons—you'll curl around the left side of Orvieto's ridge, then switchback up to the lot). While you'll pay to use this lot (€1.50/hour), it's an easier ascent into town—using either an elevator or the series of escalators, which whisk you up to the west end of the old center.

Those comfortable driving in Italian cities (and careful to avoid ZTL zones) can enter Orvieto's old center by driving up Via Postierla and Via Roma, then take your pick of short-term, pay-and-display parking areas (€1.50/hour): blue-lined spots on Piazza

Cahen; a parking lot on Via Roma northwest of Piazza Cahen; blue-lined spots on Piazza Marconi, behind the cathedral; and the private, tree-lined lot with an attendant next to the cathedral (a central choice for overnight stays in the center—€17/day).

HELPFUL HINTS

Bike Rental and Bag Check: The bright and helpful **Info Point,** run by Valerio, welcomes visitors just below and behind the train station at the tour bus depot/big free parking lot. They offer pay WCs and rent electric bikes (€20/day), and have a secure bag check—the only one in town (daily 9:00-18:00). In the upper town, you can rent bikes at the **St. Patrick's Well** ticket office, next to the upper funicular station (details under "Sights in Orvieto," later).

Market Days and Festivals: On Thursday and Saturday mornings, Piazza del Popolo becomes a busy **farmers market.**

The city's biggest event is **Corpus Domini** (June 14 in 2020), a medieval procession and festival celebrating a miraculous relic (described in the Duomo tour later in this chapter). Corpus Domini events include flag tossing, concerts, and a giant chess game with costumed people as pieces.

Laundry: The central **Lavagettone** self-service launderette is handy for travelers (daily 7:00-22:00, Via Garibaldi 30, www. lavagettone.it).

After Dark: In the evening, there's little going on other than strolling and eating. The big *passeggiata* scene is down Via del Duomo and Corso Cavour. The recommended **Bar Duomo,** filling a little square along Via del Duomo with outdoor tables, is lively late.

Tours in Orvieto

Walking Tours

Guided walks of about 1.5 hours are the specialty of **David Tordi** and his colleagues (€12, 3/week, April-Oct only, schedule at www. teseotur.com/en/shared-tours; buy ticket from guide, meet at Underground Orvieto ticket office at Piazza Duomo 23). They also offer €10, one-hour cathedral tours (3/week, does not include entrance ticket).

Local Guide

A good choice is **Manuela del Turco** (€130/2.5-hour tour, mobile 333-221-9879, manueladel@virgilio.it). **David Tordi** (listed above) also organizes custom tours focused on food and culture (€250/ half-day, €350/day, tel. 0763-300-491, www.teseotur.com, info@ teseotur.com).

Taxi Excursions

For excursions to Civita, **Giuliotaxi,** run by English-speaking Giulio and his sister, Maria Serena, offers two options from Orvieto for Rick Steves readers: to and from Civita with a one-hour wait (€100/car for up to 4 people, €130/minibus for up to 8), or a two-hour visit to Civita and Lake Bolsena (5 hours total, €160/car, €200/minibus, mobile 349-690-6547, giuliotaxi@libero.it). **Taxis** hang around the Orvieto train station ready to negotiate a little excursion to Civita, likely for a better price than Giuliotaxi.

Orvieto Walk

This quickie L-shaped self-guided walk takes you from the Duomo through Orvieto's historic center to the ramparts above the original Etruscan part of town, with vast Umbrian views. Each evening, this route is the scene of the local *passeggiata*.

❶ Piazza del Duomo: Start at the cathedral and admire its attention-grabbing facade (see the "Duomo" listing under "Sights in Orvieto" for a full explanation). Imagine how, as World War II raged around Orvieto, the fine reliefs gracing the front of the cathedral were encased in protective *tufa* walls. (Orvieto and its cathedral were spared destruction, perhaps thanks to a "safe cities" designation by a Nazi general who appreciated the town—or one of its women.)

As you face the cathedral, the papal palace (now hosting various museums) is to your right, and the TI and shuttle bus to the funicular are over your right shoulder. A nice gelato shop is around the church to the left.

• *Head left a few steps to the...*

❷ Clock Tower and **Via del Duomo:** Also known as the Maurizio Tower, this was built in the 14th century and equipped with an early mechanized clock, originally used to keep track of workers' time while building the cathedral.

The tower marks the start of Via del Duomo, lined with shops selling ceramics. The tradition of fine ceramics in Orvieto goes way back—the clay from the banks of the nearby Tiber is ideal for pottery. During the Renaissance, the town's pottery was brightly painted and highly prized.

• *Stroll down Via del Duomo.*

At the second left, The Wizard of Oz (Il Mago di Oz) shop awaits a few steps down Via dei Magoni (at #3). This shop is a wondrous toy land created by eccentric Giuseppe Rosella. Have Giuseppe push a few buttons, and you're far from Kansas.

Back on Via del Duomo, about 30 yards before the next tower is Emilio's meat-and-cheese shop (on the right, at #11). Pop in for a fragrant reminder that wild boar is an Umbrian specialty—and they love their other meats and cheeses, too.

• *Follow Via del Duomo to Orvieto's main intersection, where it meets Corso Cavour. Here you'll find the tall, stark, 11th-century...*

❸ **Tower of the Moor** (Torre del Moro): Eighty such towers, each the pride and security of a powerful noble family, once

decorated the town's skyline. Today only a few survive. This tower marks the center of town, serves as a handy orientation tool, and is decorated by the coats of arms of past governors. An elevator leaves you with 173 steps still to go to earn a commanding view (€2.80, daily March-Oct 10:00-19:00, May-Aug until 20:00, shorter hours off-season).

This crossroads divides the town into four quarters (notice the *Quartiere* signs on the corners). In the past, residents of the four districts competed in a lively equestrian competition, parading all over town during the annual Corpus Domini celebration. Historically, the four streets led from here to four landmarks: Piazza del Popolo with its market and fine palazzo, St. Patrick's Well, the Duomo, and the City Hall.

• *Before heading left down Corso Cavour, side-trip a block farther ahead, behind the tower, for a look at the striking...*

❹ **Palazzo del Popolo:** Built of local *tufo*, this is a textbook example of a fortified medieval public palace: a fortress designed to house the city's leadership and military (built atop an Etruscan temple), with a market at its base, fancy meeting rooms upstairs, and aristocratic living quarters on the top level. A lively market still bustles here Thursday and Saturday mornings, selling food, clothes, and household goods.

• *Return to the tower, turn right, and head down Corso Cavour past classic storefronts to...*

❺ **Piazza della Repubblica** and the **Church of Sant'Andrea:** The original vision—though it never came to fruition—was for the City Hall to have five arches flanking the central arch (marked by the flags today). The Church of Sant'Andrea (left of City Hall) sits atop the Etruscan forum that was likely the birthplace of Orvieto, centuries before Christ. Inside is an interesting architectural progression: 11th-century Romanesque (with few frescoes surviving), Gothic (the pointy vaults over the altar), and a Renaissance barrel vault in the apse (behind the altar)—all dimly lit by alabaster windows.

On this spot, visitors can track a layer cake of history: Under the Christian church lie the remains of the Etruscan city, destroyed

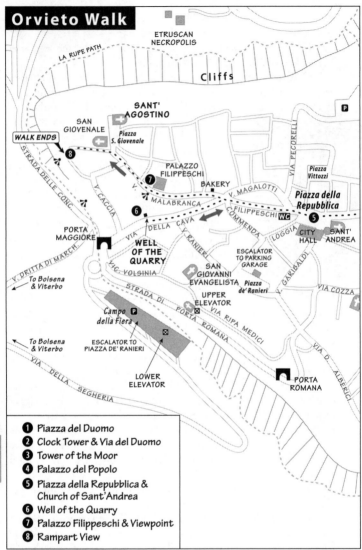

Orvieto Walk

ETRUSCAN NECROPOLIS

Cliffs

LA RUPE PATH

SANT' AGOSTINO

SAN GIOVENALE

Piazza S. Giovenale

WALK ENDS

8

STRADA DELLE CONC

V. CACCIA

PALAZZO FILIPPESCHI

7

V. MALABRANCA

BAKERY

V. MAGALOTTI

6

VIA DELLA CAVA

V. RANIERI

PORTA MAGGIORE

V. DRITTA DI MARCH.

To Bolsena & Viterbo

V.C. VOLSINIA

WELL OF THE QUARRY

SAN GIOVANNI EVANGELISTA

FILIPPESCHI

COMMENDA

LOGGIA

WC

5

Piazza della Repubblica

CITY HALL

SANT' ANDREA

VIA PECORELLI

Piazza Vittozzi

P

Piazza de' Ranieri

ESCALATOR TO PARKING GARAGE

UPPER ELEVATOR

VIA GARIBALDI

VIA COZZA

STRADA DI

PORTA ROMANA

VIA RIPA MEDICI

Campo della Fiera

P

To Bolsena & Viterbo

ESCALATOR TO PIAZZA DE' RANIERI

LOWER ELEVATOR

VIA DELLA SEGHERIA

VIA D. ALBERICI

PORTA ROMANA

ORVIETO & CIVITA

by the Romans. The ruins, currently accessible only with a tour, give you a sense of the history stacked beneath your feet throughout Orvieto (€5/person, call archaeologist Francesco Pacelli to book, tel. 328-191-1316).

• *From Piazza della Repubblica, continue straight downhill on Via Filippeschi—passing a public WC on the left—for 100 yards until you reach a fork. Check out the friendly, traditional Galleria del Pane **bakery** on the right (at Via Malabranca 6; we'll return to this intersec-*

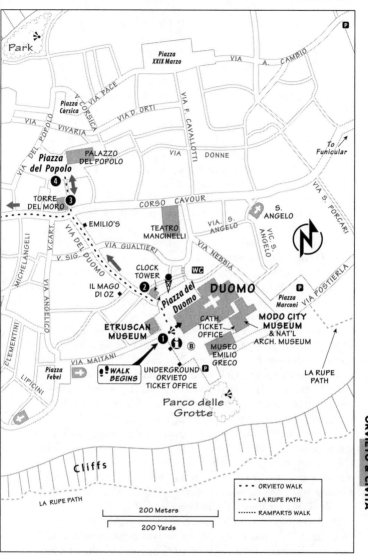

tion after a short detour). Walk downhill along Via della Cava about 70 yards to a restaurant with a green sign (at #26, on the right) to find the...

❻ **Well of the Quarry** (Pozzo della Cava): While renovating their trattoria here in the oldest part of town, an Orvieto family discovered a vast underground network of Etruscan-era caves, wells, and tunnels. The excavation started in 1984 and continues to this day. A visit to the well makes for a fun subterranean wander (see more details in "Underground Orvieto," later in this chapter), keeping in mind that the whole city sits on top of a honeycomb of tunnels like these.

Outside, Via della Cava, meaning "Quarry Street," was a main source for building material for Orvieto's predecessor, Etruscan Velzna. The street kept getting lower and lower as more and more stones were cut out of it. Downhill is the site of the town's original gate.

• Climb back up to the fork (with the bakery) and do a sharp U-turn left up Via Malabranca. After about 70 yards, at #22, you'll reach…

❼ Palazzo Filippeschi and Viewpoint: The friendly, noble Filippeschi family sometimes leaves their big green door open so visitors can peek into their classic medieval courtyard, with black travertine columns scavenged from nearby ancient Roman villas. Enjoy a moment of exquisite medieval tranquility. (If the door is closed, just move along.)

Immediately across from the palazzo, belly up to the viewpoint overlooking a commotion of faded red-tile roofs. This tradition goes back to Etruscan times, when such tiles were molded on a seated tile-maker's thigh—wide to narrow. They nest so that water flows without leaking—handy for both rooftops and plumbing.

• Continue on, downhill now, as the street crests.

Over the next 200 yards notice faded frescoes on stucco walls, arches from previous iterations of buildings (left for structural and nostalgic reasons), built-in letterboxes, and the three local building stones—basalt white, black travertine, and brown tufa.

On the left (at Via del Caccia), you'll pass an innovative-in-1991 green defibrillator station (one of 15 in town, the first such project in Europe). Soon you'll reach a square with the Church of Sant'Agostino, which hosts a museum displaying the Baroque statues that once lined the cathedral's nave (covered by your MoDo City Museum ticket). Just beyond, on the right, is the Church of San Giovenale—the oldest in town, with 11th-century frescoes.

• Finally you'll pop out at a commanding…

❽ Rampart View: You're at the end of Orvieto. The fertility of the land (with its olives, vines, and fruit orchards) is clear. The manicured little forest of cypress trees straight ahead marks the Orvieto cemetery. In the distance to the right is Mount Cetona, guarding the south end of Tuscany.

Go 50 yards along the rampart to the left for the best view of the natural fortification that made this town the choice of Etruscans before the rise of ancient Rome, of stability-starved peasants after the fall of Rome, and of several popes in the high Middle Ages. From this perch you can understand why the city was never taken by force.

• The walk is over. From here, you can retrace your steps or follow the *rampart farther left, down and up, over the original Etruscan town gate and circle back to the center from there.*

Sights in Orvieto

▲▲▲Duomo

Orvieto's cathedral has Italy's liveliest facade. This colorful, prickly Gothic facade, divided by four pillars, has been compared to a medieval altarpiece. The optical-illusion interior features some fine art, including Luca Signorelli's lavishly frescoed Chapel of San Brizio.

Cost and Hours: €4, €5 combo-ticket with MoDo City Museum; buy ticket in building to the right as you face the facade (also covered by various combo-tickets described under "Tourist Information," earlier); April-Sept Mon-Sat 9:30-19:00, Sun 13:00-17:30; closes one hour earlier March and Oct; shorter hours Nov-Feb; sometimes closes for religious services, www.opsm.it.

◆ Self-Guided Tour

• *After buying your ticket, return to the front of the church. Begin by viewing the...*

Exterior Facade: Study this gleaming mass of mosaics, stained glass, and sculpture (c. 1300, by Lorenzo Maitani and others). Note how it's literally just a facade, ornamenting an otherwise very plain, mostly Romanesque exterior.

At the base of the cathedral, the four broad **marble pillars** carved with biblical scenes tell the history of the world in four acts, from left to right. The relief on the far left shows the ❶ **Creation** (see God creating Eve from Adam's rib, Cain clubbing Abel, the snake tempting Eve, and a dramatic expulsion). Next is the ❷ **Tree of Jesse** (Jesus' family tree—with Jesus on top, and Mary just below, flanked by Old Testament stories). Look up at the roaring lion of St. Mark and the grand facade filling your view—awe-inspiring as intended. In the third panel, with scenes from the ❸ **New Testament,** look for the unique manger scene, and other events from the life of Christ. On the far right is the ❹ **Last Judgment;** see Christ judging on top, with a commotion of sarcophagi popping open and all hell breaking loose at the bottom.

Each pillar is topped with a bronze symbol of one of the Evangelists (left to right): angel (Matthew), lion (Mark), eagle (John),

ORVIETO & CIVITA

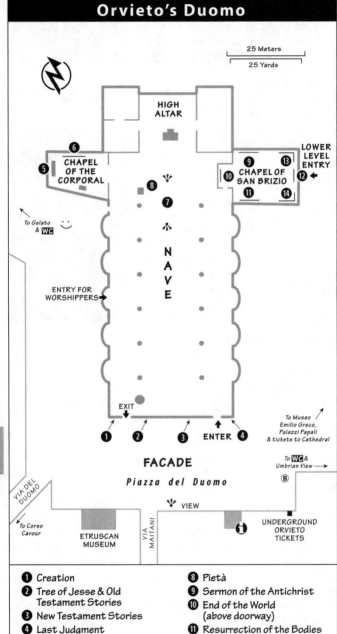

Orvieto's Duomo

ORVIETO & CIVITA

1 Creation
2 Tree of Jesse & Old Testament Stories
3 New Testament Stories
4 Last Judgment
5 "Corporal" (Linen Cloth)
6 Miracle of Bolsena Fresco
7 Marble Floor Patch

8 Pietà
9 Sermon of the Antichrist
10 End of the World (above doorway)
11 Resurrection of the Bodies
12 Last Judgment
13 Elect in Heaven
14 Damned in Hell

and ox (Luke). The bronze doors are modern, by the Sicilian sculptor Emilio Greco. (A gallery devoted to Greco's work is to the immediate right of the church; see "Museums Near the Duomo," later.)

Stand back and survey the facade, looking for the central theme—it's clear the church is dedicated to the ascension of Mary. In the mosaic below the rose window, Mary is transported to heaven. In the uppermost mosaic, Mary is crowned.

• *Ticket in hand, step inside.*

Nave: The nave feels spacious and less cluttered than most Italian churches. Until 1877, it was much busier, with statues of the apostles at each column and fancy chapels. Then the people decided they wanted to "un-Baroque" their church. (The original statues are now on display in the Church of Sant'Agostino, at the west end of town.) Bits of medieval fresco survive in the niches—once covered by altars and confessionals. From the back of the nave you can appreciate the fine stained glass above

the altar—it's original from the 14th century and some of the oldest in Italy. The stripes of the church are purely decorative, made of locally quarried basalt and black travertine.

The interior is warmly lit by **alabaster windows,** highlighting the black-and-white striped stonework. Why such a big and impressive church in such a little town? First of all, it's not as big as it looks. By lining the nave with striped columns and opening up the side aisles with arcaded chapels, the architect made the space seem longer and bigger than it is. Still, it's a big and rich cathedral—the seat of a bishop.

The cathedral's historic importance and wealth is thanks to a miracle that happened nearby in 1263. According to the story, a skeptical priest named Peter of Prague passed through the town of Bolsena (12 miles from Orvieto) while on a pilgrimage to Rome. He had doubts that the bread used in communion could really be transformed into the body of Christ. But during Mass, as he held the host aloft and blessed it, the bread began to bleed, running down his arms and dripping onto a linen cloth (a "corporal") on the altar. That miraculously bloodstained cloth is now kept here, in the Chapel of the Corporal.

• *We'll tour the church's interior. First, find the chapel in the north transept, left of the altar.*

Chapel of the Corporal: The ❺ **bloody cloth** from the mir-

ORVIETO & CIVITA

Italy Is Made of Tuff Stuff

Tuff (*tufo* in Italian) is a light-colored volcanic rock that is common in Italy. A part of Tuscany is even called the "Tuff Area."

The seven hills of Rome are made of tuff, and quarried blocks of this stone can be seen in the Colosseum, Pantheon, and Castel Sant'Angelo. Just outside of Rome, the catacombs were carved from tuff. Sorrento rises above the sea on a tuff outcrop. Orvieto, Civita di Bagnoregio (pictured), and many other hill towns perch on bluffs of tuff.

Italy's early inhabitants, including the Etruscans and Romans, carved caves, tunnels, burial niches, and even roads out of tuff. Blocks of this rock were quarried to make houses and walls. Tuff is soft and easy to carve when it's first exposed to air, but hardens later, which makes it a good building stone.

Italy's tuff-producing volcanoes resulted from a lot of tectonic-plate bumping and grinding. This violent geologic history is reflected in Italy's volcanoes, like Vesuvius and Etna, and earthquakes such as the 2009 quake in the L'Aquila area northeast of Rome.

Tuff is actually just a big hardened pile of old volcanic ash. When volcanoes hold magma that contains a lot of water, they erupt explosively (think heat + water = steam = POW!). The exploded rock material gets blasted out as hot volcanic ash, which settles on the surrounding landscape, piles up, and over time welds together into the rock called tuff.

So when you're visiting an area in Italy of ancient caves or catacombs built out of this material, you'll know that at least once (and maybe more) upon a time, it was a site of a lot of volcanic activity.

acle is displayed in the turquoise frame atop the chapel's altar. It was brought from Bolsena to Orvieto, where Pope Urban IV happened to be visiting. The amazed pope proclaimed a new holiday, Corpus Domini (Body of Christ), and the Orvieto cathedral was built (begun in 1290) to display the miraculous relic. For centuries, the precious linen was paraded through the streets of Orvieto in an ornate reliquary (now in the MoDo City Museum).

The room was frescoed in the 14th century with scenes attesting to Christ's presence in the communion wafer and offering a vivid peek at life here at that time. The ❻ **miracle of Bolsena** (here set in 13th-century Orvieto) is depicted on the chapel's right wall.

• *Now walk to the middle front of the church, where (just before the two steps) you'll see a decorative area in the floor the size of a Turkish carpet.*

❼ **Marble Floor Patch:** This patch in the marble floor marks where the altar stood before the Counter-Reformation. It's a reminder that as the Roman Catholic Church countered the Reformation, it made reforms of its own. For instance, altars were moved back so that the congregation could sit closer to the spectacular frescoes and stained glass. (These decorations were designed to impress commoners by illustrating the glory of heaven—and the Catholic Church needed that propaganda more than ever during the Counter-Reformation.)

Enjoy the richness that surrounds you. This cathedral put Orvieto on the map, and with lots of pilgrims came lots of wealth. The town—perched on its easy-to-defend hilltop—was used off and on for a couple centuries as a papal refuge, whenever the current pope's enemies forced him to flee Rome. Over the altar, the brilliant stained glass is the painstakingly restored original, from the 14th century. The fine organ, high on the left, has more than 5,000 pipes. Look high up in the right transept at the alabaster rose window. Then turn and face down the nave, the way you came in. Note how the architect's trick—making the church look bigger from the rear—works in reverse from here. From this angle, the church appears stubbier than it actually is.

• *A few steps to your left as you face the altar, near the first pillar, is a beautiful white-marble statue.*

❽ *Pietà:* The marble pietà (statue of Mary holding Jesus' just-crucified body) was carved in 1579 by local artist Ippolito Scalza. Clearly inspired by Michelangelo's *Pietà*, this exceptional work, with four figures, was sculpted from one piece of marble. Walk around it to notice the texture that Scalza achieved, and how the light plays on the sculpture from every angle.

• *Now face the main altar. To the right is Orvieto's one must-see artistic sight, the...*

Chapel of San Brizio: This chapel features Luca Signorelli's brilliantly lit frescoes of the Day of Judgment and Life after Death (painted 1499-1504). Step into the chapel and you're surrounded by vivid scenes crammed with figures. Although the frescoes refer to themes of resurrection and salvation, they also reflect the turbulent political and religious atmosphere of late-15th-century Italy.

The chapel is decorated

ORVIETO & CIVITA

in one big and cohesive story. Start with the panel on your left as you enter, and do a quick counterclockwise spin to get oriented to the basic plot: Antichrist (a false prophet), end of the world (above the arch leading to the nave), Resurrection of the Bodies, hell, Judgment Day (Fra Angelico—who worked on the chapel 50 years before Signorelli—painted Jesus above the window), and finally heaven.

Now do a slower turn to take in the full story: In the ❾ **Sermon of the Antichrist** (left wall), a crowd gathers around a man preaching from a pedestal. It's the Antichrist, who comes posing as Jesus to mislead the faithful. This befuddled Antichrist forgets his lines midspeech, but the Devil is on hand to whisper what to say next. Notice how the arm in front of the Antichrist is attached to both figures, suggesting they are joined as one. His words sow wickedness through the world, including executions (upper right). The worried woman in red and light blue (foreground, left of pedestal) gets money from a man for something she's not proud of (perhaps receiving funds from a Jewish moneylender—notice the Stars of David on his purse). Many of the faces in the crowd are probably actual portraits.

Most likely, the Antichrist himself is a veiled reference to Savonarola (1452-1498), the charismatic Florentine monk who defied the pope, drove the Medici family from power, and riled the populace with apocalyptic sermons. Many Italians—including the painter Signorelli—viewed Savonarola as a tyrant and heretic, the Antichrist who was ushering in the Last Days.

In the upper left, notice the hardworking angel. He looks as if he's at batting practice, hitting followers of the Antichrist back to earth as they try to get through the pearly gates. In the bottom left is a self-portrait of the artist, **Luca Signorelli** (c. 1450-1523), well-dressed in black with long golden hair. Signorelli, from nearby Cortona, was at the peak of his powers, and this chapel was his masterpiece. He looks out proudly as if to say, "I did all this in just a few years, on time and on budget," confirming his reputation as a speedy, businesslike painter. Next to him (also in black) is the artist Fra Angelico, who started the chapel decoration five decades earlier but completed only a small part of it: the Last Judgment over the window and the angels around it.

Compare the style of painting between these two masters—Angelico's angels stacked like little wooden dolls next to Signorelli's intertwined naked bodies. You can clearly see the huge effect the Renaissance had on painting in just a few decades.

Around the arch opposite the windows are signs of the ❿ **end of the world:** eclipse, tsunami, falling stars, earthquakes, violence in the streets, and a laser-wielding gray angel.

On the right wall (opposite the Antichrist) is the ⓫ **Resurrec-**

tion of the Bodies. Trumpeting angels blow a wake-up call, and the dead climb dreamily out of the earth to be clothed with new bodies, some of the randy skeletons finding time for flirting. On the same wall (below the action, at eye level) is a gripping pietà. Also by Signorelli, this pietà gives insight into the artist's genius and personality. Look at the emotion in the faces of the two Marys and consider that Signorelli's son had just died. The small black-and-white Deposition scene (behind Jesus' leg) seems inspired by ancient Greek scenes of a pre-Christian hero's death. In the confident spirit of the Renaissance, the artist incorporates a pagan scene to support a Christian story. This 3-D realism in a 2-D sketch shows the work of a talented master.

The altar wall (with the windows) features the ⓬ **Last Judgment.** To the left of the altar (and continuing around the corner,

filling half the left wall) are the ⓭ **Elect in Heaven.** They spend eternity posing like bodybuilders while listening to celestial Muzak. To the right (and continuing around the corner on the right wall) are the ⓮ **Damned in Hell,** in the scariest mosh pit ever. Devils torment sinners in graphic detail, while winged demons control the airspace overhead. In the center, one lusty demon turns to tell the frightened woman on his back exactly what he's got planned for their date. (According to legend, this was Signorelli's lover, who betrayed him...and ended up here.) Signorelli's ability to tell a story through human actions and gestures, rather than symbols, inspired his younger contemporary, Michelangelo, who meticulously studied the elder artist's nudes.

In this chapel, Christian theology sits physically and figuratively upon a foundation of lassical logic. Below everything are Greek and Latin philosophers, plus Dante, struggling to reconcile Classical truth with Church doctrine. You can see the intellectual challenge on their faces as they ponder the puzzle of theology that survives the test of reason.

The figures are immersed in fanciful Grotesque (that is, grotto-esque) decor. Dating from 1499, this is one of the first uses of the frilly, nubile, and even sexy "wallpaper pattern" so popular in the Renaissance. (It was inspired by the decorations found in Nero's Golden House in Rome, which had been discovered under street level just a few years earlier and was mistaken for an underground grotto.)

ORVIETO & CIVITA

During the Renaissance, nakedness symbolized purity. When attitudes changed during the Counter-Reformation, the male figures in Signorelli's frescoes were given penis-covering sashes. In a 1982 restoration, most—but not all—of the sashes were removed. A little of that prudishness survives to this day, as those in heaven were left with their sashes modestly in place.

• *Our tour is finished. As you step outside the church, you're surrounded by great sights. Across the square is the Etruscan Museum, the TI, and the ticket office for Underground Orvieto tours. Around the side of the church (near the cathedral ticket office) are the MoDo City Museum and the National Archaeological Museum. And just beyond that, you can keep going (passing a small parking lot and WC) to reach a park that affords a fine Umbrian view.*

MUSEUMS NEAR THE DUOMO
▲▲MoDo City Museum (Museo dell'Opera del Duomo)

This museum is an ensemble of three different sights scattered around town: the Emilio Greco collection (in Palazzo Soliano, next to the cathedral); the Cathedral Art Collections, immediately behind the cathedral (enter through the lower level of the right transept); and, at the far end of town, the Church of Sant'Agostino.

Cost and Hours: €4 MoDo ticket covers all MoDo sights, €5 combo-ticket includes the Duomo; also covered by La Piazza dei Musei and Carta Unica combo-tickets; April-Sept daily 9:30-19:00; March and Oct daily 10:00-18:00; Nov-Feb until 17:00 and closed Mon; Piazza Duomo, tel. 0763-343-592, www.opsm.it.

Visiting the MoDo City Museum Branches: You'll buy your ticket for the MoDo (and for the cathedral) inside Palazzo Soliano. It's the building marked *MUSEO*, to the right as you face the cathedral. This building also houses the Museo Emilio Greco. A good plan is to buy a ticket, visit the Greco collection while you're there, then tour the cathedral interior (described earlier). Afterward, enter the Cathedral Art Collections. If you want to also see the National Archaeological Museum, its entrance hides between the Cathedral Art Collections and the Museo Emilio Greco.

Museo Emilio Greco: This fresh little collection—filling a space behind the MoDo and cathedral ticket desk—shows off the work of Emilio Greco (1913-1995), a Sicilian artist who designed the modern doors of Orvieto's cathedral. His sketches and about 30 of his bronze statues are on display here, showing his absorption with gently twisting and turning nudes. Greco's sketchy outlines of women are simply beautiful. The artful installation of his work in this palazzo, with walkways and a spiral staircase up to the ceiling, is designed to let you view his sculptures from different angles.

• *To find the Cathedral Art Collections, enter the lower level of the right transept—around the right side as you face the cathedral's main facade.*

Cathedral Art Collections: Behind the Duomo, a complex of medieval palaces called the Palazzi Papali (Papal Palaces) shows off the city's best devotional art. This is the main attraction of the MoDo City Museum and well worth a visit.

Entering through the cathedral's right transept, you'll walk through the striped cellars. Under the vaults is equipment used for working on the cathedral (giant pulley mechanisms) and neatly stacked fragments of sculptures and tiles.

Follow signs right (to *Museum* and *Popes Palace*) to reach the main part of the museum. The ground floor features a skippable exhibit of frescoes. But from here, you can head outside, then go up the metal staircase to a delightful collection.

The highlight is just inside the upstairs entrance: a marble Mary and Child who sit beneath a bronze canopy, attended by exquisite angels. This proto-Renaissance ensemble, dating from around 1300, once filled the niche in the center of the cathedral's facade (where a replica sits today).

Now proceed through several art-filled rooms on this floor. Entering the first large room, look left to see an exquisite *Madonna and Child* from 1322 by the Sienese great Simone Martini, who worked in Orvieto. Nearby are saintly wooden statues and fine in-laid woodwork from the original choir. Farther along, you'll find Luca Signorelli's *Mary Magdalene* (1504), then a large room of Baroque paintings from the late 1500s that decorated the side chapels with a harsh Counter-Reformation message. (Think about how dramatically church art evolved in the 200 years from Martini's almost 2-D medieval style, to Signorelli's Renaissance humanism, to the bombast of Baroque.)

In the hall with the Baroque paintings, step into the smaller side-room. This is the Albèri Library, with delicate black-and-white frescoes done by Signorelli's workshop while he was in town working on the cathedral's Chapel of San Brizio. This hall displays items from the cathedral treasury, including the reliquary used to parade a holy bloodstained cloth on Corpus Domini.

Continuing through the main collection, go back past the entry to one more large hall, with statues of St. Michael and the dragon, more altarpieces and statues, and sinopias (preliminary drawings for the frescoes decorating the cathedral's Chapel of the Corporal, with a roughed-up surface so the wet plaster would stick).

Church of Sant'Agostino: At the west end of town (a 15-minute walk), this church has statues of the 12 apostles that were added to the Duomo in the Baroque Age (c. 1700) and removed in the late 1800s. It's skippable for most visitors, but those taking my "Orvieto Walk" can drop in with their MoDo ticket.

ORVIETO & CIVITA

National Archaeological Museum of Orvieto
(Museo Archeologico Nazionale di Orvieto)

This small five-room collection, immediately behind the cathedral in the ground floor of Palazzi Papali (under MoDo), beautifully shows off a trove of well-preserved Etruscan bronzes, terra-cotta objects, and ceramics—many from the necropolis at the base of Orvieto, and some with painted colors surviving from 500 BC. To see the treasure of this museum, ask an attendant for the Golini tombs (named after the man who discovered them in 1836). You'll be escorted to the reconstructed, fourth-century BC tombs, frescoed with scenes from an Etruscan banquet in the afterlife.

Cost and Hours: €4, €5 combo-ticket with Etruscan Necropolis, also covered by La Piazza dei Musei and Carta Unica combo-tickets, daily 8:30-19:30, tel. 0763-341-039, www.archeopg.arti.beniculturali.it. For background on the Etruscans, see page 62.

▲Etruscan Museum (Museo Claudio Faina e Museo Civico)

This 19th-century, Neoclassical nobleman's palace stands on the main square facing the cathedral. Its elegantly frescoed rooms hold an impressive Etruscan collection. The ground floor features the "Museo Civico," with fragments of Etruscan sculpture. On the first floor is the "Collezione Conti Faina," with Etruscan jewelry and an extensive array of Roman coins (push the brass buttons and the coins rotate so you can see both sides). The top floor features the best of the Etruscan and proto-Etruscan (from the ninth century BC) vases and bronzes, lots of votives found buried in nearby tombs, and fine views of the Duomo.

Cost and Hours: €4.50, also covered by La Piazza dei Musei and Carta Unica combo-tickets; April-Sept daily 9:30-18:00, Oct-March Tue-Sun 10:00-17:00, closed Mon Nov-Feb; tel. 0763-341-511, www.museofaina.it.

Teatro Mancinelli

A short walk from the cathedral, on the main drag, Teatro Mancinelli is a fine 19th-century Italian theater (from 1866) with 500 seats, elegant boxes, and frilly Romantic ceiling paintings—all well-described in English. Visitors are welcome to climb upstairs to the foyer for a chance to peek into a private box. The theater hosts the recommended Café del Teatro—buy a drink and you can wander the theater without paying the €2 entry fee (typically open Mon-Sat 8:00-14:00, closed Sun, Corso Cavour 122, www.teatromancinelli.com).

UNDERGROUND ORVIETO

These sights—showing off the remarkable bounty of history beneath your feet—are scattered around (and outside) the old center. For locations, see the main "Orvieto" map at the start of this chapter.

▲▲St. Patrick's Well (Pozzo di San Patrizio)

Modern engineers are impressed by this deep well—175 feet deep and 45 feet wide—designed in the 16th century with a double-helix pattern. The two spiral stairways allow an efficient one-way traffic flow: intriguing now, but critical then. Imagine if donkeys and people, balancing jugs of water, had to go up and down the same stairway. At the bottom is a bridge that people could walk on to scoop up water. Touring the well requires hiking 248 (awkwardly spaced) steps down, then back up. That's lots of exercise (allow 20-30 minutes round-trip) and not much to see...other than some mesmerizing 16th-century engineering.

The well was built because a pope got nervous. After Rome was sacked in 1527 by renegade troops of the Holy Roman Empire, the pope fled to Orvieto. He feared that even this little town (with no water source on top) would be besieged. He commissioned a well, which was started in 1527 and finished 10 years later. It was a huge project. (As it turns out, the town was never besieged, but supporters believe that the well was worth the cost and labor because of its deterrence value—attackers would think twice about besieging a town with a reliable water source.) Even today, when a local is faced with a difficult task, people say, "It's like digging St. Patrick's Well."

Cost and Hours: €5, interesting €2 audioguide, daily May-Aug 9:00-20:00, shorter hours off-season, ticket office immediately to your right as you exit the funicular, you'll walk a few minutes down the path to enter the well, Viale Sangallo, tel. 0763-343-768.

▲Well of the Quarry (Pozzo della Cava)

A five-minute walk west of Piazza della Repubblica, this complex of Etruscan-era caves, wells, and tunnels leads down to a fat, cylindrical, beautifully carved 2,500-year-old well. Go ahead, spit (or drop a coin 100 feet down—coins are collected each Christmas for a local charity). Your visit is capped with a review of local pottery-making.

Cost and Hours: €4, RS%—€2.50 with this book, Tue-Sun 9:00-20:00, closed Mon, enter through restaurant at Via della Cava 26, tel. 0763-342-373, www.pozzodellacava.it.

Orvieto Underground Tours (Parco delle Grotte)

Beginning from a ticket office next to the TI, guides weave archaeological history into a good look at about 100 yards of Etruscan and medieval caves. You'll see the remains of an old olive press, an impressive 130-foot-deep Etruscan well shaft, what's left of a primitive cement quarry, and an extensive dovecote (pigeon coop) where the birds were reared for roasting (pigeon dishes are still featured on many Orvieto menus; look for—or avoid—*piccione*).

Cost and Hours: €7; one-hour English tours depart daily at 11:15, 12:30, 16:15, and 17:30; book in advance and confirm schedule for English guide, book tour and depart from ticket office facing the cathedral at Piazza Duomo 23, tel. 0763-340-688, www.orvietounderground.it.

Etruscan Necropolis
(Necropoli Etrusca di Crocifisso del Tufo)

Below town, at the base of the cliff, is a remarkable "city of the dead" that dates back to the sixth to third century BC. The tombs,

which are laid out in a kind of street grid, are empty, and there's precious little to see here other than the basic stony construction. But it is both eerie and fascinating to wander the streets of an Etruscan cemetery.

Cost and Hours: €3, €5 combo-ticket with National Archaeological Museum; Wed-Sat 10:00-19:00, Oct-March until 18:00, also open the first two Sun of the month, closed Mon-Tue year-round; drivers will find it on the ring road below town, hikers can reach it via the Rupe path (see next); tel. 0763-343-611, www.archeopg.arti.beniculturali.it.

VIEW WALKS
▲Hike Around the City on the Rupe

Orvieto's Rupe is a peaceful path that completely circles the town at the base of the cliff upon which it sits. With the help of the TI's

Anello della Rupe map, you'll see there are five access points from the town for the three-mile walk, which includes a series of sightseeing stops along the way (allow about two hours round-trip). From the access points, you'll walk or take stairs down, down, down to the trail that hugs the

cliff. The easy-to-follow path is wide and partially paved, though it has some steep, gravelly descents—wear good shoes and be prepared for a climb. On one side you have the cliff, with the town high above. On the other side you have Umbrian views stretching into the distance. The path is peaceful, with few other people and only the sound of the wind and birds to accompany you. It makes for a delightful evening walk (not lit after dark).

I'd leave Orvieto at Piazza Marconi and walk left (counterclockwise) three-quarters of the way around the town (there's a fine view down onto the Etruscan Necropolis midway), and ride the escalator and elevator back up to the town from the big Campo della Fiera parking lot. If you're ever confused about the path, follow signs for *Anello della Rupe.*

▲Shorter Romantic Rampart Stroll

Thanks to its dramatic hilltop setting, several fine little walks wind around the edges of Orvieto. My favorite after dark, when it's lamp-lit and romantic, is along the ramparts at the far west end of town. Start at the Church of Sant'Agostino (near the end of my self-guided Orvieto Walk). With your back to the church, go a block to the right to the end of town. Then head left along the ramparts, with cypress-dotted Umbria to your right, and follow Vicolo Volsinia to the Church of San Giovanni Evangelista, where you can reenter the old-town center near several recommended restaurants.

NEAR ORVIETO
Wine Tasting

Orvieto Classico wine is justly famous. Two inviting wineries sit just outside Orvieto on the scenic Canale route to Bagnoregio; if you're side-tripping to Civita, it's easy to stop at either or both for a tasting (call ahead for a reservation). Two more wineries lie to the north where the soil changes from *tufo* to clay, which changes the character of the wines. For locations, see the "Orvieto and Civita Area" map near the beginning of this chapter.

Between Orvieto and Bagnoregio: For a tour of a historic winery with Etruscan cellars, make an appointment to visit **Tenuta Le Velette,** where English-speaking Corrado, Cecilia (cheh-CHEEL-yah), and Teresa Bottai offer a warm welcome. Their wines are considered to be some of the best in the region (€8-25 for tour and tasting, price varies depending on wines, number of people, and food requested; Mon-Fri 8:30-12:00 & 14:00-17:00, Sat 8:30-12:00, closed Sun; also has accommodations—see listing later in this chapter, tel. 0763-29090, mobile 348-300-2002, www.levelette.it). From their sign (5-minute drive past Orvieto at top of switchbacks just before Canale, on road to Bagnoregio), cruise

ORVIETO & CIVITA

down a long tree-lined drive, then park at the striped gate (must call ahead; no drop-ins).

Custodi is another respected family-run winery that produces Orvieto Classico, grappa, and olive oil on a modern 140-acre estate. Helpful Chiara and Laura Custodi speak English. Reserve ahead for a tour of their cantina, an explanation of the winemaking process, and a tasting of four wines. An assortment of *salumi* and local cheeses to go with your wine tasting is available on request (€13/person for wines only, €23/person with light lunch, daily 8:30-12:30 & 15:30-18:30 except closed Sun afternoon, Viale Venere S.N.C. Loc. Canale; on the road from Orvieto to Civita, a half-mile after Le Velette, it's the first building before Canale; tel. 0763-29053, mobile 338-316-0405, www.cantinacustodi.com).

To the North: In the rolling hills just north of Orvieto, **Neri** rests amid postcard-pretty estate grounds, with an ancient manor house and grand views of Orvieto and the countryside. Their wines are simple and traditional (tour and tastings from €10, reservations preferred, daily 9:30-17:00; just down the road from recommended Agriturismo Cioccoleta at Località Bardano 28—head north from Orvieto following signs to *Sferracavallo* and *Bardano;* tel. 0763-316-196, mobile 393-331-3844, www.neri-vini.it, visite@neri-vini.it, Enrico).

Sleeping in Orvieto

Orvieto's high season (with higher hotel prices) is roughly May to early July, September, and October. You'll save a little money off-season.

IN THE TOWN CENTER

$$$ Grand Hotel Italia is businesslike, with a stay-awhile lobby and terrace. While not as "grand" as it once was, it brings predictable modern amenities to this small town. The 46 overpriced rooms are well located in the heart of Orvieto, a block off the main drag and near the market square (RS%, air-con, elevator, off-site pay parking—reserve ahead, Via di Piazza del Popolo 13, tel. 0763-342-065, www.grandhotelitalia.it, hotelita@libero.it).

$$$ Hotel Virgilio is small, cheery, modern, and a bit pricey, renting 13 rooms facing the side of the cathedral (air-con, elevator, Piazza Duomo 5, tel. 0763-394-937, www.orvietohotelvirgilio.com, booking@orvietohotelvirgilio.com).

$$ Hotel Duomo is centrally located and modern, with splashy art in 17 rooms and a friendly welcome. It's tucked a few steps off the cathedral square, but double-paned windows keep the sound of the church bells well-muffled (RS%, family rooms, air-con, elevator, private pay parking, sunny terrace, a block from the Duomo at

Vicolo di Maurizio 7, tel. 0763-341-887, www.orvietohotelduomo. com, orvietohotelduomo@gmail.com; Gianni and Maura Massaccesi don't speak English, daughter Elisa and son-in-law Diego do). They also run a three-room B&B 50 yards from the hotel (lower prices, breakfast at the main hotel).

$$ Hotel Corso is friendly, with 18 frilly and flowery rooms— a few with balconies and views. Their sunlit little terrace is enjoyable, but the location—halfway between the center of town and the funicular—is less convenient than others (RS%, family rooms, ask for quieter room off street, air-con, elevator, reserved pay parking, Corso Cavour 339, tel. 0763-342-020, www.hotelcorso.net, info@ hotelcorso.net, Carla).

$ La Magnolia B&B has lots of fancy terra-cotta tiles, a couple of rooms with frescoed ceilings, terraces, and other welcoming touches. Its seven unique rooms—some of them mini-apartments with kitchens—are cheerfully decorated and on the town's main drag. The three units facing the busy street are air-conditioned and have double-paned windows (RS%, family rooms, no elevator, washing machine, Via del Duomo 29, tel. 0763-342-808, mobile 349-462-0733, www.bblamagnolia.it, info@bblamagnolia.it, Serena).

$ B&B Michelangeli offers two comfortable and well-appointed apartments hiding along a residential lane a few blocks from the tourist scene. It's run by eager-to-please Francesca, who speaks limited English but provides homey touches and free tea, coffee, and breakfast supplies. From the Corso, follow Via Michelangeli, a street full of wood sculptures made by her famous artistic family (family rooms, fully equipped kitchen, washing machine, private pay parking, Via dei Saracinelli 20—ring bell labeled *M. Michelangeli,* tel. 0763-393-862, mobile 347-089-0349, www. bbmichelangeli.com).

$ Affittacamere Valentina rents six clean, airy, well-appointed rooms, all with big beds and antique furniture. It's in the heart of Orvieto, on a quiet street behind the palace on Piazza del Popolo (RS%, no breakfast, family rooms, air-con, pay parking, Via Vivaria 7, tel. 0763-341-607, mobile 393-970-5868, www.bandbvalentina. com, camerevalentina@gmail.com). Welcoming Valentina also rents four apartments in the center.

$ Hotel Posta is a centrally located, long-ago-elegant palazzo renting 20 quirky, clean, cheap rooms with dark wood floors and vintage furniture. It feels a little institutional, but it's well-run, and the rooms without private bath are among the cheapest in town (breakfast extra, elevator, Via Luca Signorelli 18, tel. 0763-341-909, www.hotelpostaorvieto.it, hotelposta@orvietohotels.it, Alessia).

$ Villa Mercede, a good value and excellent location, is owned

ORVIETO & CIVITA

Orvieto Hotels & Restaurants

ETRUSCAN NECROPOLIS

LA RUPE PATH

Cliffs

SANT' AGOSTINO

SAN GIOVENALE

Piazza S. Giovenale

PALAZZO FILIPPESCHI

BAKERY

V. MAGALOTTI

Piazza Vittozzi

13

Piazza della Repubblica

STRADA DELLE CONC.

V. CACCIA

MALABRANCA

FILIPPESCHI

COMMENDA

19

WC

LOGGIA

CITY HALL

SANT' ANDREA

VIA DELLA CAVA

PORTA MAGGIORE

WELL OF THE QUARRY

V. RANIERI

SAN GIOVANNI EVANGELISTA

ESCALATOR TO PARKING GARAGE

31

GARIBALDI

12

V. DRITTA DI MARCH.

VIC. VOLSINIA

Piazza de' Ranieri

VIA COZZA

To Bolsena & Viterbo

STRADA DI

UPPER ELEVATOR

VIA RIPA MEDICI

6

Campo della Fiera

PORTA ROMANA

To Bolsena & Viterbo

ESCALATOR TO PIAZZA DE' RANIERI

VIA D. ALBERICI

VIA DELLA SEGHERIA

11

LOWER ELEVATOR

PORTA ROMANA

V. PECORELLI

SAN GIOVENALE

Accommodations
- **1** Grand Hotel Italia
- **2** Hotel Virgilio
- **3** Hotel Duomo
- **4** Hotel Corso
- **5** La Magnolia B&B
- **6** B&B Michelangeli
- **7** Affitacamere Valentina
- **8** Hotel Posta
- **9** Villa Mercede
- **10** Istituto SS. Salvatore
- **11** Casa Sèlita B&B

Eateries & Other
- **12** Trattoria la Palomba
- **13** L'Antica Trattoria dell'Orso
- **14** Trattoria la Pergola
- **15** Trattoria del Moro Aronne

ORVIETO & CIVITA

by a religious institution and offers 26 cheap, simple, mostly twin-bedded rooms, each with a big modern bathroom and many with glorious Umbrian views (elevator, free parking, a half-block from Duomo at Via Soliana 2, reception upstairs, tel. 0763-341-766, www.villamercede.it, info@villamercede.it).

$ Istituto SS. Salvatore rents nine spotless twin rooms and five singles in their convent, which comes with a peaceful terrace and garden, great views, and a 24:00 curfew. Though the nuns don't speak English, they have mastered Google Translate, and will hap-

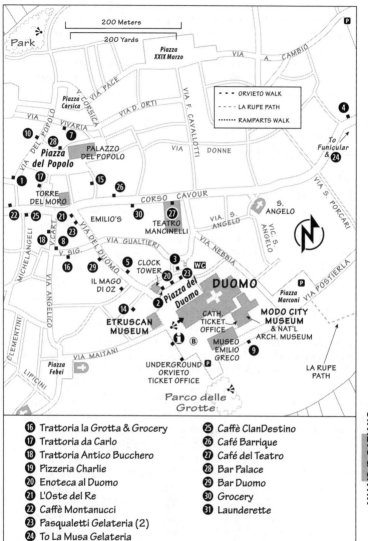

16 Trattoria la Grotta & Grocery
17 Trattoria da Carlo
18 Trattoria Antico Bucchero
19 Pizzeria Charlie
20 Enoteca al Duomo
21 L'Oste del Re
22 Caffè Montanucci
23 Pasqualetti Gelateria (2)
24 To La Musa Gelateria
25 Caffè ClanDestino
26 Café Barrique
27 Café del Teatro
28 Bar Palace
29 Bar Duomo
30 Grocery
31 Launderette

pily use it to answer your questions (cash only, no breakfast, elevator, Wi-Fi in common areas only, free parking, just off Piazza del Popolo at Via del Popolo 1, tel. 0763-342-910, istitutosansalvatore@tiscali.it).

Just Outside the Town Center: A peaceful country house, **$ Casa Sèlita B&B** offers easy access to Orvieto (best for drivers, but workable for adventurous train travelers who want an *agriturismo*-style experience). It's nestled in an orchard just below the town cliffs; to get to town, you'll climb an uphill path through their olive orchard (with a view terrace along the way) to reach the Campo della Fiera parking lot, with its handy escalator taking you the rest of the way up into Orvieto. Its five rooms with terraces are airy and fresh, with dark hardwood floors, fluffy down comforters, and modern baths. Enjoy the views from the relaxing garden. Conscientious Sèlita, her husband, Ennio, and daughter Elena are gracious hosts (RS%, cash preferred, air-con, free parking, closed mid-Nov-Easter, Strada di Porta Romana 8, ask for directions— GPS can be tricky, mobile 339-225-4000 or 328-611-2052, www. casaselita.com, info@casaselita.com).

NEAR ORVIETO

All of these (except the last one) are within a 20-minute drive of Orvieto, in different directions, and require a car—see the "Orvieto and Civita Area" map, near the beginning of this chapter.

$$$ Alta Rocca Wine Resort, run by Emiliano and Sabrina, is a fancy "country resort" and spa, located 15 minutes north of Orvieto. They produce their own olive oil and wine, and rent 30 modern and air-conditioned rooms and a few apartments. Popular on weekends as a wedding location, this place has *luna di miele* (honeymoon) written all over it (2 pools, panoramic view restaurant, wellness center with Jacuzzi and steam room, massages and spa treatments available, visit to winery and wine tasting upon request, gym, mountain bikes, bocce court, hiking paths to private lake, tel. 0763-344-210 or 0763-393-437, www.altaroccawineresort.com, info@altaroccawineresort.com).

$$$ Agriturismo Locanda Rosati, where you'll be greeted by friendly host Giampiero Rosati, rents 10 tastefully decorated rooms in a pleasant, homey atmosphere. The peaceful, flower-lined grounds are perfect for a retreat (RS%, family rooms, full traditional dinners for €40 on request, air-con, swimming pool, 5 miles from Orvieto on the road to Viterbo, tel. 0763-217-314, www. locandarosati.it, info@locandarosati.it).

$$ Agriturismo Poggio della Volara, located between Todi and Orvieto (12 miles from either), has seven apartments (sleeping from two to five people) and five rooms in two buildings overlooking a swimming pool. Along with keeping rabbits, geese, dogs, and ducks, Marco produces wine, olive oil, and salami made from wild boar that he hunts. If you're looking for a real farmhouse experience far out in the countryside, this is it (air-con, €30-35 dinners on request, mobile 347-335-2523, www.poggiodellavolara.it, info@ poggiodellavolara.it).

$$ Tenuta Le Velette is a sprawling, historic, family-run estate and winery. Cecilia and Corrado Bottai rent six fully furnished apartments and villas scattered over their family's expansive and scenic grounds. Rooms range wildly in size—accommodating from

2 to 14 people—but they all nestle in perfect Umbrian rural peace and tranquility. See the website for details on their various villas (2-night minimum, discount for weekly stay, pool, bocce court, 10 minutes from Orvieto—drive toward Bagnoregio-Canale and follow *Tenuta Le Velette* signs, tel. 0763-29090, mobile 348-300-2002, www.levelette.it, cecilialevelette@libero.it). They also offer wine tastings (see description under "Near Orvieto," earlier in this chapter).

$$ Agriturismo Cioccoleta ("Little Stone") has eight rooms with cozy country decor, each named after one of the grapes grown in the *agriturismo*'s vineyards. It's family run and offers sweeping views of Orvieto and the pastoral countryside (RS%, fans, 3 miles north of Orvieto at Località Bardano 34 in Bardano, tel. 0763-316-011, mobile 349-860-9780, www.cioccoleta.it, info@cioccoleta.it, Angela Zucconi).

Farther Out: Northeast of Orvieto, **$$$ Agriturismo Fattoria di Vibio** produces olive oil and honey, sells organic products, and offers classes and spa services. In August, its 14 rooms rent at peak prices and have a minimum-stay requirement. The rest of the year, no minimum stay is required, although rates drop dramatically for longer visits. Its two cottages sleep from four to six people and rent only by the week (panoramic pool, expensive restaurant, farthest cottage is 20 miles from Orvieto, www.fattoriadivibio.com, info@fattoriadivibio.com).

Eating in Orvieto

TRATTORIAS IN THE CENTER

$$$ Trattoria la Palomba features excellent game and truffle specialties in a wood-paneled dining room. Giampiero, Enrica, and the Cinti family enthusiastically take care of their diners, offering a fine value, high quality, and classy conviviality. Truffles are shaved right at your table—try the *umbricelli al tartufo* (homemade pasta with truffles) or *spaghetti dell'Ascaro* (with truffles). Their *filetto alla cardinale* and mixed-cheese plates are popular. As slow-foodies, they use organic and locally sourced ingredients (Thu-Tue 12:30-14:15 & 19:30-22:00, closed Wed and July, reservations smart, off Piazza della Repubblica at Via Cipriano Manente 16, tel. 0763-343-395).

$$$ L'Antica Trattoria dell'Orso offers well-prepared Umbrian cuisine paired with fine wines in a homey, bohemian-chic, peaceful atmosphere. Owner Stefano and chef Hania offer a good deal for my readers: €30 for two people—my vote for the best dining value in town (Wed-Mon 12:00-14:30 & 19:30-22:00, closed Tue and Feb, just off Piazza della Repubblica at Via della Misericordia 18, tel. 0763-341-642).

$$$ Trattoria la Pergola, run by chef Enrico and family, with a serious kitchen in back next to a covered patio, offers a small, accessible menu of seasonal Umbrian specialties. Closer to the center, this spot is touristy, but the food is tasty and lovingly presented (reservations smart, air-con, Thu-Tue 12:15-15:00 & 19:15-22:00, closed Wed, Via dei Magoni 9, tel. 0763-343-065).

$$ Trattoria del Moro Aronne is a long-established family bistro run by Cristian and his mother, Rolanda, who lovingly prepare homemade pasta and market-fresh Umbrian specialties. Consider their *nidi*—folds of fresh pasta enveloping warm, gooey pecorino cheese sweetened with honey. Three small and separate dining areas make the interior feel intimate. While touristy and not particularly atmospheric, this place is known locally as an excellent value (Wed-Mon 12:30-14:30 & 19:30-22:00, closed Tue, Via San Leonardo 7, tel. 0763-342-763).

$$ Trattoria la Grotta prides itself on serving only the freshest food and finest wine. The decor is Signorelli-mod, and the ambience is quiet, with courteous service. They've been at it for more than 50 years, and promise diners a free coffee, grappa, *limoncello,* or vin santo with this book (Wed-Mon opens at 12:00 for lunch and at 19:00 for dinner, closed Tue, Via Luca Signorelli 5, tel. 0763-341-348).

$$ Trattoria da Carlo, hiding on its own little *piazzetta* between Via Corso Cavour and Piazza del Popolo, is a cozy spot with a bright, white-tiled interior and inviting tables outside. Animated and opinionated Carlo—a young, likeable loudmouth—holds court, chatting up his diners as much as he cooks, while his mama scuttles about taking orders, busing dishes, and lovingly rolling her eyes at her son's big personality. Carlo likes big flavors and putting a modern twist on traditional dishes (daily 12:00-15:00 & 19:00-24:00, often closed Sun dinner, Vicolo del Popolo 1, tel. 0763-343-916).

$$ Trattoria Antico Bucchero, elegant under a big, white vault, makes for a nice memory with its delicious food—especially game and wild boar (daily 12:00-15:00 & 19:00-23:00 except closed Wed Nov-March, seating indoors and on a peaceful square in summer, air-con, a half-block south of Corso Cavour, between Torre del Moro and Piazza della Repubblica at Via de Cartari 4, tel. 0763-341-725; Piero and Silvana, plus sons Fabio and Pericle).

$$ Pizzeria Charlie is a local favorite. Its noisy dining room and stony courtyard are reminiscent of a beer hall, and popular with families and students for casual dinners of wood-fired gourmet pizzas. In a quiet courtyard guarded by a medieval tower, it's a block southwest of Piazza della Repubblica (Wed-Mon 19:00-23:00, closed Tue, Via Loggia dei Mercanti 14, tel. 0763-344-766).

$$$ Enoteca al Duomo is to the left of the Duomo and has pleasant outdoor seating with a cathedral view. They serve wines by the glass and a vast selection of Italian wines by the bottle, and a full menu of local dishes in a contemporary wine-bar atmosphere (daily 10:00-22:00, closed Feb, Piazza del Duomo 13, tel. 0763-344-607).

FAST AND CHEAP EATS

$ L'Oste del Re is a simple osteria on Corso Cavour, where Maria Grazia and Claudio offer pasta, bruschetta, enticing meat-and-cheese plates, and hearty, made-to-order sandwiches to eat in or take out (good gluten-free options, daily 11:00-15:30 & 19:00-22:00—but usually closed for dinner Nov-May, Corso Cavour 58, tel. 0763-343-846).

$ Caffè Montanucci, the dominant hangout on the main street—for good reason—lays out an appetizing display of pastas and main courses behind the counter. Choose one (or two—called a *bis*), find a seat in the modern interior or sunny courtyard, and they'll bring it out on a tray. You'll eat among locals on lunch break. They also have good *caffè*, simple sandwiches, and tasty sweets all day (daily 7:00-24:00, meals for lunch only—though they may be open for dinner in summer, Corso Cavour 21, tel. 0763-341-261).

Panini **and a Picnic:** Scattered around town you'll find many *alimentari* (grocers) selling cured meats, cheese, and other staples. If you're feeling gamey, order prosciutto or salami made from *cinghiale* (cheen-gee-AH-lay; wild boar), a surprisingly mild-tasting local favorite. They're usually willing to make you a simple sandwich of bread, cold cuts, and/or cheese for a few euros.

Elsewhere along the Corso Cavour, you'll find places selling fruit, vegetables, and other picnic items. The fortress/garden, to the right as you face the funicular, is a great spot to enjoy your meal.

Groceries: While a small *alimentari* might have what you need for a picnic, two slightly larger **Pam Local** markets are tucked away two minutes from the Duomo (both Mon-Sat 8:00-20:00, Sun from 9:00, one at Corso Cavour 100 and the other just past recommended Trattoria la Grotta at Via Luca Signorelli 23).

Gelato: For dessert, *gelateria* **Pasqualetti,** next to the cathedral, is a favorite (daily, may close in cold weather, closed Dec-Feb; one location is next to left transept of church, Piazza del Duomo 14; another branch is a few steps off the main drag at Via del Duomo 10). Closer to the funicular, **La Musa** has a nice variety of creative flavors (daily, Corso Cavour 351).

CAFÉ SCENE ON CORSO CAVOUR AND NEARBY

Orvieto has a charming, traffic-free, pedestrian-friendly vibe. To enjoy it, be sure to spend a little time savoring *la dolce far niente*—the art of doing nothing—while sitting at a café. There are inviting places all over town, but these are either on or very near Corso Cavour, the main strolling drag, and offer the best people-watching.

Caffè Montanucci is the town's venerable place for a coffee and pastry, but has no on-street seating (Corso Cavour 21, described earlier for lunch). **Caffè ClanDestino** is well-located, with plenty of streetside seating and endless little bites served with your drink (Corso Cavour 40). **Café Barrique** is less crowded, less trendy, and quieter, with nice outdoor tables and good free snacks with your drink (Corso Cavour 111).

Café del Teatro, at Teatro Mancinelli (described earlier), can be a fun experience. While entry to the historic theater is normally €2, if you buy a drink, you're free to wander around on your own. Drink streetside, at the bar, or in the theater lobby (Mon-Sat 8:00-14:00, closed Sun, may be open later when there's a show, Corso Cavour 122, tel. 0763-531-502).

On Piazza del Popolo: A sunny, relaxed perch, **Bar Palace** faces a big square that's generally quiet (except on market day), with quality coffee and pastries.

Cafés Facing the Cathedral: Several cafés on Piazza del Duomo invite you to linger over a drink with a view of Orvieto's amazing cathedral.

Orvieto Connections

From Orvieto by Train to: Rome (every 1-2 hours, 1-1.5 hours), **Florence** (6/day, 2.5 hours, use Firenze S.M.N. train station), **Siena** (12/day, 2.5 hours, change in Chiusi), **Assisi** (roughly hourly, 2-3 hours, 1 or 2 transfers), **Milan** (2/day direct, 5.5 hours; otherwise about hourly with a transfer in Florence, Bologna, or Rome, 4.5-5 hours). The train station's Buffet della Stazione is surprisingly good if you need a quick focaccia sandwich or pizza picnic for the train ride.

Tip for Drivers: If you're thinking of driving to Rome, consider stashing your car in Orvieto instead. You can easily park the car, safe and free, in the big lot below the Orvieto train station (for up to a week or more), and zip effortlessly into Rome by train (roughly hourly, 1-1.5 hours).

Civita di Bagnoregio

Perched on a pinnacle in a grand canyon, the 2,500-year-old, traffic-free village of Civita di Bagnoregio is Italy's ultimate hill town. Civita's only connection to the town of Bagnoregio (ban-yoh-REH-joh)—and the world—is a long pedestrian bridge. In the last decade, the old, self-sufficient Civita (chee-VEE-tah) has died—the last of its lifelong residents have passed on, and the only employment here is in serving gawking sightseers. But Civita remains an amazing place to visit. And it remains popular as a backdrop for movies, soap operas, and advertising campaigns.

Civita's history goes back to Etruscan and ancient Roman times. In the early Middle Ages, Bagnoregio was a suburb of Civita, which had a population of about 4,000. Later, Bagnoregio surpassed Civita in size—especially following a 1695 earthquake, after which many residents fled Civita to live in Bagnoregio, fearing their houses would be shaken off the edge into the valley below. Bagnoregio is dominated by Renaissance-style buildings, while architecturally, Civita remains stuck in the Middle Ages.

Despite being a "dead city," Civita can be very crowded—especially on the weekends and at lunchtime. The best way to enjoy Civita is early or late in the day, when you have the village to yourself. While Bagnoregio lacks the pinnacle-town romance of Civita, it's a healthy, vibrant community. In Bagnoregio, get a haircut, sip a coffee on the square, and walk down to the old laundry (ask, *"Dov'è la lavanderia vecchia?"*).

Planning Your Time: In high season—and especially on weekends—little Civita can be uncomfortably jammed; for a better experience, treat it like a major museum and visit either early or late in the day. If side-tripping by bus from Orvieto, it works well to get up early, take the 7:50 bus, and see Civita in the cool morning calm. The next bus after 7:50 is at 12:45. If you take this later one, you can make the last bus back (around 17:20), but your time in Civita may feel a little rushed. Note that the buses connecting Orvieto to Bagnoregio (and Civita) do not run on Sundays or holidays.

GETTING THERE

To reach Civita from Orvieto, you'll first head for the adjacent town of Bagnoregio. From there, it's a 30-minute walk or 5-minute drive to the base of Civita's pedestrian bridge, followed by a steep 10-minute hike up to the town's main square.

By Bus to Bagnoregio: The blue Cotral bus runs to Bagnoregio about 10 times each day, including some very early departures and a long break mid-morning; get the detailed schedule at the TI or at www.cotralspa.it (Italian only; no bus on Sundays or holidays). The

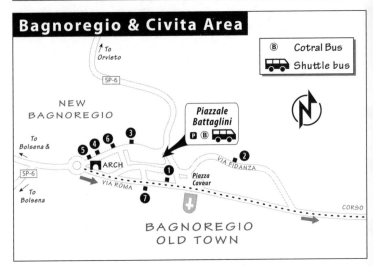

Bagnoregio & Civita Area

Ⓑ Cotral Bus
🚐 Shuttle bus

To Orvieto

SP-6

NEW BAGNOREGIO

To Bolsena &

❺ ❹ ❻ ❸

SP-6

To Bolsena

ARCH

VIA ROMA

❼

Piazzale Battaglini
Ⓟ Ⓑ 🚐

❶

Piazza Cavour

VIA FIDANZA

❷

CORSO

BAGNOREGIO OLD TOWN

trip takes about 45 minutes, and tickets are €2.20 one-way if bought in advance at a bar or tobacco shop, or €7 one-way if purchased from driver. In Orvieto's upper town, buy your ticket from Silvia at the tobacco shop at Corso Cavour 306, a block up from the funicular (daily 7:00-13:00 & 16:00-20:00)—otherwise you'll pay the premium ticket price on board the bus. If you'll be returning to Orvieto by bus, buy two tickets now (they're harder to get in Bagnoregio).

Buses depart from a courtyard within the former military barracks, a short walk from the upper funicular station at the east end of Orvieto. It's tricky to find: With your back to the funicular, walk to the right, bear left (uphill) with the street, then go right under the arch marked *Caserma Piave*. Angle left through the parking lot to find the blue Cotral bus, under and behind the tall trees. (Note: Lots of buses marked *Umbria Mobilità* stop in front of the funicular, but Civita is served by a different bus company, Cotral.)

Buses departing the barracks stop five minutes later at Orvieto's train station—to catch the bus there, wait to the left of the funicular station (as you're facing it); schedule and tickets are available in the tobacco shop/bar in the train station.

For information on buses returning to Orvieto, see "Bagnoregio Connections," later.

Getting from Bagnoregio Bus Stop to Civita: By Cotral bus from Orvieto, you'll arrive in Bagnoregio at Piazzale Battaglini, at the opposite

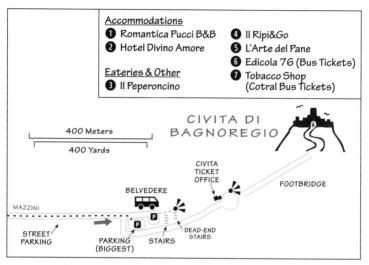

Accommodations
1 Romantica Pucci B&B
2 Hotel Divino Amore

Eateries & Other
3 Il Peperoncino

4 Il Ripi&Go
5 L'Arte del Pane
6 Edicola 76 (Bus Tickets)
7 Tobacco Shop
  (Cotral Bus Tickets)

CIVITA DI
BAGNOREGIO

400 Meters
400 Yards

CIVITA
TICKET
OFFICE

FOOTBRIDGE

BELVEDERE

MAZZINI

STREET
PARKING

PARKING
(BIGGEST)

STAIRS

DEAD-END
STAIRS

end of the old center from Civita. To get to Civita's bridge, it's a 20- to 30-minute, mostly downhill **walk** through the middle of Bagnoregio. The walk itself is enjoyable, as it offers a delightful look at a workaday Italian town. To walk, take the road going uphill, Via Garibaldi (overlooking the big parking lot), then jog a block over to the main drag, Via Roma, which changes names a few times as it takes you all the way to Civita.

If you'd rather not walk, you can take a **shuttle.** It runs to Civita from near the Piazzale Battaglini bus stop—look for white minibuses labeled *EPF Tours.* The shuttle is especially handy for the uphill return—it drops you right at the Orvieto-bound bus stop (usually 1-2/hour, 5 minutes, 7:30-18:15 but few buses 13:15-15:00 or on Sun Oct-March, €0.70 one-way, €1 round-trip, pay driver).

By Taxi or Shared Taxi to Civita: If you can share the cost with other travelers, a 30-minute taxi ride from Orvieto to Civita is a reasonable value (basic rate: €50 one-way, €80 round-trip with an hour wait). Giuliotaxi can take groups by car or minibus (see "Tours of Orvieto," earlier in this chapter).

By Car to Bagnoregio and Civita: Driving from Orvieto to Civita takes about 30 minutes. Orvieto overlooks the autostrada (and has its own exit). From the Orvieto exit, the shortest way to Civita is to turn left (below Orvieto), and then simply follow the signs to *Lubriano* and *Bagnoregio.*

A more winding and scenic route takes a few minutes longer: From the Orvieto exit on the autostrada, go right (toward *Orvieto*), then at the first big roundabout, follow signs to *Bolsena* (passing under hill-capping Orvieto on your right). Take the first left (direction: Bagnoregio), winding up past great Orvieto views and the recommended Tenuta Le Velette and Custodi wineries (reservations required) en route to Canale, and through farms and fields of giant shredded wheat to Bagnoregio.

Whichever route you take, for a breathtaking view of Civita, just before Bagnoregio follow signs left to *Lubriano,* head into that village, turn right as you enter town, and pull into the first little square by the yellow church (on the left). You'll find an even better view farther into the town, from the tiny square at the next church (San Giovanni Battista). Then return to the Bagnoregio road.

Once in Bagnoregio, you'll drive right up the main street—which seems pedestrian-only, but isn't (follow yellow *Civita* signs). As you approach Civita, you'll begin to see pay-and-display parking lots and blue-painted lines along the side of the road (all charge €2/hour). The closest you can get is the lot at the end of the tree-lined stretch of road, right in front of the belvedere—but this is often full, in which case the larger lot farther back likely has space.

Walking Across the Bridge to Civita: Whether arriving by foot, shuttle bus, or car, first head out to the belvedere at the very end of Bagnoregio for a superb viewpoint (through the little garden). From there, backtrack a few steps (the staircase next to the viewpoint is a dead end) and take the stairs down to the road leading to the bridge. You'll first head downhill, then pay the admission fee and hike up the narrow bridge into town.

Orientation to Civita

Civita charges a €5 **admission fee** to enter the old town (waived for overnight guests). The revenue helps with its extensive maintenance expenses. Buy your ticket from the brown kiosk, just before the bridge, on the left.

HELPFUL HINTS

Market Day: A lively market fills the Bagnoregio bus-station parking lot each Monday.

Orvieto Bus Tickets: Because the Orvieto-Bagnoregio bus ticket is much cheaper purchased in advance (€2.20 one-way) than from the driver (€7), ideally you'll buy both tickets in Orvieto. But if you wind up in Bagnoregio needing a ticket, only two places sell them—and both are closed for several hours in the afternoon. Buy one on arrival so you have it when you need it later. One option is the newsstand (named Edicola 76) across from the gas station near the Bagnoregio bus stop (look for the white awning at #47; daily 7:00-13:00 & 17:00-20:00 except closed Sun and Thu afternoons). The other option is the tobacco shop up along the main drag of Bagnoregio, directly uphill from the big parking lot, next to the GemminOro shop (Mon-Sat 8:00-13:00 & 17:00-20:00, closed Sun, Larga Fidenza 6).

Civita di Bagnoregio

Note: Map not to scale;
a walk across Civita
takes approx. 5 minutes—
but don't rush it!

To Lubriano Town

Cliffs

Cliffs

OSTERIA
AL FORNO
DI AGNESE

ANTICO FORNO TRATTORIA
& CIVITA B&B

LOCANDA
DELLA BUONA
VENTURA

CAMPANILE
(BELL TOWER)

ANTICO FRANTOIO
OLIVE PRESS
& BRUSCHETTERIA

L'ARCO DEL GUSTO

WC

Piazza

CHURCH

OLD LAUNDRY

ETRUSCAN
COLUMNS

ALMA
CIVITA

ARCH

MAIN   STRADA

FOOTBRIDGE

To
Bagnoregio

BAR LA
PIAZZETTA

WINE BAR
D'ANDREA

TRATTORIA LA
CANTINA
DE ARIANNA

ANTICA
CIVITA
MUSEUM

WINE BAR
DA PEPPONE
& GEOLOGICAL
MUSEUM

PALACE
(PRIVATE)

CAVES &
CHAPEL
CARVED
IN ROCK

Cliffs

RUINS OF HOUSE
OF ST. BONAVENTURE

Trail to Etruscan
tunnel under Civita

Civita Walk

Civita was once connected to Bagnoregio, before the saddle between the separate towns eroded away. Photographs around town show the old donkey path—the original bridge. It was bombed in World War II and replaced in 1966 with the footbridge that you're climbing today.

• *Entering the town, you'll pass through* **Porta Santa Maria,** *a 12th-century Romanesque arch. This stone passageway was cut by the Etruscans 2,500 years ago, when this town was a stop on an ancient trading route. Inside the archway, you enter a garden of stones. Stand in the little square—the town's antechamber—facing the Bar La Piazzetta. Over your right shoulder are the remains of a...*

Renaissance Palace

The wooden door and windows (above the door) lead only to thin air. They were part of the facade of one of five palaces that once graced Civita. Much of the palace fell into the valley, riding a chunk of the ever-eroding rock pinnacle. Today, the door leads to a remaining section of the palace—complete with Civita's first hot

ORVIETO & CIVITA

tub. It was once owned by the "Marchesa," a countess who married into Italy's biggest industrialist family.

• *A few steps uphill, farther into town (on your left, beyond the Bottega souvenir store), notice the two shed-like buildings.*

Old WC and Laundry (Vecchio Lavatoio)

In the nearer building (covered with ivy), you'll see the town's old laundry, which dates from just after World War II, when water was finally piped into the town. Until a few years ago, this was a lively village gossip center. Now, locals park their mopeds here. Just behind that is another stone shed, which houses a poorly marked and less-than-pristine WC.

• *The main square is just a few steps farther along, but we'll take the scenic circular route to get there, detouring around to the right. Walk past the ruined palace and belly up to the...*

Canyon Viewpoint

Lean over the banister and listen to the sounds of the birds and the bees. Survey old family farms, noticing how evenly they're spaced. Historically, each one owned just enough land to stay in business. Turn left along the belvedere and walk a few steps to the site of the long-gone home of Civita's one famous son, St. Bonaventure, known as the "second founder of the Franciscans" (look for the small plaque on the wall).

• *From here, a lane leads past delightful old homes and gardens, and then to...*

Civita's Main Square

The town church faces Civita's main piazza. Grab a stone seat along the biggest building fronting the square (or a drink at Peppone's bar) and observe the scene. They  say that in a big city you can see a lot, but in a small town like this you can feel a lot. The generous bench is built into the long side of the square, reminding me of how, when I first discovered Civita back in the 1970s and 1980s, the town's old folks would gather here every night.

The piazza has been integral to Italian culture since ancient Roman times. While Civita is humble today, imagine the town's former wealth, when mansions of the leading families faced this square, along with the former City Hall (opposite the church, to your left). The town's history includes a devastating earthquake in 1695. Notice how stone walls were reinforced with thick bases, and how old stones and marble slabs were recycled and built into walls.

Here in the town square, you'll find **Bar Da Peppone** (open daily, local wines and microbrews, inviting fire in the winter) and two restaurants. There are wild donkey races on the first Sunday of June and the second Sunday of September. At Christmastime, a living Nativity scene is enacted in this square, and if you're visiting at the end of July or beginning of August, you might catch a play here. The pillars that stand like giants' bar stools are ancient Etruscan. The church, with its campanile (bell tower), marks the spot where an Etruscan temple, and then a Roman temple, once stood. Across from Peppone's, on the side of the former City Hall, is a small, square stone counter. Old-timers remember when this was a meat shop, and how one day a week the counter was stacked with fish for sale.

The humble **Geological Museum,** next to Peppone's, tells the story of how erosion is constantly shaping the surrounding "Bad Lands" valley, how landslides have shaped (and continue to threaten) Civita, and how the town plans to stabilize things (€3; June-Aug Tue-Sun 9:30-13:30 & 14:00-18:30, closed Mon; Sept-May Fri-Sun 10:00-13:30 & 14:00-19:30, closed Mon-Thu; www.museogeologicoedellefrane.it, mobile 328-665-7205).

• *Now step inside...*

Civita's Church

A cathedral until 1699, the church houses records of about 60 bishops that date back to the seventh century (church open daily 10:00-13:00 & 15:00-17:00, often closed Feb). Inside you'll see Romanesque columns and arches with faint Renaissance frescoes peeking through Baroque-era whitewash. The central altar is built upon the relics of the Roman martyr St. Victoria, who once was the patron saint of the town. St. Marlonbrando served as a bishop here in the ninth century; an altar dedicated to him is on the right. The fine crucifix over this altar, carved out of pear wood in the 15th century, is from the school of Donatello. It's remarkably expressive and greatly venerated by locals. Jesus' gaze is almost haunting. Some say his appearance changes based on what angle you view him from: looking alive from the front, in agony from the left, and dead from the right. Regardless, his eyes follow you from side to side. On Good Friday, this crucifix goes out and is the focus of the midnight procession.

On the left side, midway up the nave above an altar, is an intimate fresco known as *Madonna of the Earthquake,* given this name because—in the great shake of 1695—the whitewash fell off and revealed this tender fresco of Mary and her child. (During the Baroque era, a white-and-bright interior was in vogue, and churches such as these—which were covered with precious and historic frescoes—were simply whitewashed over. Look around to see examples.) On the same wall—just toward the front from the *Madonna*—find the faded portrait of Santa Apollonia, the patron saint of your teeth; notice the scary-looking pincers.

• *From the square, you can follow...*

The Main Street

A short walk takes you from the church to the end of the town. Along the way, you'll pass a couple little eateries (described later, under "Eating in Civita"), olive presses, gardens, a rustic town museum, and valley views. The rock below Civita is honeycombed with ancient tunnels, caverns (housing olive presses), cellars (for keeping wine at a constant temperature all year), and cisterns (for collecting rainwater, since there was no well in town). Many date from Etruscan times.

Wherever you choose to eat (or just grab a bruschetta snack), be sure to take advantage of the opportunity to poke around—every place has a historic cellar. At the trendy **Alma Civita,** notice the damaged house facing the main street—broken since the 1695 earthquake and scarred to this day. Just beyond, the rustic **Antico Frantoio Bruschetteria** serves bruschetta in an amazing old space. Whether or not you buy food, venture into their back room to see

an interesting collection of old olive presses (if you're not eating here, a €1 donation is requested). The huge olive press in the entry is about 1,500 years old. Until the 1960s, blindfolded donkeys trudged in the circle here, crushing olives and creating paste that filled the circular filters and was put into a second press. Notice the 2,500-year-old sarcophagus niche. The hole in the floor (with the glass top) was a garbage hole. In ancient times, residents would toss their jewels down when under attack; excavations uncovered a windfall of treasures.

In front is the wellhead of an ancient cistern—designed to collect rainwater from neighboring rooftops—carved out of *tufo* and covered with clay to be waterproof.

• *Across the street and down a tiny lane, find...*

Antica Civita

This is the closest thing the town has to a history museum. The humble collection is the brainchild of Felice, the old farmer who hung black-and-white photos, farm tools, olive presses, and local artifacts in a series of old caves. Climb down to the "warm blood machine" (another donkey-powered grinding wheel) and a viewpoint. You'll see rooms where a mill worker lived until the 1930s. Felice wants to give visitors a feeling for life in Civita when its traditional economy was strong (€1, daily 10:00-19:00, until 17:00 in winter, some English explanations, tel. 320-110-4279).

• *Another few steps along the main street take you to...*

The End of Civita

Here the road is literally cut out of the stone, with a dramatic view of the Bad Lands opening up. To savor the scene, consider popping into the cute **"Garden of Poets"** (immediately on the left just outside town; they'll ask for a donation, or you can purchase something at their little local-products shop). Then, look back up at the end of town and ponder the precarious future of Civita. There's a certain stillness here, far from the modern world and high above the valley.

Continue along the path a few steps toward the valley below the town, and you come to some shallow caves used as stables until a few years ago. The third cave, cut deeper into the rock, with a barred door, is the **Chapel of the Incarcerated** (Cappella del Carcere). In Etruscan times, the chapel—with a painted tile depicting the Madonna and child—may have been a tomb, and in medieval times, it was used as a jail (which collapsed in 1695).

Although it's closed to the public now, an Etruscan tunnel just beyond the Chapel of the Incarcerated cuts completely through the hill. Tall enough for a woman with a jug on her head to pass through, it may have served as a shortcut to the river below. It was widened in the 1930s so that farmers could get between their scattered fields more easily. Later, it served as a refuge for frightened villagers who huddled here during WWII bombing raids.

• *Hike back into town, taking some time to explore the peaceful back lanes before returning to the modern world.*

Sleeping in Civita or Bagnoregio

Civita has nine B&B rooms up for grabs. Bagnoregio has larger lodgings, and there are plenty of *agriturismi* nearby; otherwise, there's always Orvieto. Off-season, when Civita and Bagnoregio are deadly quiet—and cold—I'd side-trip in from Orvieto rather than spend the night here.

IN CIVITA

$$ Alma Civita is a classic old stone house that has been renovated by a sister-and-brother team, Alessandra and Maurizio (hence the name: Al-Ma). These are Civita's two most comfortable, modern, and warmly run rooms and they also have a recommended restaurant (tel. 0761-792-415, mobile 347-449-8892, www.almacivita. com, prenotazione@almacivita.com).

$$ Locanda della Buona Ventura rents four overpriced rooms, up narrow stairs, decorated in medieval rustic-chic, and overlooking Civita's piazza. You're not likely to see the owner—the Dallaiti shop across the square functions as the reception (tiny bathrooms, skimpy breakfast, tel. 0761-792-025, mobile 347-627-5628, www. locandabuonaventura.com, info@locandabuonaventura.com).

$ Civita B&B, run by gregarious Franco Sala, has three little rooms above Trattoria Antico Forno, each overlooking Civita's main square. Two are doubles with private bath. The third is a triple (with one double and one kid-size bed), which has its own bathroom across the hall (RS%, family rooms, continental breakfast, Piazza del Duomo Vecchio, tel. 076-176-0016, mobile 347-611-5426, www.civitadibagnoregio.it, fsala@pelagus.it). Franco also rents a few apartments in Civita, Bagnoregio, and nearby.

IN BAGNOREGIO

$ Romantica Pucci B&B is a haven for city-weary travelers. Its five spacious rooms are indeed romantic, with canopied beds and flowing veils (air-con, free parking, along the main drag at Piazza Cavour 1, tel. 0761-792-121, www.hotelromanticapucci.it, info@ hotelromanticapucci.it).

$ Hotel Divino Amore has 23 bright, modern rooms, four with perfect views of a miniature Civita. These view rooms, and the seven rooms with air-conditioning, don't cost extra—but they book up first (closed Jan-March, a block below the main drag at Via Fidanza 25-27, tel. 076-178-0882, mobile 329-344-8950, www. hoteldivinoamore.com, info@hoteldivinoamore.com, Silvia).

Eating in Civita or Bagnoregio

IN CIVITA

Note that opening hours are highly unpredictable in this little town—when it's quiet, places can close unexpectedly. Take the hours listed here as rough estimates.

$$ Osteria Al Forno di Agnese is a delightful spot where Manuela and her friends serve visitors simple yet delicious meals and a good selection of local wines on a covered patio just off Civita's main square or in a little dining room in gloomy weather (daily at 12:00 for lunch, June-Sept also at 19:00 for dinner, closed sometimes in bad weather, tel. 0761-792-571, mobile 340-1259-721).

$$ Trattoria Antico Forno serves up rustic dishes, homemade pasta, and salads at affordable prices. Try their homemade pasta with truffles (daily 12:30-15:30 & 19:00-22:00—but not always open for dinner, on main square, also rents rooms—see Civita B&B listing earlier, tel. 076-176-0016, Franco, daughter Elisabetta, and assistants Nina and Daniela).

$$ Trattoria La Cantina de Arianna is a family affair, with a busy open fire specializing in grilled meat and wonderful bruschetta. It's run by Arianna, her sister, Antonella, and their parents, Rossana and Antonio. After eating, wander down to their cellar, where you'll see traditional winemaking gear and provisions for rolling huge kegs up the stairs. Tap on the kegs in the bottom level to see which are full (daily 12:00-16:30, Sat also dinner from 19:30, tel. 0761-793-270).

$$ Alma Civita feels like a fresh, new take on old Civita, owned by a sister-and-brother team of longtime residents: Alessandra (an architect) and Maurizio (who runs the restaurant). Choose from one of three seating areas: outside on a stony lane, in the modern and trendy-feeling main-floor dining room, or in the equally modern but atmospheric cellar. Even deeper is an old Etruscan tomb that's now a wine cellar (April-Oct lunch Wed-Mon 12:00-15:15, dinner Fri-Sat only 19:00-21:30, closed Tue; Nov-March Thu-Sun only for lunch plus Sat for dinner; they also rent recommended rooms, tel. 0761-792-415).

$ Antico Frantoio Bruschetteria, the last place in town, is a rustic, super-atmospheric spot for a bite to eat. The specialty here: delicious bruschetta toasted over hot coals. Peruse the menu, choose your toppings (chopped tomato is super), and get a glass of wine for a fun, affordable snack or meal (roughly 10:00-18:00— sometimes later in summer, mobile 328-689-9375, Fabrizio).

Sandwich Shop: If you just want a quick bite, **$ L'Arco del Gusto** can make you a sandwich using local products (daily 10:30-16:30, tucked in an archway near the start of town).

IN BAGNOREGIO

The recommended **$$ Romantica Pucci B&B** offers a small restaurant with tables in its private garden (closed Mon, see contact details earlier). For good gelato, on your walk to Civita you'll go right past a branch of Orvieto's **Pasqualetti**, on the main drag at Mazzini 32.

Near the Bagnoregio Bus Stop: Several basic eateries are along Via Giacomo Matteotti just below the bus stop in Bagnoregio, including **$ Il Peperoncino,** selling pizza by the slice (closed Wed, #49); **$$ Il Ripi&Go,** a sit-down eatery serving traditional food (closed Wed, #35); and—a half-block past Il Ripi&Go— fresh pastries at **$ L'Arte del Pane** (#5).

ORVIETO & CIVITA

Bagnoregio Connections

From Bagnoregio to Orvieto: Cotral buses connect Bagnoregio to Orvieto (about 10/day Mon-Sat only—no buses Sun or holidays, 45 minutes, €2.20 one-way if purchased in advance, €7 one-way from driver). For information, call 06-7205-7205 or 800-174-471 (press 7 for English), or see www.cotralspa.it (click "Orari," then fill in "Bagnoregio" and "Orvieto" in the trip planner—Italian only). For info on coming from Orvieto, see "Getting There" near the start of this section.

From Bagnoregio to Points South: Cotral buses also run to **Viterbo,** which has good train connections to Rome (about 10/day Mon-Fri, fewer Sat, no buses Sun, 35 minutes).

ORVIETO & CIVITA

PRACTICALITIES

This section covers just the basics on traveling in Italy (for much more information, see *Rick Steves Italy*). You'll find free advice on specific topics at www.ricksteves.com/tips.

MONEY

Italy uses the euro currency: 1 euro (€) = about $1.20. To convert prices in euros to dollars, add about 20 percent: €20 = about $24, €50 = about $60. (Check www.oanda.com for the latest exchange rates.)

The standard way for travelers to get euros is to withdraw money from an ATM (known as a *bancomat*) using a debit card, ideally with a Visa or MasterCard logo. To keep your cash, cards, and valuables safe, wear a money belt.

Before departing, call your bank or credit-card company: Confirm that your card(s) will work overseas, ask about international transaction fees, and alert them that you'll be making withdrawals in Europe. Also ask for the PIN number for your credit card—you may need it for Europe's "chip-and-PIN" payment machines. Allow time for your bank to mail your PIN to you.

European cards use chip-and-PIN technology (most chip cards issued in the US instead have a signature option). Some European card readers may generate a receipt for you to sign, while others may prompt you to enter your PIN (so it's important to know the code for each of your cards). US credit cards may not work at some self-service payment machines (transit-ticket kiosks, parking, etc.). If your card won't work, look for a cashier who can process the transaction manually—or pay in cash.

Dynamic Currency Conversion: If merchants offer to convert your purchase price into dollars (called dynamic currency conversion, or DCC), refuse this "service." You'll pay extra in fees for the expensive convenience of seeing your charge in dollars. If an ATM offers to "lock in" or "guarantee" your conversion rate, choose "proceed without conversion." Other prompts might state, "You can be charged in dollars: Press YES for dollars, NO for euros." Always choose the local currency.

STAYING CONNECTED

The simplest solution is to bring your own device—mobile phone, tablet, or laptop—and use it just as you would at home (following the money-saving tips below, such as connecting to free Wi-Fi whenever possible).

To call Italy from a US or Canadian number: Whether you're phoning from a landline, your own mobile phone, or a Skype account, you're making an international call. Dial 011-39 and then the local number. (The 011 is our international access code, and 39 is Italy's country code.) If dialing from a mobile phone, you can enter + in place of the international access code—press and hold the 0 key.

To call Italy from a European country: Dial 00-39 followed by the local number. (The 00 is Europe's international access code.)

To call within Italy: Just dial the local number.

To call from Italy to another country: Dial 00 followed by the country code (for example, 1 for the US or Canada), then the area code and number. If you're calling European countries whose phone numbers begin with 0, you'll usually omit that 0 when you dial.

Tips: If you bring your own mobile phone, consider signing up for an international plan; most providers offer a global calling plan that cuts the per-minute cost of phone calls and texts, and a flat-fee data plan.

Use Wi-Fi whenever possible. Most hotels and many cafés offer free Wi-Fi, and you'll likely also find it at tourist information offices, major museums, and public-transit hubs. With Wi-Fi you can use your phone or tablet to make free or inexpensive domestic and international calls via a calling app such as Skype, FaceTime, or Google Hangouts. When you can't find Wi-Fi, you can use your cellular network to connect to the Internet, send texts, or make voice calls. When you're done, avoid further charges by manually switching off "data roaming" or "cellular data."

It's generally not possible to dial Italian toll or toll-free numbers from a US mobile or landline (although you can sometimes get through using a calling app such as Skype). Look for a direct-dial number instead.

Without a mobile device, you can make calls from your hotel and get online using public computers (there's usually one in your hotel lobby or at local libraries). Most hotels charge a high fee for international calls—ask for rates before you dial.

For more on phoning, see www.ricksteves.com/phoning. For a one-hour talk on "Traveling with a Mobile Device," see www.ricksteves.com/travel-talks.

Sleep Code

Hotels in this book are categorized according to the average price of a standard double room with breakfast in high season.

$$$$	**Splurge:**	Most rooms over €170
$$$	**Pricier:**	€130-170
$$	**Moderate:**	€90-130
$	**Budget:**	€50-90
¢	**Backpacker:**	Under €50
RS%	**Rick Steves discount**	

Unless otherwise noted, credit cards are accepted, hotel staff speak basic English, and free Wi-Fi is available. Comparison-shop by checking prices at several hotels (on each hotel's own website, on a booking site, or by email). For the best deal, *book directly with the hotel.* Ask for a discount if paying in cash; if the listing includes **RS%,** request a Rick Steves discount.

SLEEPING

I've categorized my recommended accommodations based on price, indicated with a dollar-sign rating (see sidebar). I recommend reserving rooms in advance, particularly during peak season. Once your dates are set, check the specific price for your preferred stay at several hotels. You can do this either by comparing prices on Hotels.com, Booking.com, or the hotels' own websites. After you've zeroed in on your choice, book directly with the hotel itself. Contact small family-run hotels directly by phone or email. When you go direct instead of a website, the owner avoids any third-party commission, giving them wiggle room to offer you a discount, a nicer room, or free breakfast. If you prefer to book online or are considering a hotel chain, it's to your advantage to use the hotel's website.

For complicated requests, send an email with the following information: number and type of rooms; number of nights; arrival date; departure date; and any special requests. Use the European style for writing dates: day/month/year. Hoteliers typically ask for your credit-card number as a deposit.

While most taxes are included in the price, a variable city tax of €3-7/person per night is often added to hotel bills in Italy. Some hoteliers will ask to collect the city tax in cash to make their book-keeping simpler.

EATING

I've categorized my recommended eateries based on the average price of a typical main course, indicated with a dollar-sign rating (see sidebar). Italy offers a wide array of eateries. A *ristorante* is a formal restaurant, while a *trattoria* or *osteria* is usually more

Restaurant Price Code

Eateries in this book are categorized according to the average cost of a typical main course (pasta or *secondi*). Drinks, desserts, and splurge items (steak and seafood) can raise the price considerably.

$$$$	**Splurge:** Most main courses over €20
$$$	**Pricier:** €15-20
$$	**Moderate:** €10-15
$	**Budget:** Under €10

In Italy, pizza by the slice and other takeaway food is **$**; a basic trattoria or sit-down pizzeria is **$$**; a casual but more upscale restaurant is **$$$**; and a swanky splurge is **$$$$**.

traditional and simpler (but can still be pricey). Italian "bars" are not taverns, but small cafés selling sandwiches, coffee, and other drinks. An *enoteca* is a wine bar with snacks and light meals. Take-away food from pizza shops and delis *(rosticcería)* makes an easy picnic.

Italians eat dinner a bit later than we do; better restaurants start serving around 19:00. A full meal consists of an appetizer (antipasto), a first course (*primo piatto,* pasta, rice, or soup), and a second course (*secondo piatto,* expensive meat and fish/seafood dishes). Vegetables *(verdure)* may come with the *secondo*, but more often must be ordered separately as a side dish (*contorno*). Desserts *(dolci)* can be very tempting. The euros can add up in a hurry, but you don't have to order each course. My approach is to mix anti-pasti and *primi piatti* family-style with my dinner partners (skipping *secondi*). Or, for a basic value, look for a *menù del giorno*, a three- or four-course, fixed-price meal deal (avoid the cheapest ones, often called a *menù turistico*).

At bars and cafés, getting a drink while standing at the bar *(banco)* is cheaper than drinking it at a table *(tavolo)* or sitting outside *(terrazza)*. This tiered pricing system is clearly posted on the wall. Sometimes you'll pay at a cash register, then take the receipt to another counter to claim your drink.

Good service is relaxed (slow to an American). You won't get the bill until you ask for it: *"Il conto?"* Many (but not all) restaurants in Italy add a cover charge *(coperto)* of €1-3.50 per person to your bill.

Tipping: A 10- to 15-percent service charge—called *servizio*—is most likely added to your bill in locations with lots of tourists. Look carefully at your check to see if you've already paid a tip—there's no need to leave a tip beyond this.

If there is no *servizio* on the bill, a common tip at a simple restaurant or pizzeria is €1 per person at the table (or simply round up the bill). At a finer restaurant, leave a few euros per person—hand the cash directly to the server.

TRANSPORTATION

By Train: To see if a rail pass could save you money, check www. ricksteves.com/rail. To research train schedules, visit Germany's excellent all-Europe website, www.bahn.com, or Italy's www. trenitalia.com. A private company called Italo also runs fast trains on major routes in Italy; see www.italotreno.it.

It's easy to buy tickets online or download the Trenitalia or Italo app to your smartphone—both have English versions. It's also easy to buy tickets at train stations (at the ticket window or at machines with English instructions) or from travel agencies. If your ticket includes a seat reservation *(biglietto con prenotazione),* you're all set and can just get on board. The same is true for any ticket bought online or with the Trenitalia or Italo smartphone apps; these tickets are considered already validated.

An open ticket (generally for a slower, regional train) bought from a ticket desk or machine must be validated (date-stamped) before you board (the ticket may say *da convalidare* or *convalida).* To validate it, before getting on the train, stamp your ticket in the small green machine on your way to the platform.

Strikes *(sciopero)* are common and generally announced in advance (but a few sporadic trains still run—ask around).

By Bus: Long-distance buses are catching on in Italy as an alternative to the train. They are usually cheaper, modern, and often have free Wi-Fi. Some of the operators you'll see are Flixbus (http://global.flixbus.com) and Marozzi (www.marozzivt.it).

By Car: It's cheaper to arrange most car rentals from the US. For tips on your insurance options, see www.ricksteves.com/ cdw, and for route planning, consult www.viamichelin.com. Theft insurance is mandatory in Italy ($15-20/day). In Italy, most car-rental companies' rates automatically include Collision Damage Waiver (CDW) coverage. Even if you try to decline CDW when you reserve your Italian car, you may find when you show up at the counter that you must buy it after all.

It's also required that you carry an International Driving Permit (IDP), available at your local AAA office ($20 plus two passport-type photos, www.aaa.com).

Italy's superhighway *(autostrada)* system is slick and speedy, but you'll pay a toll. Be warned that car traffic is restricted in many city centers—don't drive or park in any area that has a sign reading *Zona Traffico Limitato (ZTL,* often shown above a red circle). If you do, your license plate will be photographed and a hefty (€80-plus) ticket mailed to your home.

Italians love to tailgate; otherwise, local road etiquette

is similar to that in the US. Ask your car-rental company for details, or check the US State Department website (www.travel. state.gov, select "International Travel," search for your country in the "Learn about your destination" box, then click "Travel and Transportation").

A car is a worthless headache in cities—park it safely (get tips from your hotelier). When you park, be sure your valuables are out of sight and locked in the trunk, or even better, with you or in your hotel room.

HELPFUL HINTS

Emergency Help: For any emergency service—ambulance, police, or fire—call **112** from a mobile phone or landline. For passport problems, call the **US Embassy** (in Rome, 24-hour line—tel. 06-46741) or a **US Consulate** (Milan—tel. 02-290-351, Florence—tel. 055-266-951, Naples—tel. 081-583-8111), see http://it.usembassy.gov; or the **Canadian Embassy** (in Rome, tel. 06-854-442-911) or **Canadian Consulate** (in Milan, tel. 02-6269-4238), see www.italy.gc.ca. If you have a minor illness, do as the locals do and go to a pharmacist for advice. Or ask at your hotel for help—they'll know of the nearest medical and emergency services.

ETIAS Registration: Beginning in 2021, US and Canadian citizens may be required to register online with the European Travel Information and Authorization System (ETIAS) before entering certain European countries (quick and easy process, $8 fee, valid 3 years). A useful private website with more details is www.schengenvisainfo.com/etias.

Theft or Loss: Italy has particularly hardworking pickpockets—wear a money belt. Assume beggars are pickpockets and any scuffle is simply a distraction by a team of thieves. If you stop for any commotion or show, put your hands in your pockets before someone else does.

To replace a passport, you'll need to go in person to an embassy or consulate (see above). Cancel and replace your credit and debit cards by calling these 24-hour US numbers with a mobile phone: Visa (tel. +1 303/967-1096), MasterCard (tel. +1 636/722-7111), and American Express (tel. +1 336/393-1111). From a landline, you can call these US numbers collect by going through a local operator. File a police report either on the spot or within a day or two; you'll need it to submit an insurance claim for lost or stolen rail passes or travel gear, and it can help with replacing your passport or credit and debit cards. For more information, see www.ricksteves.com/ help.

Business Hours: Many businesses have now adopted the government's recommended 8:00 to 14:00 workday (although in tourist areas, shops are open longer). Still, expect small towns and villages to be more or less shut tight during lunch. Stores are also usually closed on Sunday, and often on Monday.

Sights: Opening and closing hours of sights can change unexpectedly; confirm the latest times with the local tourist information office or its website. Some major churches enforce a modest dress code (no bare shoulders or shorts) for everyone, even children.

Holidays and Festivals: Italy celebrates many holidays, which can close sights and attract crowds (book hotel rooms ahead). For information on holidays and festivals, check Italy's website: www.italia.it. For a simple list showing major—though not all—events, see www.ricksteves.com/festivals.

Numbers and Stumblers: What Americans call the second floor of a building is the first floor in Europe. Europeans write dates as day/month/year, so Christmas 2021 is 25/12/21. Commas are decimal points and vice versa—a dollar and a half is 1,50, and there are 5.280 feet in a mile. Italy uses the metric system: A kilogram is 2.2 pounds; a liter is about a quart; and a kilometer is six-tenths of a mile.

RESOURCES FROM RICK STEVES

This Snapshot guide is excerpted from my latest edition of *Rick Steves Italy*, one of many titles in my ever-expanding series of guidebooks on European travel. I also produce a public television series, *Rick Steves' Europe*, and a public radio show, *Travel with Rick Steves*. My website, www.ricksteves.com, offers free travel information, a forum for travelers' comments, guidebook updates, my travel blog, an online travel store, and information on European rail passes and our tours of Europe. If you're bringing a mobile device, my free Rick Steves Audio Europe app features dozens of self-guided audio tours of the top sights in Europe—including sights in Rome, Florence, Venice, Milan, Naples, Pompeii, Siena, and Assisi—plus radio shows and travel interviews about Italy. For more information, see www.ricksteves.com/audioeurope.

ADDITIONAL RESOURCES

Tourist Information: www.italia.it
Passports and Red Tape: www.travel.state.gov
Packing List: www.ricksteves.com/packing
Travel Insurance: www.ricksteves.com/insurance
Cheap Flights: www.kayak.com or www.google.com/flights
Airplane Carry-on Restrictions: www.tsa.gov
Updates for This Book: www.ricksteves.com/update

Italian Survival Phrases

English	Italian	Pronunciation
Good day.	*Buongiorno.*	bwohn-**jor**-noh
Do you speak English?	*Parla inglese?*	**par**-lah een-**gleh**-zay
Yes. / No.	*Sì. / No.*	see / noh
I (don't) understand.	*(Non) capisco.*	(nohn) kah-**pees**-koh
Please.	*Per favore.*	pehr fah-**voh**-ray
Thank you.	*Grazie.*	**graht**-see-ay
You're welcome.	*Prego.*	**preh**-go
I'm sorry.	*Mi dispiace.*	mee dee-spee-**ah**-chay
Excuse me.	*Mi scusi.*	mee **skoo**-zee
(No) problem.	*(Non) c'è problema.*	(nohn) cheh proh-**bleh**-mah
Good.	*Va bene.*	vah **beh**-nay
Goodbye.	*Arrivederci.*	ah-ree-veh-**dehr**-chee
one / two	*uno / due*	**oo**-noh / **doo**-ay
three / four	*tre / quattro*	tray / **kwah**-troh
five / six	*cinque / sei*	**cheeng**-kway / **seh**-ee
seven / eight	*sette / otto*	**seh**-tay / **oh**-toh
nine / ten	*nove / dieci*	**noh**-vay / dee-**ay**-chee
How much is it?	*Quanto costa?*	**kwahn**-toh **koh**-stah
Write it?	*Me lo scrive?*	may loh **skree**-vay
Is it free?	*È gratis?*	eh **grah**-tees
Is it included?	*È incluso?*	eh een-**kloo**-zoh
Where can I buy / find...?	*Dove posso comprare / trovare...?*	**doh**-vay poh-soh kohm-**prah**-ray / troh-**vah**-ray
I'd like / We'd like...	*Vorrei / Vorremmo...*	voh-**reh**-ee / voh-**reh**-moh
...a room.	*...una camera.*	**oo**-nah **kah**-meh-rah
...a ticket to ____.	*...un biglietto per ____.*	oon beel-**yeh**-toh pehr ____
Is it possible?	*È possibile?*	eh poh-**see**-bee-lay
Where is...?	*Dov'è...?*	doh-**veh**
...the train station	*...la stazione*	lah staht-see-**oh**-nay
...the bus station	*...la stazione degli autobus*	lah staht-see-**oh**-nay **dehl**-yee ow-toh-boos
...tourist information	*...informazioni per turisti*	een-for-maht-see-**oh**-nee pehr too-**ree**-stee
...the toilet	*...la toilette*	lah twah-**leh**-tay
men	*uomini / signori*	**woh**-mee-nee / seen-**yoh**-ree
women	*donne / signore*	**doh**-nay / seen-**yoh**-ray
left / right	*sinistra / destra*	see-**nee**-strah / **deh**-strah
straight	*sempre dritto*	**sehm**-pray **dree**-toh
What time does this open / close?	*A che ora apre / chiude?*	ah kay **oh**-rah ah-**pray** / kee-**oo**-day
At what time?	*A che ora?*	ah kay **oh**-rah
Just a moment.	*Un momento.*	oon moh-**mehn**-toh
now / soon / later	*adesso / presto / tardi*	ah-**deh**-soh / **preh**-stoh / **tar**-dee
today / tomorrow	*oggi / domani*	**oh**-jee / doh-**mah**-nee

In an Italian Restaurant

English	Italian	Pronunciation
I'd like...	Vorrei...	voh-**reh**-ee
We'd like...	Vorremmo...	vor-**reh**-moh
...to reserve...	...prenotare...	preh-noh-**tah**-ray
...a table for one / two.	...un tavolo per uno / due.	oon **tah**-voh-loh pehr **oo**-noh / **doo**-ay
Is this seat free?	È libero questo posto?	eh **lee**-beh-roh **kweh**-stoh **poh**-stoh
The menu (in English), please.	Il menù (in inglese), per favore.	eel meh-**noo** (een een-**gleh**-zay) pehr fah-**voh**-ray
service (not) included	servizio (non) incluso	sehr-**veet**-see-oh (nohn) een-**kloo**-zoh
cover charge	pane e coperto	**pah**-nay ay koh-**pehr**-toh
to go	da portar via	dah **por**-tar **vee**-ah
with / without	con / senza	kohn / **sehnt**-sah
and / or	e / o	ay / oh
menu (of the day)	menù (del giorno)	meh-**noo** (dehl **jor**-noh)
specialty of the house	specialità della casa	speh-chah-lee-**tah deh**-lah **kah**-zah
first course (pasta, soup)	primo piatto	**pree**-moh pee-**ah**-toh
main course (meat, fish)	secondo piatto	seh-**kohn**-doh pee-**ah**-toh
side dishes	contorni	kohn-**tor**-nee
bread	pane	**pah**-nay
cheese	formaggio	for-**mah**-joh
sandwich	panino	pah-**nee**-noh
soup	zuppa	**tsoo**-pah
salad	insalata	een-sah-**lah**-tah
meat	carne	**kar**-nay
chicken	pollo	**poh**-loh
fish	pesce	**peh**-shay
seafood	frutti di mare	**froo**-tee dee **mah**-ray
fruit / vegetables	frutta / legumi	**froo**-tah / lay-**goo**-mee
dessert	dolce	**dohl**-chay
tap water	acqua del rubinetto	**ah**-kwah dehl roo-bee-**neh**-toh
mineral water	acqua minerale	**ah**-kwah mee-neh-**rah**-lay
milk	latte	**lah**-tay
(orange) juice	succo (d'arancia)	**soo**-koh (dah-**rahn**-chah)
coffee / tea	caffè / tè	kah-**feh** / teh
wine	vino	**vee**-noh
red / white	rosso / bianco	**roh**-soh / bee-**ahn**-koh
glass / bottle	bicchiere / bottiglia	bee-kee-**eh**-ray / boh-**teel**-yah
beer	birra	**bee**-rah
Cheers!	Cin cin!	cheen cheen
More. / Another.	Di più. / Un altro.	dee pew / oon **ahl**-troh
The same.	Lo stesso.	loh **steh**-soh
The bill, please.	Il conto, per favore.	eel **kohn**-toh pehr fah-**voh**-ray
Do you accept credit cards?	Accettate carte di credito?	ah-cheh-**tah**-tay **kar**-tay dee **kreh**-dee-toh
tip	mancia	**mahn**-chah
Delicious!	Delizioso!	day-leet-see-**oh**-zoh

For more user-friendly Italian phrases, check out *Rick Steves Italian Phrase Book & Dictionary* or *Rick Steves French, Italian & German Phrase Book*.

PRACTICALITIES

INDEX

A

Accademia Musicale Chigiana (Siena): 19

Accommodations: *See Agriturismo; Sleeping*

Agriturismo: 6, 85–88; near Assisi, 165, 167; near Montalcino, 88; near Montelpuciano, 88; near Orvieto, 198–199; near Pienza, 86–87; near San Gimignano, 79; near Volterra, 65–66

Airport, Perugia/Assisi: 168

Air travel, resources: 220

Alab'Arte (Volterra): 60

Alabaster Museum (Volterra): 57

Alabaster Workshop (Volterra): 55, 60

Altesino: 118

Ambulances: 220

Amphitheaters (theaters): Assisi, 134–135; Volterra, 57–58

Antica Civita: 210–211

Aperitivo: 43, 61, 64

Archaeological museums: Montalcino Museums, 114; Museo Claudio Faina (Orvieto), 190; National Archaeological Museum of Orvieto, 190; Siena Archaeological Museum, 34–35. *See also* Etruscan Museums

Archaeological sites: Volterra Archaeological Park, 61. *See also* Etruscans; Roman sites

"Artisan Lane" (Volterra): 51–52

Assisi: 4, 128–168; arrival in, 130–131; eating, 165–167; helpful hints, 131–133; maps, 130, 132–133, 136–137, 162–163; orientation, 129; planning tips, 129; shopping, 131, 142–143; sights, 145–161; sleeping, 162–165; tourist information, 129; transportation, 130–131, 134, 167–168; walking tour, 134–144

Assisi Diocesan Museum: 139

Assisi Olive Wood: 142

Assisi Pinacoteca: 158

ATMs: 215–216

Audio Europe, Rick Steves: 220

B

Bagnoregio: *See* Civita di Bagnoregio

Bagno Vignoni: 87, 123, 125–126; eating, 126

Banchi di Sopra (Siena): 23–24

Banchi di Sotto (Siena): 23–24

Baptistery of San Giovanni (Siena): 12, 33

Basilica di San Francesco (Assisi): *See* St. Francis Basilica

Basilicas: *See* Churches and cathedrals

Baths, in Bagno Vignoni: 126

Beccafumi, Domenico: 27

Bernini, Gian Lorenzo: 30–31

Bike rentals, in Orvieto: 175

Bishop's Palace (Pienza): 107

Bookstores: Assisi, 146; Siena, 11

Borgia Palace (Pienza): 107

Bravio delle Botti (Montepulciano): 88, 92

Brunello di Montalcino: 87, 111, 113, 115–119, 123

Buses (bus travel): 5, 219; Assisi, 131, 134, 168; Bagnoregio, 203–205, 214; heart of Tuscany, 83; map, 5; Montalcino, 112, 120; Montepulciano, 90, 102; Orvieto, 174; Pienza, 104, 111; San Gimignano, 70, 72, 80; Siena, 8–10, 10, 46; Volterra, 49, 68

Business hours: 220–221

C

Cabs: *See* Taxis

Caffè Poliziano (Montepulciano): 93–94

Campatelli Tower House (San Gimignano): 77

Cantina della Talosa (Montepulciano): 99

Cantuccini: 55

Car insurance: 219

Car rentals: 219

Car travel (driving): 5–6, 219–220; Assisi, 131; Civita di Bagnoregio, 205–206; distances and time, 6; heart of Tuscany, 83, 120–127; Montalcino, 112; Montepulciano, 89–90; Orvieto, 174–175, 202;

INDEX

INDEX

Explore Europe

At ricksteves.com you can browse through thousands of articles, videos, photos and radio interviews, plus find a wealth of money-saving travel tips for planning your dream trip. And with our mobile-friendly website, you can easily access all this great travel information anywhere you go.

TV Shows

Preview the places you'll visit by watching entire half-hour episodes of *Rick Steves' Europe* (choose from all 100 shows) on-demand, for free.

your travel dreams into affordable reality

Radio Interviews

Enjoy ready access to Rick's vast library of radio interviews covering travel tips and cultural insights that relate specifically to your Europe travel plans.

Travel Forums

Learn, ask, share! Our online community of savvy travelers is a great resource for first-time travelers to Europe, as well as seasoned pros.

Travel News

Subscribe to our free Travel News e-newsletter, and get monthly updates from Rick on what's happening in Europe.

Classroom Europe

Check out our free resource for educators with 400+ short video clips from the *Rick Steves' Europe* TV show.

Rick's Free Travel App

Get your FREE **Rick Steves Audio Europe**™ app to enjoy…

- Dozens of self-guided tours of Europe's top museums, sights and historic walks
- Hundreds of tracks filled with cultural insights and sightseeing tips from Rick's radio interviews
- All organized into handy geographic playlists
- For Apple and Android

With Rick whispering in your ear, Europe gets even better.

Find out more at ricksteves.com

Gear up for your next adventure at ricksteves.com

Light Luggage

Pack light and right with Rick Steves' affordable, custom-designed rolling carry-on bags, backpacks, day packs and shoulder bags.

Accessories

From packing cubes to moneybelts and beyond, Rick has personally selected the travel goodies that will help your trip go smoother.

Shop at ricksteves.com

Save time and energy

This guidebook is your independent-travel toolkit. But for all it delivers, it's still up to you to devote the time and energy it takes to manage the preparation and logistics that are essential for a happy trip. If that's a hassle, there's a solution.

Rick Steves Tours

A Rick Steves tour takes you to Europe's most interesting places with great

with minimum stress

guides and small groups of 28 or less. We follow Rick's favorite itineraries, ride in comfy buses, stay in family-run hotels, and bring you intimately close to the Europe you've traveled so far to see. Most importantly, we take away the logistical headaches so you can focus on the fun.

Join the fun

This year we'll take 33,000 free-spirited travelers—nearly half of them repeat customers—along with us on 50 different itineraries, from Athens to Istanbul. Is a Rick Steves tour the right fit for your travel dreams?

Find out at ricksteves.com, where you can also request Rick's latest tour catalog. Europe is best experienced with happy travel partners. We hope you can join us.

BEST OF GUIDES

Full-color guides in an easy-to-scan format. Focused on top sights and experiences in the most popular European destinations

Best of England
Best of Europe
Best of France
Best of Germany
Best of Ireland
Best of Italy
Best of Scotland
Best of Spain

COMPREHENSIVE GUIDES

City, country, and regional guides printed on Bible-thin paper. Packed with detailed coverage for a multi-week trip exploring iconic sights and venturing off the beaten path

Amsterdam & the Netherlands
Barcelona
Belgium: Bruges, Brussels, Antwerp & Ghent
Berlin
Budapest
Croatia & Slovenia
Eastern Europe
England
Florence & Tuscany
France
Germany
Great Britain
Greece: Athens & the Peloponnese
Iceland
Ireland
Istanbul
Italy
London
Paris
Portugal
Prague & the Czech Republic
Provence & the French Riviera
Rome
Scandinavia
Scotland
Sicily
Spain
Switzerland
Venice
Vienna, Salzburg & Tirol

THE BEST OF ROME

POCKET GUIDES

Compact color guides for shorter trips

Amsterdam	Paris
Athens	Prague
Barcelona	Rome
Florence	Venice
Italy's Cinque Terre	Vienna
London	
Munich & Salzburg	

SNAPSHOT GUIDES

Focused single-destination coverage

Basque Country: Spain & France
Copenhagen & the Best of Denmark
Dublin
Dubrovnik
Edinburgh
Hill Towns of Central Italy
Krakow, Warsaw & Gdansk
Lisbon
Loire Valley
Madrid & Toledo
Milan & the Italian Lakes District
Naples & the Amalfi Coast
Nice & the French Riviera
Normandy
Northern Ireland
Norway
Reykjavík
Rothenburg & the Rhine
Sevilla, Granada & Southern Spain
St. Petersburg, Helsinki & Tallinn
Stockholm

CRUISE PORTS GUIDES

Reference for cruise ports of call

Mediterranean Cruise Ports
Scandinavian & Northern European
  Cruise Ports

Complete your library with...

TRAVEL SKILLS & CULTURE

*Study up on travel skills and gain
insight on history and culture*

Europe 101
Europe Through the Back Door
Europe's Top 100 Masterpieces
European Christmas
European Easter
European Festivals
For the Love of Europe
Travel as a Political Act

PHRASE BOOKS & DICTIONARIES

French
French, Italian & German
German
Italian
Portuguese
Spanish

PLANNING MAPS

Britain, Ireland & London
Europe
France & Paris
Germany, Austria & Switzerland
Iceland
Ireland
Italy
Spain & Portugal

Photo Credits